Genre Publics

Emma Baulch

GENRE PUBLICS

Popular Music, Technologies,

and Class in Indonesia

Wesleyan University Press   Middletown, Connecticut

Wesleyan University Press
Middletown CT 06459
www.wesleyan.edu/wespress
© 2020 by Emma Baulch

Manufactured in the United States of America
Designed by Mindy Basinger Hill
Typeset in 10/14 pt Minion Pro.

Library of Congress Cataloging-in-Publication Data

Names: Baulch, Emma, [date] author.

Title: Genre publics : popular music, technologies, and class
in Indonesia / Emma Baulch.

Description: Middletown : Wesleyan University Press, [2020] |
Includes bibliographical references and index. | Summary: "An
exploration of how pop music's increasing popularity helped to
develop Indonesia as a global center, recognized both by other global
powers and Indonesians themselves"—Provided by publisher.

Identifiers: LCCN 2020022359 (print) | LCCN 2020022360 (ebook) |
ISBN 9780819579645 (cloth) | ISBN 9780819579638 (trade paperback) |
ISBN 9780819579652 (ebook)

Subjects: LCSH: Popular music—Social aspects—Indonesia. |
Popular music—Political aspects—Indonesia. | Music trade—Social
aspects—Indonesia. | Music trade—Political aspects—Indonesia. |
Culture and globalization—Indonesia.

Classification: LCC ML3917.15 B38 2020 (print) | LCC ML3917.15
(ebook) | DDC 306.4/842309598—dc23

LC record available at https://lccn.loc.gov/2020022359
LC ebook record available at https://lccn.loc.gov/2020022360

Hardcover ISBN: 978-0-8195-7964-5
Paperback ISBN: 978-0-8195-7963-8
Ebook ISBN: 978-0-8195-7965-2

5 4 3 2 1

FOR HENNY AMELIA DEBORA LAULANG
AND PAULINA RAJA

CONTENTS

Illustrations follow page 118.

Genre Publics

Introduction

At the end of the twentieth century a profound change took place in Indonesian popular music. Sales of Indonesian pop, or "pop Indonesia," suddenly increased, overtaking for the first time sales of those from the West (Sopiann 2002; SWAOnline 2007, 2008). This increase in sales—generally referred to in Indonesia as the "local music boom"—accompanied an expansion of pop Indonesia's presence in the Indonesian public sphere. Pop Indonesia musicians began to appear as endorsers of the most ubiquitous commodities, such as cigarettes, instant noodles, and energy drinks. Record labels began to develop brand identities based on their pop Indonesia repertoires. Artist management companies mushroomed. Television networks began to devote ever-larger segments of airtime to pop performances. Festivals and competitions for amateur pop performances blossomed all over the archipelago.

At first glance, Indonesia's local music boom appears to resemble similar instances of brand nationalism (Iwabuchi 2002, 2010) in Japan, the UK (Street 2004, 2012; Oakley 2004), and Korea (Fuhr 2016). Iwabuchi avers that brand nationalism emerged from "a new collaborative relationship between the state and media cultural industries" (2010, 90), citing government policy in the UK, Korea, Singapore, Taiwan, China, and Japan as examples. But in Indonesia, it took some time for the cogs of state policy to draw the music industry into rhetoric about the need for national branding (Pangestu 2009a, b), and not until 2014 did pop Indonesia musicians begin to appear in election campaigns as ambassadors for a new style of leadership (in the manner that — candidate Tony Blair used the band Blur, for example; see Street 2012, 348). At its height, the local music boom, together with a renaissance of Indonesian literature and filmmaking, appeared to fill something of an ideological vacuum left by the demise of the authoritarian New Order regime (1966–1998). Books celebrating women's sexual power became best sellers, Indonesian films in which teens read modern Indonesian poets with a fan-like fondness became box office extravaganzas, bands that had called on their young followers to be critical of the New Order's president, Suharto, found enormous commercial success, and others declared their love for the national flag in catchy tunes that, for many years thereafter, blasted from boom boxes during neighborhood independence day celebrations.

But it would be wrong to interpret this fervent outpouring as a consequence of regime change. The term "ideological vacuum" is also misleading, for while the local music boom was certainly not the result of a concerted, state-led brand nationalism, it did emerge from ideological transformation taking place prior to regime change. This book understands the local music boom as a function of the reconfiguration of global cultural flows after the end of the Cold War. Such reconfigurations were prompted by shifts in media policy frameworks, specifically the move away from "developmentalist" models, in which states played dominant roles, and toward deregulated or liberalized models in which media industries in Asia achieved heightened levels of global integration. As Fuhr notes (2016) in his study of K-pop, such integration did not have the effect of orienting Asian media productions ever more forcefully to a single, dominant global aesthetic. Rather, it promoted the aesthetic diversification of global modern ideals. Deregulation, that is, yielded new kinds of content that identified Asia as a prime site of the global modern (rather than derivative of a global modernity with its source elsewhere), as well as new domestic and in some cases transnational markets for such content. These new markets reconfigure global cultural flows when they exceed in size the market for Anglophone content that once dominated.

The reconfigured flows prompted by globalization had both centripetal and centrifugal effects. Undeniably, new regional soft power centers have emerged, reorienting Asian audiences away from a Western elsewhere to new Asian elsewhere. The best documented examples of such centers include Japan and Korea (Iwabuchi 2010; Fuhr 2016), and both Jpop and K-pop cultivated enthusiastic fan bases in Southeast Asia in the 1990s and 2000s. But J-pop and K-pop spread regionally in contexts also being reconfigured by growing local popular music industries, with varying degrees of state involvement in promotion and nation branding, as well as varying degrees of transnational mobility. Consumption of home-grown popular culture, as well as that of K-pop, has become increasingly key to both articulations of citizenship and membership in the global modern in many places in Southeast Asia, including Indonesia.

Genre Publics explores this phenomenon in late twentieth- and early twenty-first-century Indonesia through a focus on the local music boom. In it, I consider how notions of "the local" are being produced in a context of increasingly layered global interconnection. I examine the ideological, institutional, and technological conditions that enabled this boom, and inquire into their links with those prompting the expansion of consumerism elsewhere in Asia, as well as with a more specific context of Indonesian democratization. How has the local music boom reshaped the ways Indonesian people form distinct senses of the modern, as "Asia" plays an ever more influential role in defining what it means to be modern? What can it tell us about the contexts of consumer capitalism's unfolding in Indonesia, and of the particular kinds of class politics it engenders? The book explores such questions through a case-by-case analysis of the performances, technologies, and fans that constitute the local music boom, revealing both the ways big media capital is forcefully shaping Indonesians' cultural identities and the new solidarities budding from popular-music consumers' ethical proclivities.

The local music boom can be situated at a complex juncture featuring change on a number of fronts: media deregulation, regime change, and heightened consumerism. This set of changes provides the context for the intensified contests over preferred meanings of "the local" chronicled in the book. As homegrown popular music became increasingly important in a commercial sense, actors representing distinct popular music genres launched various kinds of authenticity claims. Such claims commonly retrieved long-standing genre categories distinguished by the terms "Melayu" and "Indonesia" and associated with a village-metropolis (*kampungan-gedongan*) dichotomy. Dangdut, which employs elements of Indian film music such as the bamboo flute and the tabla, is recognized as a *kampungan*/Melayu form. Genres associated with the *gedongan* assignation typically employ Western musical idioms and are designated by the term "Indonesia." In a literal sense, *kampungan* means "of the slums" or "of the village," and *gedongan* means "of the buildings," but *kampungan-gedongan* also invokes a taste hierarchy that reflects the particular imaginaries at play in the cultural constitution of Indonesia as a post-colony. After 1966, genres associated with the West (pop Indonesia and rock) gained cultural ascendance and were considered proximate to modernity, while *kampungan*/Melayu signified its lack (Weintraub 2006).

In the twenty-first century, *kampungan-gedongan* endures as a key conceptual resource in Indonesians' efforts to develop senses of belonging that feel apt to the new democratic, digitally equipped, and increasingly consumerist context. The continued salience of *kampungan-gedongan* serves the book as an entry point to inquire into the relationship between popular music and class formation in the context of Indonesia's capitalist development. In this pursuit I am indebted to a body of work on Indonesia popular music examining the links between performance and consumption of popular musical aesthetics and people's class position (Barendregt and van Santen 2002; Baulch 2007a; Browne 2000; David 2003; Frederick 1982; Gjelstad 2003; Heins 1975; Heryanto 2008; Luvaas 2009; Murray 1991; Pioquinto 1995; Piper and Jabo 1987; Wallach 2002 and 2007; Weintraub 2006; Yampolsky 1989). The book builds on these works by conceptualizing the class-genre relationship through recourse to the concept of publics. Popular music genres, I argue, are not superstructural manifestations of class, but rather the "stuff" on which class formations are based. In context of Indonesia's "capitalist revolution" (Robison 1986, 1) enabled by the New Order's establishment, genres played a crucial part in the 1970s' formation of the middle classes and masses, both as modes of addressing classed subjects and as virtual spaces for their imagined assembly.

Popular music's structuring force arose from the ways categories of musical sound and performance forged relationships with particular media technologies in a rearranged media landscape in the late 1960s and 1970s. As discussed in chapter 1, in the 1970s rock relied largely on print media to circulate, and this reliance shaped its meaning in particular ways. A sense of *gedongan*-ness began to coalesce around a print publication devoted to rock music, while dangdut was marked as *kampungan* and did not represent itself in print for the first twenty-five years of the New Order regime. The relationships between the generic marking of popular music texts and their modes of circulation gave rise to presences and absences from media spaces that worked to produce popular music audiences as classed subjects, and afforded proponents of genre categories differing degrees of media power and "voice" in positing forms of citizenship that were variously privileged and devalued.

Since the publication of Anderson's *Imagined Communities* and Habermas's *The Transformation of the Public Sphere*, it has become increasingly common for scholars to consider how mass mediation shapes political subjectivity by employing the concept of publics (Anderson 1983; Cody 2011; Dean 2001; Habermas 1991; Hirschkind 2006; Warner 2002a, b). At the heart of this body of scholarship lies an understanding that texts in circulation possess a social power deriving from their ability to address people in a way that enables them to imagine themselves as members of a community of strangers (publics) who, although physically distant from one another, act collectively by inhabiting the texts' paths of circulation.

Moreover, media technologies not only circulate texts in an instrumental way, but also confer meaning upon them, shaping their inherent modes of address and therefore the qualities of publics (Warner 2002b). The book argues that Indonesian class formations emerge in this manner from relationships between popular music texts and their modes of circulation, and can therefore be conceptualized as genre publics: virtual social entities arising from the twinning of particular mediating technologies with particular kinds of address.

Conceptualizing class formations as genre publics is productive for two reasons. First, it recasts notions of class structure underpinning debates about the forces implicated in regime change in Indonesia in 1998 (Hadiz 2013b; Ford and Pepinsky 2013). These debates, between political economists and those advocating pluralist interpretations of contemporary Indonesian politics, explore the role class formations have played in ensuring continuity of, or bringing about change within, power relations in post–New Order Indonesia. Some scholars argue that the middle class that emerged in the New Order period was a product of the establishment of the New Order state, not of a longer process of industrialization. This rendered it ineffectual as a force for democratization. When regime change did occur in 1998, it was not the result of middle-class demands for the rule of law and social justice, but was prompted by exogenous factors, especially the 1998 monetary crisis. Rather than democratization, the post–New Order period has entailed the consolidation of the "predatory state and private oligarchies" (Hadiz and Robison 2005, 220–241; Hadiz and Robison 2013; Winters 2013). Others have argued that there is much that this argument omits. Heryanto avers that rather than using abstract, macro-structural concepts as a measure of middle-class political agency, scholars ought to be attuned to micro-level processes and whether "democratisation-friendly consciousness, ideas, practices and institutions have already found fertile ground in various forms, including in offices, schools, families or social organisations" (2003, 25). Aspinall (2013) argues that political economists have accorded too much importance to patterns of capital accumulation and too little importance to ideas, and this has led to erroneous predictions of the likelihood of democratic change and then, when democratic change did occur, caused scholars to proffer erroneous readings of its causes and of its quality.

An approach using the concept of publics to understand social change can contribute to these debates about middle-class agency. Studying texts in circulation make possible new perspectives on the origins of the middle class, and publics also provide a conceptual framework by which the social force of ideas can be theorized. Political economists describe the middle class as a child of the New Order state, but this interpretation underestimates the role circulating texts play in assembling people and endowing them with agency. The new Anglophone and Anglophone-oriented popular musical forms that played important roles in public life in the 1970s certainly addressed a middle class that in general terms endorsed the New Order regime's pro-us orientation. However, the intricate interplay between these new popular musical texts and new mediating technologies spawned subjectivities that retrieved long-standing tropes of the revolutionary male to articulate notions of middle-class critique and sovereignty, in spite of the middle class's political-economic disempowerment. Such subjectivities were striking features of the pro-democracy movement in the lead-up to the New Order's downfall in 1998, revealing the cultural arena born of the capitalist revolution to be fertile grounds for the growth of political ideas that came to underpin the movement to overthrow the regime.

Second, any account of political and social change that attends to the evolution of publics necessarily foregrounds the roles media technologies play in forging that change, for such technologies are key elements in publics' formation. Therefore, conceptualizing class formations as genre publics prompts inquiry into the technological forces at play in the local music boom; this book traces the links between a changing technological environment and the new contests that produce locality. Drawing on Castells, I historicize the local music boom as a feature of a "new technological paradigm" (Castells 2010, 5), featuring the spread of commercial television and also of digital technologies. These new technologies set cultural forms marked as "local" (such as *kampungan* and *gedongan*) on new circulatory paths, disrupting long-standing modes for the articulation of class and prompting new contests over notions of ideal Indonesian-ness.

By employing the concept of technological paradigms to historicize the local music boom, the book posits a reimagining of the conditions shaping contemporary public life in Indonesia. Post-authoritarianism and democratization remain the dominant frame for analyzing present-day Indonesia, but I propose that the processes of democratizing and decentralizing the public sphere were profoundly shaped by post–Cold War media deregulation, featuring the expansion of commercial television and also of digital technologies, including mobile phones and compact discs. At major points of media change, the technological assemblages that constitute popular music genres are significantly altered and therefore so are the imagined assemblies that undergird public life. By arguing thus, the book not only reveals developments within popular music itself, but also draws attention to unnoticed historical turning points that are alternate to those identified in prevailing frames that predominate in the study of Indonesia. It shows how experimentations with popular music genres flag important points of rupture in the country's cultural history and how studying popular music contributes in important ways to a broader remapping of the contemporary.

HISTORIES AND GENEALOGIES

Genre Publics situates the local music boom at a historical juncture featuring three overlapping developments. First, the far-reaching effects of media deregulation, which has changed the way in which pop artists realize their exchange value, caused pop to become a much more firmly televisual phenomenon, and resulted in an advertising boom, heightening the role of consumerist ideology in articulations of nationality and making it possible to locate the Indonesian case in a broader context of the expansion of consumerism in Asia. Second is the end of the Suharto-led New Order regime in 1998, and the ensuing process of democratizing (and decentralizing) the formal political sphere. Third is the spread of digital technologies, which has expanded the range of technologies responsible for mediating popular musical sounds and images.

This juncture complicates the task of historicizing the local music boom, and in order to pursue questions about the processes of locality production and their historical context, I employ an Appaduraian approach of "doubly historicizing" (Appadurai 1996, 74). In *Modernity at Large*, Appadurai (73) advises, "What we need to avoid is the search for pre-established sequences of institutional change, axiomatically defined as constitutive of the consumer revolution. What this might encourage is a multiplication of scenarios concerning the appearance of consumer society, in which the rest of the world will not simply be seen as repeating, or imitating, the conjunctural precedents of England or France." Appadurai argues that such scenarios come to light when one perceives in them the possibility of multiple histories. He proposes "doubly historicizing" as a method for uncovering both the "historical" and "genealogical" dimensions of consumer societies, and writes that "history leads you outward, to link patterns of change to increasingly larger universes of interaction; and genealogy leads you inward, towards cultural dispositions and styles that might be stubbornly embedded in both local institutions and the history of the local habitus" (1996, 74). By "doubly historicizing" in this way, I aim to tease out the regional flows that the local music boom inhabits, without disavowing important national-level developments that also shape its evolution. On the one hand, the book locates the local music boom within a *history* of policy, technological, and cultural changes that conjoin various places in the region in an epochal sense and render Asian consumerism a plausible object of study. On the other hand, it shows how Asian consumerism unfolds at various conjunctures, marking specific *genealogies* and making it possible to speak of it as one now does of modernity—in the plural.

Histories: Technological Paradigms

The twenty-first century has seen the publication of a sizable body of work investigating the cultural dimensions of consumerism in Asia (Fuhr 2016; Iwabuchi 2002; Liechty 2003; Lewis, Martin, and Sun 2016; Lukose 2009; Mazzarella 2003). These works, especially those of Fuhr, Iwabuchi, and Lewis et al., paint a picture that makes it possible to identify two features that mark an Asianized archive of global modernity as distinct from earlier resources for delineating national modernities in the region. The first is a tendency to blur rigid East-West dichotomies that once so forcefully shaped notions of postcolonial modernity. The second is a valorization of consumption as vital to the articulation of citizenship. These two features—the fracturing of East-West dichotomies and the rise of consumer citizenship—commonly inflect Asians' experiences of the various iterations of Asia as a source (rather than mere recipient) of the new global modern.

These features are manifest in the local music boom, itself an assertion of Indonesia as a source of the global modern. They can be seen in several well-documented phenomena, such as the rise of Muslim fashion and pop culture, as well as the enthusiastic consumption of K-pop, both of which orient audiences toward non-Western ideals (Barendregt 2006; Beta 2016, 2014; Heryanto 2014; Hoesterey 2016; Jones 2010; Jones and Slama 2017; Jung and Shim 2014; Schmidt 2017; Weintraub 2011). They can also be found in the emergence of pop acts that blur once separate categories of popular music, Melayu (drawing on Indian film music) and Indonesia (drawing on a Western pop idiom). As discussed in chapters 3 and 6, in the mid-2000s, a wave of pop Melayu acts propelled new conceptions of Indonesian modernity, which idealized the lower-class "little man" into the public culture.

Drawing on Castells, I position these developments—the rise of consumerism and the transformation of long-standing orienting dichotomies—as part of a "new technological paradigm" (Castells 2010, 5). In *The Rise of Network Society* (2010, 5), Castells argues that different modes of development yield different forms and structures of communication, which in turn shape modes of production. Modes of development refer to the "technological arrangements" responsible for generating surpluses, and modes of production determine "rules for the appropriation, distribution and use of surpluses" (2010, 16). In this sense, modes of development, or technological arrangements, are paradigmatic. They produce logics that infuse society at large. In informational societies, "information generation, processing and transmission become fundamental sources of productivity and power" (2010, 21). The communicative logic prevalent in informational societies is that of the network, distinct from the logics of orality and literacy that pervade agrarian and industrial societies respectively.

The new technological paradigm that accommodated the local music boom broke with earlier paradigms marked by the presence of the press, which was considerably reorganized on the advent of the New Order regime in 1966, and state television, Televisi Republik Indonesia (TVRI), established in 1962. During this period, particularly after the establishment of the New Order, a strong sense of a society constituted by two social forces—the middle class and the masses—emerged. US soft power and an orientation to the West played an important role in the constitution of the Indonesian middle class, and an orientation to nominally "Eastern" cultural forms such as dangdut played a pivotal role in constituting a sense of the masses (Baulch 2016; Wallach 2007; Weintraub 2006; Yampolsky 1989). The second technological paradigm—this book's main focus—emerged after the end of the Cold War and featured the expansion of advertising television and, slightly later, the proliferation of digital technologies. The notion of consumer sovereignty began to play an increasingly influential role in the formation of Indonesian subjectivities. In chapter 3 I discuss how new kinds of pop music programming on newly established private television stations in the mid-1990s advanced notions of identity as flexible, ephemeral, detached from nationalist narratives of youth as *pemuda* (literally, "young man"), and shaped more forcefully by audience measurement regimes that television producers employ to categorize their audiences and sell them to advertisers. Conspicuous consumption and wealth became increasingly accepted features of "authentic" Indonesian-ness, but more aggressively celebratory articulations of lower-classness also emerged in this period (Baulch 2007a; Heryanto 2014).

While Castells's notion of technological paradigms is indispensable to the historical revision I pursue in the book, regional particularities challenge his periodizing of such paradigms' evolution by evoking of a world history altered primarily by the spread of digital technologies. By linking informational capitalism so closely to post-Keynesianism, Castells limits its use to those places where particular modes of governance were at play between the mid-1940s and the mid-1970s, delivering stability and economic growth following World War II. For Indonesians, this period was one of independence and upheaval. Stability and economic growth were not delivered until the 1970s, a period of economic decline and restructuring in much of the Global North. The oil price rises that sparked rampant inflation and reform in the US were a windfall to an Indonesian authoritarian state overseeing the consolidation, rather than fragmentation, of class formations and the outlawing of labor unions. Nor was the ensuing paradigm marked by a break with the broadcast mode. Rather it involved, quite crucially, the expansion of commercial television, which formed the basis for the rise of notions of consumer sovereignty that informed in important ways ideas about a good, post-authoritarian society.

The technological paradigms examined in this book are more akin to the "developmental" and "post-developmental" eras invoked by Lewis, Martin, and Sun than they are of Keynesianism and post-Keynesianism. Lewis et al. aver that Taiwan's engagement with neoliberalism manifests post-developmental features—a mixture of the structural legacies of the developmental state and the neoliberal ideals that tug away from developmentalism (2016, 14). Similar dynamics are manifest in Indonesia, where key orienting dichotomies established in the developmental era, *kampungan-gedongan*, endure into the present. They help afford meaning to new developments, such as celebrity politics and the rise of fan organizations, just as they become inflected with values associated with neoliberalism, such as individuality, mobility, and flexibility. In this sense, neoliberal values rearticulate and distort the legacies of the developmental era rather than replace them outright.

Genealogies: A Rigid Genre System

As well as positioning the local music boom in the context of broader changes that swept Asia in the post–Cold War period, precipitating the rise of consumerism, the book highlights the particularities of Indonesian consumerism; the local music boom yielded post–Cold War formulations of citizenship and global modernity that were distinct from those predominating in other emerging Asian centers of media production. Fuhr argues that the term "consumerist Asianism" captures the decentralization of global popular cultural flows as they orient away from Euro-America, apparent in the development of South Korean industries

(Fuhr 2016, 8). By contrast, in Indonesia, complex relationships developed between particular media technologies (print) and preexisting tropes of masculinity that prepared a certain category of popular music (rock) to assume the mantle of the local music boom's primary cultural form and, by extension, to posit itself as a model of post-authoritarian citizenship. The Indonesian local music boom therefore elevated categories that oriented toward the West, appearing to reinstate the idea of a Euro-American core and to indicate the boom's roots in the orienting dichotomies established in the Cold War period.

The all-male rock band assumed a privileged role in the signification of "the local" in the context of the local music boom, and this reflects the enduring primacy since the early New Order of middle-class cultural forms in the delineation of preferred meanings of a local modernity. Over the decade following the establishment of the New Order regime on March 11, 1966, three distinct genres emerged. In the early 1970s, a new sound—which subsequently became known as dangdut—emerged, mixing elements derived from Indian film music (bamboo flute, a two-headed drum, and a *cengkok* vocal ornamentation) with a rock aesthetic. Contrasting the secular proclivities of rock and pop Indonesia, dangdut's consumption came to be closely linked to Islam (Weintraub 2010, 27). Scholarship on dangdut is varied in its interpretations of the genre—a point I will discuss in chapter 3. Suffice it to note here something on which several writers agree: throughout the New Order period, dangdut served as a convenient trope signifying the unknowing and vulgar masses that aided the construction of middle-classness (Browne 2000; Pioquinto 1995; Wallach 2007; Weintraub 2006). Pop Indonesia and rock developed along a similar trajectory, although there were also important distinctions between them. Both were commonly associated with middle-class, metropolitan lifestyles (Wallach 2007; Yampolsky 1989), but while pop Indonesia was associated with pro-regime performances, rock attained significant ideological force for its ability to combine two important tropes of masculinity—both denoted by the term *pemuda*: the wild, heroic revolutionary man and the literate, well-educated critic.

This genre landscape is remarkable not only for its difference from that which preceded it, but also for the rigidity of the semiotic values of its constituent categories. As mentioned, the genres that populated the post-1965 landscape were assigned social qualities according to the *kampungan-gedongan* dichotomy. Attendant binaries—high-low and East (Melayu)-West (Indonesia)—helped sustain *kampungan-gedongan*, and particular media technologies inhered in these sets of associations, helping them to crystallize as part of people's lived realities.

This genre system—both the constituent categories and their semiotic values—has remained fairly consistent from the late twentieth century to the present, revealing a rigidity that stands in contrast to the mutability of genres in the preceding period, as discussed in Yampolsky's 2013 article "Three Genres of Indonesian Popular Music." The article documents a generic landscape experiencing a high degree of flux; aesthetic structures and social meanings of genres changed frequently. Yampolsky's discussion of keroncong is particularly striking in this regard.

In the late nineteenth century, keroncong had a loose lyrical form and simple musical structure (technical rules), which lent it to reproduction by amateur street musicians (semiotic rules) who used it to articulate satire, which identified the form and spaces of its performance and consumption with a certain political morality. In the 1920s the recording of keroncong had removed the genre from the realm of orality and "satirical comment and repartee between singers" (Yampolsky 2013, 29) and paved the way for the transformation of the formal qualities of the genre. Once recorded, the accompanying lyrics or pantun attained a degree of fixity and lost some of their satirical and comic power. Recording also gave rise to a certain elaboration and complication of the keroncong style, causing it to move out of the streets and professionalize. The mid-1920s, Yampolsky writes, witnessed "the flowering of melody and . . . the development of a distinctive accompaniment idiom featuring interlocking figuration (often called cakcuk) played on a small plucked lute, single strong 'walking guitar,' and a pizzicato cello imitating the drumming characteristic of Central Javanese and Sundanese gamelan music" (2013, 29). As a recorded product, keroncong began to "appeal to the audience that could afford to buy gramophones and records" (30). The sheer cost of gramophone ownership limited keroncong to a wealthy class of people and a certain way of life. Recording channeled keroncong to these costly objects and the people who owned them. By the 1950s and '60s, keroncong, a genre that in the late 1800s was an "urban folk music, particularly associated with Batavia and . . . performed by Eurasians at Chinese New Year festivities," had become identified as the expressive form of veterans of the Indonesian revolution, and by the 1970s it was being linked to an exclusionary militaristic nationalism (Yampolsky 2013, 28, 34).

By contrast, the genre system that evolved in the subsequent period displayed a high degree of *im*mutability. In the introduction to their special issue on Indonesian popular music genres in the journal *Asian Music*, Wallach and Clinton argue that it harbored a "tripartite structure," including dangdut, pop, and underground/indie (2013, 3), and in his 2007 book Wallach contends that these genres articulate competing visions of modernity: pop "domesticated the megarhetoric of developmental modernization," while dangdut "interrogated" it, and underground rock "vernacularized" it (Wallach 2007, 252). Wallach and Clinton argue for the rigidity of this genre system. While acknowledging "the agency, often audacity, of creative, individual musicians to innovate and challenge genre boundaries in spite of formidable constraints," they assert that "it is vitally important to understand the historical and cultural dimensions of such constraints . . . [including] . . . the underlying rigidity of Indonesia's genre system" (Wallach and Clinton 2013, 6).

I concur with Wallach and Clinton's arguments for rigidity, but the generic landscape I present in this book departs from their tripartite structure. This structure can only apply to the period from the early 1990s when underground music first emerged.[1] Indeed, the body of scholarship chronicling the development of Indonesian popular music, which has grown substantially in the twenty-first century, focuses largely on this period. Barendregt and van Santen (2002) noted that little work had been undertaken on Indonesian popular music. Nearly twenty years later, this situation has changed enormously. At least five scholarly monographs on the topic have been published (Baulch 2007b; Luvaas 2013a; Richter 2012; Wallach 2007; Weintraub 2010), and too many theses, book chapters, and journal articles to mention here, but estimated to number around fifty. Most of these works study the early twenty-first century, including a number of works on underground music (Wallach 2007; Martin-Iverson 2012, 2014; Karib 2007; Saefullah 2010; Baulch 2002a, 2002b, 2007b), indie (Moore 2013a, b; Juliastuti 2018; Luvaas 2013a, b), rock (Baulch 2010, 2012, 2016), dangdut (David 2014; Weintraub 2006, 2010, 2013, 2014) (building on seminal works by Browne 2000; Frederick 1982; and Pioquinto 1995), and pop Melayu (Baulch 2013; Weintraub 2014).

I argue that rather than forming a tripartite structure, contemporary genre categories are accommodated within a series of dichotomies, including urban-rural, but also high-low, East-West, and masculine-feminine, and condensed within the master dichotomy, *kampungan-gedongan*. The positions that various genres occupy on the *kampungan-gedongan* spectrum have also remained fairly stable. Above, I touched on Yampolsky's discussions of keroncong's social mobility—originally a lower-class form, it entered the social worlds of the wealthy when it was recorded and could be played on gramophones, which were costly (Yampolsky 2013). No such mobility can be perceived in the generic landscape of the last fifty years. For various reasons, pop Indonesia and rock have both dispersed in different ways (chapter 3, 6, and 7) and been appropriated into lower-class cultural expressions, but they have not ceased to be prime signifiers of a middle-class cultural ascendance. What we see are new developments in genres that destabilize Melayu-Indonesia, East-West dichotomies, but high-low distinctions appear to be fairly rigidly maintained.

THEORIZING GENRE

By arguing that Indonesian popular music genres articulate a series of binaries condensed within the *kampungan-gedongan* dichotomy, the book extends existing scholarship theorizing genre. Since the birth of popular music studies as a recognized area of study in the early 1980s, the publication of works analyzing processes of genre construction in popular music studies has been sporadic, and in the forty years of the discipline's existence, only around seven works (two of which are journal articles) have been published (Fabbri 1981; Finnegan 1989; Frith 1996; Holt 2007; Negus 1999; Toynbee 2000, Wallach 2007). This list includes works that seek to conceptualize genre in general, as opposed to those that are focused studies of particular genres.

Most of those to have written about the topic agree, genres are much more than the organization of particular types of musical sound into particular categories. They have powerful social meanings and efficacies, which are enforced through spatial, visual, and corporeal, as well as sonic, means. In one of the earliest works on popular music genre, Fabbri (1981) argues that genre distinctions are drawn by sets of rules that come into play in various realms of musical production, circulation, and consumption: "a musical genre is a set of musical events (real or possible) whose course is governed by a definite set of socially acceptable rules" (Fabbri 1981, 1).

First, formal or technical rules come into play in the production and recording of musical sound. Such rules include the kinds of instruments used, the ways they are used, and their relationship to one another, but also the expected level of skill and the quality of sound recording, and are responsible for our ability to sense the social sonically.

Second, semiotic rules enable particular musical sounds to mean something; they enable particular sonic arrangements to articulate particular dimensions of social life—for instance, queer culture or high culture or blackness.

Third, there are behavioral rules, which govern the particular ways performers and audiences comport themselves in various settings — not only while performing or consuming music, but also in a more general sense. It is behavioral rules that enable performers and audiences to embody semiotic rules and therefore contribute to their further elaboration and penetration into the social.

Fourth, economic or juridical rules come into play when the cohesion of certain categories of musical sound assume the force of law or policy (for example, efforts to ban or promote certain kinds of music). Fabbri is brief in his discussion of this dimension of genre, but his statement that "these rules, the importance of which has actually been transformed into state laws, can be concealed behind the artist's independence or 'the anger of a generation'" (Fabbri [1981] 2004, 14), suggesting that he is referring specifically to how policy frameworks can bolster the authenticity claims of particular musical communities. In his review of Fabbri's typology, Frith proffers a looser interpretation, stating that "commercial and juridical rules . . . refer to the means of production of a music genre, to questions of ownership, copyright, financial reward and so on" (1996, 93).

A final set of rules identified by Fabbri are social and ideological rules, which derive from the ways various rules are ordered and codified in different genres. According to Fabbri, this ordering is determined by hyper-rules, which position the genre ideologically by arranging systems of ideas that help constitute it. These hyper-rules can be understood as ideological because they organize genres into ideas that present particular interpretations of the social, and ways of acting. The foregrounding of certain rules and the backgrounding of others work to articulate certain ideologies. For example, Luvaas (2013b) argues that Indonesian indie foregrounds technical and behavioral rules (the importance of musical eclecticism and affecting the looks and sounds) and backgrounds economic rules (by refraining from codifying an ideal "indie" position vis-à-vis major labels. This relative positioning of economic and technical rules can be seen as ideological because it proposes that one's autonomy and agency (i.e., indie-ness) can be discerned in expressive forms, rather than one's political-economic position vis-à-vis media capital.

Just as Fabbri's essay seeks to establish the coherence of genre categories as attributable to much more than the formal or technical qualities of musical sound, so have other authors drawn attention to the important non-sonic dimensions of popular music genres. Holt and Frith identify genre categories as emerging from mass mediation and the creation of markets, thereby positioning the categorizing of music into genres historically in a way that Fabbri does not. Both authors identify genre categories as a function of industrial production and mass consumption of information (i.e., modernity) and the resulting taste hierarchies that distinguish markets from one another. That is, genre is a function of popular music—music that is produced and consumed on industrial scales (and which includes but is not limited to the category of "pop"). For example, Holt states that "the very term genre emerged in the mid 19th century when processes of modernity were accelerating and new forms of modernity were beginning to emerge" (2007, 2). Frith (1996) discusses how Tin Pan Alley productions were labeled according to their imagined suitability for amateur or professional musicians. Scores produced by the same industrial processes were divided up according to the imagined contexts of their use—that is, "markets."

While Holt (2007) laments the paucity of studies on genre of popular music, and Weintraub avers that "genres remain under-researched and under-theorised" (2010, 12), we can see from the above discussion that the body of scholarship dedicated to understanding the forces implicated in genre construction is not insubstantial. It is true that among those studying Europe or North America, few have attempted to theorize how popular music genres generally (as opposed to particular genres) inform and shape the social. Rather, the common concern has been to identify the social factors implicated in processes of genre construction, to show how genres are far from natural categories, or groupings of sound objects that can objectively be placed in one category or another.

In this respect, some of the work on Indonesia advances the field of popular music genre studies, because it not only shows how genres are socially and culturally constructed, but also theorizes their foundational role in key social imaginaries, such as class. Popular music genres play important roles in pegging out broader social fields—a process that manifests itself in the ways genres attain coherence not only by adhering to certain rules, but also by constantly positioning themselves vis-à-vis one another. In particular, Richter's, Wallach's, and Weintraub's studies draw attention to the fact that the social and ideological qualities of genres are not only drawn through hyper-rules that order the technical, behavioral, semiotic, and commercial in relation to one another, but also through the position particular genres occupy in relation to others (Richter 2012; Wallach 2007; Weintraub 2010). Richter (2012) and Weintraub (2010) both argue that the aesthetic properties of genres enforce broader social effects by marking their adherents as inhabiting a place in a social hierarchy, structured by notions of high and low culture. Wallach dedicates his entire book to demonstrating how Indonesian popular music is a "metacultural field of ideological and social oppositions manifested in particular genre ideologies" (2007, 68). He avers that the assemblages of texts (spatial, visual, sonic) that work to constitute genres as metacultures index alternate ideological outlooks and "competing visions of modernity—the collectivist, egalitarian, national vision of Sukarno versus the individualist status-obsessed developmentalism of Suharto's New Order" (2007, 252).

DEVELOPMENTS IN THE GENRE SYSTEM

A number of developments have taken place in the twenty-first century that illustrate the rigidity of this genre system, as well as instances of its destabilization. The first pertains to the dispersal, appropriation (by the provincial lower classes), and subsequent recuperation of pop Indonesia in the mid-2000s as discussed in chapters 3 and 7. As advertising-funded television established itself following the deregulation of the industry in the late 1980s, and increasing numbers of Indonesians began to own television sets, pop Indonesia, a ubiquitous presence on television in the early 2000s, filtered into the everyday lives of Indonesians of all classes. As I argue in chapter 3, this represented a dispersal of the genre, which had formerly been associated with specifically middle-class musical affinities. In the mid-2000s, as evidenced by the rise to fame of Kangen Band (chapters 3 and 7), provincial poor people began to play their own versions of pop Indonesia, perceived by critics as misaligned with the proper rules of the genre—for example, slick production and a certain level of technical ability—suggesting that pop Indonesia had been appropriated by provincial dwellers as a result of its televisual circulation. This appropriation of pop was subsequently erased when forms of pop Indonesia being composed and performed by provincial dwellers were relabeled by Jakarta-based music executives who strove to explicitly associate the acts with the term *kampungan*, as pop Melayu, thus marking its distinction from pop Indonesia, a distinction exacerbated by this genre's absence from the music press (chapter 5). This reinstated the *kampungan-gedongan* / Melayu-Indonesia dichotomy that had been destabilized by the original rendering, and lends credence to arguments for the rigidity of the genre system.

A second development took place at the *kampungan* end of the scale, which will not be analyzed in this book but is worth mentioning here, for it serves to fill out the picture of the genre landscape in which this book's case studies are set. This development pertains to the splintering of dangdut and of its association with Islam, which had been established in the 1970s, through dangdut star Rhoma Irama's Islamically themed musical and filmic repertoire, as well as his political alliances (Barendregt and van Santen 2002; Frederick 1982; Weintraub 2010). However, there was also a stream of localized performances of dangdut that included sexualized performances by women (Browne 2000; Pioquinto 1995). In the 2000s, these performances began to be subjected to national circulation via digital mediation, as video compact disc recordings of such shows circulated far and wide. Weintraub (2008) discusses the case of Inul Daratista, an East Javanese woman from a poor family whose "drilling" dance style became nationally known as a result of VCD mediation, prompting Rhoma Irama to denounce her. Inul's drilling style and Irama's denunciation of it came to national attention at a time when a proposed, and highly controversial, antipornography bill was poised to pass the parliament. Support for Inul emerged among those opposed to the bill, which many saw as overreach by political Islamic groups, showing how dangdut was being used to challenge the Islamicization of social life and disrupting the genre's inherent link to Islam. At the same time, pop Indonesia, a genre that had been conventionally associated with a secular outlook, became, in the 2000s, increasingly Islamic — part of a broader Islamicization of middle-class consumer lifestyles (Schmidt 2017; Heryanto 1999; Barendregt 2006).

The picture that emerges from existing scholarship, and affirmed by the cases presented in this book, is one in which the genre system established in the Cold War period endures but is increasingly contested. On the one hand, masculinist middle-class formations continue to hold a privileged place in the delineation of the ideal local in the context of the local music boom. On the other, secular, urban-based middle-class men have begun to lose their dominant hold on chronicling national history, and Muslim women and the lower classes are playing more important roles in delineating ideal tropes.

For example, as I discuss in chapter 1, a sense of rock as more authentic than pop Indonesia, and of dangdut as entirely different from both (dangdut itself had no print media to represent it) emerged from the press of the New Order period (see also Weintraub 2006). This process of distinguishing took place in conversation with the inclusion and exclusion of particular genres from television broadcast. While pop Indonesia acts could gain exposure by appearing on the show devoted to pop aired on the state television, rock and dangdut musicians were barred from appearing on the show, which only served to entrench the idea that these were categories of popular music distinct from pop Indonesia. Moreover, rock was culturally elevated as a result of its exclusive association with the medium of print — a media form associated with the role that heroic, educated youth played in the beginnings of nationalism.

Ideals that had emerged in conversation with the evolution of popular music genres in the 1970s were afforded new life by the new technological paradigm in the twenty-first century. The expansion of commercial television accorded greater importance to audience measurement regimes in the way the public sphere was imagined, and this had the effect of reinforcing middle-class cultural ascendance (chapter 4). Licensees and branches of global print publications and recording labels translated themselves into the Indonesian context in such a way as to enable the retrieval of masculinist middle-class ideals, using the cultural form of the all-male rock band to peg out "proper" ways of producing and consuming local content (chapters 2 and 5).

At the same time, commercial television afforded rock musicians with new sources of income, enabling them to craft brand identities independently of recording labels. As they did so, they played with East-West/low-high/*kampungan-gedongan* dichotomies and, sometimes, the notions of middle-class cultural ascendance inherent to them (chapter 2). Digital recording extended access to pop Indonesia to lower-class provincial dwellers, enabling them to manipulate the genre by stretching its boundaries. Other digital technologies—mobile phones—opened lower-class markets for pop Indonesia, markets that were honed and tended by Jakarta-based intellectuals who heralded them, via television, as embodying a new kind of local ideal, the upwardly mobile Melayu/*kampungan* subject, thereby commodifying lower- classness in new ways (chapter 3). At the same time, the televisualization of pop Indonesia gave rise to a new kind of associational life—the pop fan group—whose members perform unpaid labor in the service of media capital but who also forge emergent lower-class solidarities based on affect and conspicuous consumption (not the discourse of political activism), and in which lower-class women play prominent roles (chapters 6 and 7). Chapter by chapter, the book presents cases that are revealing of both this fragmenting and of the enduring (albeit beleaguered) hold of masculinist middle-class formulations of the ideal local.

CHAPTER OUTLINES

The book is divided into three parts. Part I, "Technological Paradigms," chronicles the changes and continuities in the constitution and articulation of genre publics over the period 1965–2005. It provides a chronological account of developments in media regulation and policy, in ecologies of media technologies, and the establishment of key dichotomies structuring class (East/West, high/

low, *kampungan/gedongan*) and their subsequent fragmenting. This account unfolds through discussion of three case studies: that of *Aktuil* magazine, that of the rock band Slank, and that of the rise to national fame of the provincial Kangen Band. I use these cases to flesh out the two paradigms discussed above, by examining the media technologies and contents, and the particular kinds of class politics, that constituted them.

Chapter 1, "Establishing Class," shows how the reorganization of print media and popular music genres, as well as the important role played by state television, on the advent of the New Order enabled the imagining of the middle classes and the masses respectively. The chapter proceeds through an analysis of the rock magazine *Aktuil*, established in 1967, and argues that by addressing disparate groups of youths, the magazine enabled them to imagine their membership in an assembly of people positioned between the state and the masses. *Aktuil* drew on (and recirculated) discourses of print and rock as elevated forms to position its readers as members of a social middle. By reworking and melding two distinct preexisting notions of *pemuda* (male youth)—as highly educated pioneers of nationalism, and as raggedly attired revolutionary fighters, *Aktuil* proposed a new *pemuda* trope fit for the New Order period: the critical middle-class *pemuda* who was both highly literate and "raggedy-clad" (Peters 2009, 903) in a progressive rock kind of way.

The chapter draws on theories of publics to argue that by sketching this figure, *Aktuil* both enabled people to imagine their membership in a middle-class assembly and allowed certain kinds of materials and bodies (flared jeans, long-haired men) to serve as evidence of such an assembly's actual existence. This treatment of class formation departs from the prevailing analysis of the middle class as a function of economic growth coupled with the anticommunist ideology of the New Order regime. In the chapter, I argue that some revision of the factors responsible for the emergence of class structures in the 1970s is a necessary starting point for a history that seeks to foreground the role of technological change in the transformation of public culture. The chapter shines a light on the important role played by texts in circulation—magazines, stickers, advertisements—in the generation of a new social structure, offers a perspective that urges readers to turn away from the notion that political-economic developments are the primary determinant of social change, and paves the way for viewing the history of Indonesian capitalism as one marked by technological paradigms.

Chapters 2 and 3 chronicle the new fields of intellectual endeavor—specifically the manipulation of genres—emerging from a changed media environment resulting from media deregulation policies of the 1990s. Together, these chapters aim to establish the historical basis for the local music boom and the interplay of technological and human forces in the production of locality within it. Both chapters show how this interplay reflected broader trends emerging in consumerist Asia—the blurring of East-West dichotomies, for example. They also highlight some of the specific cultural consequences of media convergence in Indonesia. The concurrent expansion of commercial television and digital communication networks, and its coincidence with regime change, facilitated the commercial success of certain kinds of local content seen to reflect the political mood.

Chapter 2, "Consumer Citizenship," chronicles the 1990s' industrial transformation that underpinned the local music boom. It does so through a focus on the rock band Slank, which featured as a key endorser of Joko Widodo's 2014 presidential election campaign, suggesting that the band had come to be seen as iconic of the post-authoritarian moment. The chapter inquires into how Slank came to be seen as embodying the "new" Indonesia. It details how Slank pioneered the localization of rock in the early 1990s, by associating the genre with lower-class street life and *kampungan*, thereby encouraging lower-class men to embrace rock and understand it as a "local" form—previously it was considered derivative of a more authentic, Euro-American scene, as most Indonesian rock bands sang in English and played cover songs. By localizing rock in this way, Slank laid the groundwork for the predominance in the local music boom of a masculine band culture, and posited the all-male rock band as symbolic of an ideal form of national belonging. In the chapter, I discuss how Slank validated the notion of the critical male as the prime representative and chronicler of the local music boom, thereby retrieving notions of critical youth as inherently linked to print media and rock music, developed in *Aktuil*.

The chapter examines how these processes—the commercial success of Slank's *kampungan* rock, and the valorization of all-male rock bands as the epitome of a new Indonesia—were enabled by a new environment for media industries and technologies following the deregulation of television and recording in the late 1980s and early 1990s. It attributes the local music boom to the particular ways that private television and a newly arranged recording industry intersected in the 1990s, opening space for performers themselves to shape their own brand images, including, in several cases, brand images that rested on elaborate moral philosophies espousing visions for post-authoritarian futures. As the Slank case shows, these visions were often commodified when rendered as endorsements in TV ads for instant noodles, motorbikes, cigarettes, or mobile phone providers.

While the first two chapters are concerned with the constitution of a rock-related masculinity through successive technological paradigms, chapter 3 examines changes in the articulation of *kampungan*, through a study of the rise to fame of the provincial boy band Kangen Band. It explores the mainstream production of Kangen Band as a pop Melayu band, and the championing of *kampungan* that was associated with this assignation.

The chapter begins by coupling a review of works on the construction of Melayu as a genre with a musical and lyrical analysis of contemporary pop Melayu compositions to understand this new genre's place in a history of Melayu's development. I show how contemporary pop Melayu's links to dangdut are tenuous. Rather than a child of dangdut, this new genre can be understood as a function of technological change. At the time Kangen Band rose to fame, mobile phones were becoming increasingly integral to the exchange and circulation of popular music commodities, and television, telephone companies (telcos), and recording companies forged a "tactical convergence" (Mishra 2016, 103) to market lucrative musical products known as ringback tones to the lower classes, imagined now as avidly consuming. In the chapter, I show how new players in the industry, whom I refer to as "hinge occupants" (Mazzarella 2003), played key roles in this work of heralding the lower classes by using pop Melayu and *kampungan* as modes of address.

Part II, *Gedongan*, presents two chapters that examine how middle-classness is being built and represented in the context of a deregulated, post-developmental media environment that is rich in images, partly as a result of television's expansion, and harbors an array of multinational media corporations that are marked as at once global and Indonesian (for example, Sony Indonesia, MTV Indonesia, *Rolling Stone* Indonesia). It considers the role these resources—photography, moving images, and the global brand—play in the construction of new, dominant formulations of ideal citizenship. In chapter 1, I considered the roles print literacy played in evoking a sense of middle-classness in the 1970s. In this section I explore how, in the early twenty-first century, people manipulated images in order to get a sense of what it meant to be middle class in a democratizing, rapidly globalizing Indonesia.

Chapter 4 presents three cases that attest to the centrality of images to such experimentations with identity. I begin the chapter with a study of MTV Indonesia's VJ (video jockey, aka MTV presenter) competition. The channel's tag line—*Gue banget* (It's so me)—provides an instance of a broader valorization of individualism, and the competition presents young Indonesian MTV aspirants performing their individuality for the camera in the hope of winning the competition for their very *gue banget*-ness. I argue that the competition exemplifies how global corporate media brands produce locality by "settling down" on local bodies (Mazzarella 2003), making the global brand appear as a true and natural reflection of people's underlying desires. I then go on to analyze images of two pop Indonesia acts—Krisdayanti and Superman Is Dead—to show how producing the authentic local body in globalizing Indonesia is a project not limited to global media corporations. In the wake of regime change in the early twenty-first century, self-images served artists as realms of experimentation and exploration, enabling them to play with notions of self-transformation, and also authenticity, and to come to grips with how the two might feasibly be interwoven.

One of the features of the Indonesian music industry in the twenty-first century has been a concerted interest in the past. For example, *Rolling Stone* accords considerable page space to features devoted to rock heroes of the 1970s or 1980s, and newly established Indonesian branches of global recording labels frequently sponsor comebacks and tribute albums dedicated to rock heroes from the 1970s. Through a study of one such comeback, that of the rock band God Bless, chapter 5 explores this nostalgia industry, identifying it as a function of the reconfiguration of global cultural flows and the emergence of Asian sites as important sources of global popular culture. I argue that, while it brings to light and celebrates formerly unacknowledged dimensions of the archipelago's cultural history, this nostalgia industry is at the same time founded on a concerted effort of forgetting about some of the more challenging dimensions of Indonesia's political history. The chapter considers how the emerging middle spaces of consumerist globalism, in which new kinds of cultural nationalism (including the local music boom) are nurtured, are implicated in this forgetting, and the mechanisms by which certain histories are papered over so that others can be celebrated.

The third and final section of the book, *Kampungan*, traces patterns of organizational life emerging in the context of the new technological paradigm forged by both television and digital technologies. Solidarities form when global consumerism settles on bodies, both drawing them in and opening opportunities for ordinary people to find ways to exercise their agency. As television began to play an increasingly important role in the production and consumption of popular music generally, so did performers' relationships to their audiences begin to change. Official fan groups became more common and more central to the staging, watching, and consuming of popular music acts. Consequently, being a fan of popular music came to be equated with being a member of a fan group, attending regular fan gatherings, and adhering to a particular moral philosophy customized in line with the idol's brand image. Scores of such groups now honeycomb the Indonesian public sphere and serve as a new kind of associational life in and through which various notions of the civic are practiced. This section of the book includes two case studies of such fan groups coalescing around popular music performances that explicitly address the lower classes.

Chapter 6, "Television's Children," continues the discussion of Kangen Band begun in chapter 3. In that chapter, I focused on the processes by which Kangen Band came to be assigned as a Melayu act. In this chapter I discuss the public forms that emerged in response to Kangen Band both prior to and following its mainstream success. This focus affords a view of both the unnoticed, informal media economies that elude corporate production, and the new forms of associational life emerging from the televisualization of popular music. The chapter considers two new forms of collective life evident in the Kangen Band case: the uncanny counterpublic coalescing around the circulation of pirate CDs, and the fan group that is a product of corporate production processes. In different ways, both exist at a tangent to the corporate brand. Therefore, they generate meanings of *kampungan* that contest those being endorsed by big media institutions, such as recording labels and television.

The final chapter, "Provincial Cosmopolitanism," discusses Nanoe Biroe, a foremost member of a new wave of "pop Bali" performers who compose and perform their songs in Balinese. This development is seen as evidence of a shift in language ideologies as a result of administrative decentralization after the fall of Suharto. I examine how Nanoe Biroe writes low Balinese into emerging discourses of the provincial modern by drawing on Slank's pluralist moral philosophy, and study the technological assemblages that circulate Nanoe Biroe's words around the provincial cityscape. The chapter also discusses how young female fans adapt and adopt these assemblages to enhance their visibility and their mobility. By doing so, they demonstrate how the new, consumerist paradigm can be harnessed to propose novel social alternatives that accommodate lower-class women.

PART I

Technological Paradigms

ONE

Establishing Class

This chapter explores the origins of Indonesia's middle class through a focus on the pop music magazine *Aktuil* (1967–1984). *Aktuil* was established in the context of the radical reorganization of the press and of popular music on the advent of the New Order, and studying the magazine reveals how such reorganizing gave rise to the quiet evolution of Indonesia's middle class. The chapter foregrounds these processes by examining how the magazine addressed its readers in ways that allowed them to feel that they inhabited a middle social space, between the state and the masses. *Aktuil*'s circulation gave rise to a middle-class genre public—a virtual social entity heralded into being by overlapping modes of address, that touched not only on popular music genres but also a rhetoric of print.

By proposing that the middle class was a virtual entity, the imagination of which was enabled by the reorganization of the press and of popular music, the chapter departs from a dominant perspective that attributes to the state a pivotal role in the growth of the middle class in the 1970s. In the late 1980s and early 1990s, a surge of literature appeared on the subject. Many observers of the Indonesian middle class aver that the New Order provided the political and economic conditions for middle-class growth, and quite a lot of scholarly activity has focused on quantifying that growth (Hadiz and Dhakidae 2005; Lev 1990; Tanter and Young 1990; Crouch 1986; Dick 1985; Hadi Jaya 1999; Robison 1996; Zulkarnaen, Siagian, and Ida 1993). Scholars disagreed about the nature and definition of class and about the relationship between middle-class groups and democratization (Lev 1990; Liddle 1990; Mackie 1990; Robison 1990; Slamet 1990; Subianto 1999; Zulkarnaen, Siagian, and Ida 1993).

Some of these works serve as the basis for important contributions to contemporary debates about the involvement of Indonesia's middle class in overthrowing the New Order regime in 1998. Richard Robison has consistently argued that the middle class never emerged as an effective political force during the New Order period. In 1990 he wrote: "Whilst in the last decade the physical ranks of the middle classes have swelled with the inflow of oil money, its liberal elements have been hammered into political ineffectiveness by the regime on the campuses, in the media, and within the state apparatuses" (1990, 134). Consequently, Robison and others have argued, rather than democratization, regime change has entailed the consolidation of the "predatory state and private oligarchies" (Hadiz and Robison 2005, 220–241; Hadiz and Robison 2013; Winters 2013). Others have challenged these arguments. In his reappraisal of Robison's assessment of state-capitalist class relations under the New Order, for example, Aspinall concludes by stating, "Looking at capital is not enough. The Indonesian masses and middle classes too are starting to write their own history, and we need to broaden our analytical focus accordingly" (Aspinall 2013, 240).

While debates about the role of the middle class in overthrowing the New Order regime and in shaping the post-Suharto polity have blossomed, they have been very much focused on the present or recent past. The "underlying agreement" about the New Order state's pivotal role in the genesis of the Indonesian middle class remains largely unrevised, and this leaves some important questions unanswered. If Suharto's overthrow were testimony to the assertiveness of societal forces, what historical conditions enabled such forces to recognize their power? Is it possible that scholars writing in the 1980s of the evolution of the middle class missed signs of its agency and autonomy? If we are to turn our focus away from capital accumulation, what conceptual tools would be aptly applied to an exploration of such possibilities?

A study of *Aktuil* provides an opportunity to employ fresh conceptual tools to understand the genesis of the middle class in the 1970s. *Aktuil* spoke to a varied group of urban-dwelling youth, sometimes with little in common but an advanced level of print literacy.[1] To understand the political significance of these disparate groups' imagined assembly via *Aktuil*, I turn to work on publics. Membership in *Aktuil*'s middle-class genre public, I argue, served to imbue young readers with a sense of their own agency. In *Aktuil*, two figures—the female runaway and the young man with a rock sensibility—address readers as those in possession of such agency. These representations do not sit comfortably with political-economic analyses of the period, which characterize the middle class as heavily dependent on the state, and politically ineffectual. They can, however, be accommodated as features of a public emerging from the circulation of texts.

Publics are virtual assemblies resulting from a common orientation to texts in circulation. Texts, in other words, address such assemblies into being, and the modes of address of these texts are forcefully shaped by the discursive qualities of their mediating technologies. Publics have served as a key concept in scholarly considerations of the implications of the development of mass media for democracy. As Michael Warner points out, only a faith in the existence of publics can render notions of political will and consumer agency plausible. "Without a faith, justified or not, in self-organized publics, organically linked to our activity in our very existence, capable of being addressed, capable of action, we would be nothing but the peasants of capital" (Warner 2002a, 69).[2] Warner's discussion draws attention to publics' elusive power. Wherever there is mass media, there is a faith in the existence of a collective capable of being addressed by that media. In the *Aktuil* case, such politics are discernable in the way the magazine depicted youth. In particular, the dogged persistence of the notion of youth as historical agents, or *pemuda*, in the magazine, suggests that they were by no means "hammered into political ineffectiveness" (Robison 1990, 134).

Pemuda literally translates as "male youth," but the term specifically denotes youth at the forefront of social change, and does so by harking back to two distinct periods of young people's political mobilization: the 1928 generation of highly educated, nationalist youth, and the 1945 generation of revolutionary youth who took up arms against the Dutch. From *Aktuil*'s outset, *pemuda* played a crucial role in providing readers with a historical position from which to orient themselves toward the West.[3]

Pemuda refers to men, but the gendered dimensions of *Aktuil*'s portrayal of middle-class youth changed throughout the magazine's career. That portrayal reveals a progressive masculinizing of the notion of critical youth as the New Order wore on. In early editions, women featured prominently, and the figure of the mobile young woman plays a primary role in articulating the magazine's message. Later editions began to pay more attention to Indonesian men, both by putting forward the image of the young man with a rock sensibility as an ideal figure, and by directly addressing a young, male, middle-class *reading* public. In this way, *Aktuil* created a new archetype, for the overlap of rock and print in the magazine had the effect of bringing together the two distinct legacies of *pemuda* mentioned above, and of creating space for this new composite in a new world full of consumption and exchange, and of commodities.

WESTERN POP AND THE
COUNTERREVOLUTIONARY MODERN

Several writers have noted the important role Western-style music—pop Indonesia and rock—played in the military's efforts to convey a sense of ideological
rupture and cultural novelty, following the overthrow of Guided Democracy and
the violent suppression of the left (Setiyono 2001; Sopiann 2001b; Mulyadi 2009;
Sen 2003; Weintraub 2017). Such close ties can only be understood in the light of
the prohibitions placed on the airing of North American and European popular
music and film in the national public space during the course of Guided Democracy (1959–1965). In 1959, Sukarno delivered a speech in which he espoused the
need to take steps to protect national culture from foreign influences. Initially,
these steps included banning Western commercial pop on the national public
radio, Radio Republik Indonesia (RRI). Further steps to protect the national
culture were taken in 1963, when a Presidential Decision forbade any public
airing of rock and roll, and in 1964, when police operations undertaken in the
provincial city of Bandung were aimed at publicly burning Elvis Presley records
and "disciplining" young men with shaggy, Beatles-style haircuts. In 1965, members of the band Koes Bersaudara were arrested after attending a house party
where they sang the Beatles' song "I Saw Her Standing There."[4]

After September 30, 1965, the army began tactically to undermine the ban
on public performances of Western-style music. Krishna Sen notes how anti-
Sukarnoist student activists used pirate radio stations to broadcast both anticommunist messages and Western pop music, and were protected as they did
so by the military:

> One of the best known [of such pirate radio stations], Radio Ampera, set up
> by activists, including brothers Soe Hok Gie and Arief Budiman, broadcast
> for a time from the home of Mashuri, then a next-door neighbor and trusted
> political ally of Soeharto. While technically illegal, anticommunist and anti-
> Sukarno broadcasts were not just condoned but often actively aided by as-
> cendant factions of the military. While based at Mashuri's residence, Radio
> Ampera, for instance, was openly protected by pro-Soeharto troops. . . . The
> student stations also flouted RRI's ban on certain types of Western pop music,
> by broadcasting popular songs from prohibited bands like the Beatles and
> Rolling Stones. (Sen 2003, 578)

Additionally, Mulyadi states that the military used state-prohibited Western-style commercial pop music to interest people in a new regime of governance, beginning with the mass killings and arrests of 1965–1966. He contends that the Body for Cooperation between Artists and the Army Strategic Command (Badan Kerjasama Seniman-Kostrad) promoted a series of "soldier stages" (*panggung prajurit*), inviting (as part of an "effort towards moral transformation") artists to perform the kinds of songs that had been banned (Mulyadi 2009, 20), and details how, from late 1965 through the early 1970s, live and telecast (on public television, TVRI) musical events were used to associate the military uniform with pop music. The military uniform was ubiquitous on TVRI's music show *Kamera Ria*, since after 1965 senior military personnel established and played (dressed in their uniforms), or sponsored, Western pop bands. It was that kind of cultural environment that yielded the following lyric, published in RRI's magazine in 1967:

"CAMOUFLAGE-SHIRTED GUY"

Ah ah ah . . . how lovely / To sit by the shore / And dream of /
   My camouflage-shirted guy
An army man / In a camouflage shirt / With his beret on /
   Oh, he's so handsome and brave
He stole my heart / The pride of my country / I will be in awe of him /
   I will always remember your service. (Cited in Mulyadi 2009, 29)

Aktuil was established in the midst of the military's concerted incorporation of pop into its performance of newness. It was founded in 1967 as a biweekly magazine and became the first popular-music publication to emerge during the transition from Sukarno's Guided Democracy to Suharto's New Order. *Aktuil* was the brainchild of a young man named Denny Sabrie, an avid Deep Purple fan and the son of Sabrie Gandanegara, the vice governor of the province of West Java (1966–1974); and Toto Rahardja, who managed a dance troupe. The magazine *Diskorina*, where the younger Sabrie was formerly based, did not afford him the opportunity to write serious rock criticism, hence his idea to establish *Aktuil* in Bandung, West Java (Mulyadi 2009, 52). *Aktuil* survived until 1984 (Mulyadi 2009; Solihun 2004; Sopiann 2001b). At its peak, in 1973–1974, *Aktuil* boasted a circulation of 126,000 — up to triple that of *Tempo*, the celebrated news magazine, which up to the late 1970s had a circulation of "around 25,000 or 40,000" (Steele

2005).[5] By 1977, sales of *Aktuil* had dropped to thirty thousand, and by 1979 they were merely three to four thousand. In 1979, the title was sold to Sondang Pariaman Napitupulu, its headquarters moved to Jakarta, and its music-related and literary content were dropped (Sopiann 2001b).[6]

I based this chapter's analysis on 126 editions of *Aktuil* dated from 1967 to 1974. Editions 1–46 (1967–1969) are in A5 (page) format (148 × 210 mm, or about 5.8 × 8.25 inches) and priced between Rp50 and Rp75 (approximately 25–35 US cents). Editions 67–157 (1971–1974) are in A4 format (210 × 297 mm, or about 8.25 × 11.7 inches) and priced at Rp150 (approximately 40 US cents). Aside from the page size, there are other differences between earlier and later editions, which is why I discuss them separately.

In some ways *Aktuil*'s address of a new kind of youth overlapped with the military project of using pop to evince the novelty of New Order rule.[7] Reading through the first three editions of *Aktuil*, one gains a strong sense of the magazine as a space devoted to addressing a community of youths who are distinctive for their lifestyle choices, which set them apart from their parents and other authority figures. Short stories and graphic dramas recount conflicts between parents and their teenage children over their chosen partner, and some of them openly depict scenes of sex before marriage ("Aku Lahir" 1970; Purbaya 1970a, b; Didiek W 1970). Editorials criticize the authorities' education policies and corruption in the administration of schools, and refer to "our generation of schoolchildren" (Carr 1970, 8–9). Features directly align pop-music consumption with young people's inherent desire for freedom from their parents (Surya 1969, 10–11).

Additionally, both the military project and early editions of *Aktuil* focused on women. The late 1960s and early 1970s saw the rise to prominence of a number of female rock bands and soloists, and in promotional photographs these women are often shown donning military uniform or accompanied by soldiers.[8] "Camouflage-Shirted Guy," for example, was penned and performed by Lilis Suryani and was included in an album the cover of which features her in camouflage. Dara Puspita, the foremost all-female rock band of the period, was often photographed in military uniform. In 1965, the Army Strategic Command invited the Dutch band the Blue Diamonds to perform a series of shows at the Hotel Indonesia, and Dara Puspita appeared as the opening act.

Similarly, in *Aktuil*, Indonesian youth assume a distinctly female form. Early editions of the magazine were primarily devoted to celebrating Western pop and included many images of the West and Western people. They included reviews of Hollywood films, publication of Western pop songs' lyrics, gossip about Western bands, and reports of shows in the United States and the United Kingdom. Western musicians are shown to sport defiantly long hair—an antidote, perhaps, to the Indonesian military ideal, but this coiffure never settles down on the heads of Indonesian male musicians, who in fact are scarcely present in early editions of the magazine. The scarcity of images of Indonesian performers in *Aktuil* may seem to position Indonesians as spectators, rather than producers, and to more broadly infer young Indonesians as consumers of the West, rather than agents of their own destiny. But at the same time, reading these early editions is not like bathing in images of the West. Indonesian women are strikingly present.

Women, sometimes scantily clad or smoking in risqué fashion (or both), adorn the front and back covers of many early editions. They are never the subject of the much-sought-after poster in the centerfold, but Indonesian female singers appear as subjects of feature articles (Hasanta 1970; Hendrik Z 1969; Hoo 1970; Ratna Press 1969; "Tinny" 1970; Wajah 1970). In *Aktuil*, women are shown to have complex opinions and to be sexually active. They are mobile, sometimes transnationally so; they are runaways; they are theater critics; they serve alongside men as officeholders in the *Aktuil* fan club, revealing that women, too, read *Aktuil*. They also appear as the main protagonists in short stories penned by men, which explore moral considerations surrounding sex and arranged marriages. Sometimes these women are sexually active before marriage (although generally this sexual activity does not serve them well), and sometimes they enter into painful and prolonged conflicts with their mothers regarding relationships and partner choices (Purbaya 1970a, b).

Arranged marriage is a consistent theme in the struggles of the women represented in *Aktuil*. It is the main reason for their interest in premarital flight from the family home. I have no way of knowing whether they are genuine letters, or penned by the magazine's editors, but the following letters, published in the feature titled "Help" in a 1969 edition (*Aktuil* 30, p. 53), highlight how the magazine strove to use female figures to portray generational conflict:

Susie, mum and dad want you to come home. The problem is resolved. We recognize we were wrong and that you must follow your heart to find your soul mate. You should bring Herman home and immediately ask for dad's blessing. Come home Sus! Longing parents, Somatri, Bandung

Mami, Lily has left home to follow her heart. Don't try to find me. One thing is clear, I am choosing my own man. We will be responsible for ourselves now, we realize we are no longer considered part of the family. Please pray for us. Naughty child, destination somewhere.

Students, then, allied with the military in order to overthrow Guided Democracy, and all-female pop bands provided that effort with a soundtrack. Together, all-female bands and the students furnished regime change with an air of fun-loving moral elevation, helping to paper over the violent reinterpretation of modernity that proceeded with the regime's establishment. The figure of Lily — the letter-writing naughty daughter whose destination was uncertain — may be seen as consistent with the spirit of youth that was given space to blossom because it endorsed generational change and historical rupture. But this does not mean that in every respect the spirit of youth fell into step with the regime's hopes for a compliant populace. As it happens, Dara Puspita also performed shows sponsored by *Aktuil*, including their 1971–1972 "spectacular" tour of the country. *Aktuil*, however, never published photographs of military personnel or of musicians wearing military uniform. The absence of the military uniform in *Aktuil* reveals the tensions resulting from foregrounding women in the military's notion of the counterrevolutionary modern. In *Aktuil* — very much a child of the counterrevolution — women broke free of the military uniform and, wearing civilian clothes, insisted on defying their fathers.[9]

Also of interest is *Aktuil*'s choice of language to sketch the category of youth, for this, too, points to how the magazine's address worked to imbue readers with a sense of their own agency. In this respect, *Aktuil* problematizes key dimensions of New Order–era pop Indonesia as interpreted by scholars. There is a tendency in scholarship examining Western-style pop, or pop Indonesia, to interpret the cultural practices associated with this genre as either politically benign or pro-regime. According to Siegel, pop Indonesia–devoted magazines for youth propagated apolitical youth ideals that suited the regime's interest in maintaining order and stability. Based on his analysis of *Topchords* magazine, he argues that new terms were coined in the New Order period to denote ideal youth. Specifically, the term *remaja*, which means teen, came to replace that of *pemuda*, which carries political connotations "of the sort the Soeharto regime has made difficult" (Siegel 1986, 201; Wallach 2007; Yampolsky 1989, 9–10).

Aktuil, however, reveals that the term *pemuda* was very present in writing about pop music in magazines devoted to youth. For example, a 1969 feature article titled "Pop Music Yields Creativity, Art and Revolution" serves as a prime example of how *Aktuil* addressed youths as distinct from their parents, and it employs the term *pemuda* liberally. The article firmly differentiated between "the old establishment who are the pawns of the power-holders" and the young, "who want to free themselves from the imprisoning chains that so disgust them" (Surya 1969, 10–11). It calls on the young (*pemuda*) to wage a nonviolent, antiestablishmentarian war through music and fashion. Gde Putra, who assisted me with the research for this chapter, shared with me his insights into how the article attempts to redefine the term *pemuda* and to align it with consumption of Western popular culture and points of view — the article hints at pop music's function as a soft power to aid the counterrevolution. But what is equally interesting about the article is that it does not clearly detach from its *pemuda* legacy. It does attempt to associate *pemuda* with pop consumption. There is no easy distinction in *Aktuil* between Western-pop-consuming, apolitical youth and revolutionary youth, critical of Western influence of the preceding period. The magazine calls out to a hybrid: *pemuda*-teen.

Pemuda remained a consistent feature of Aktuil's address, but by 1971 the willful young female pop fans and performers had faded from its pages, reflecting changes at the magazine. In 1970, Denny Sabrie appointed the writer Remy Sylado as editor.[10] As a result, the literary content of the magazine began to change. At the same time, *Aktuil* also appointed Maman Husen Somantri as designer, and his idea to include bonuses such as stickers and iron-ons in each edition of the magazine was adopted and proved successful. Circulation soared as a result.

In addition to including bonuses inside the magazine, there were other design changes. Later editions are in the larger A4 format, and their contents are ordered into neatly arranged columns. The material still reveals a consistent interest in gazing at the West, but the way in which Indonesian performance is portrayed, especially its gender makeup, has changed. In earlier editions, female performers are prominent. However, these women are never present in national spaces. They are either highly mobile — running from their parents, touring Europe — or posing in spaces notable for their lack of geographical distinction. The "pop" feeling of early editions exists outside the spaces of the nation. In later editions, the magazine begins to accord more page space to Indonesian male rock musicians and to address readers not only as youth, distinct from the authorities and their parents, but also as young rock fans, distanced from mass production and consumption of pop music.

PRODUCING ROCK, PRODUCING MIDDLENESS

Over the decade following the New Order's establishment, three distinct genres emerged: dangdut, pop Indonesia, and rock. Pop and rock developed separately along similar trajectories, but there were also distinctions between them. As mentioned, Western-style pop music was incorporated into the "effort towards moral transformation" required immediately after 1965 (Mulyadi 2009, 20). Subsequently, many of those performing this genre became quite closely associated with the ruling group, Golkar (Partai Golongan Karya, Party of the Functional Groups), and state media channels in general. Some pop Indonesia musicians took part in 1971 and 1977 in a so-called "artists' safari," part of Golkar's campaign to win elections. By virtue of their participation, artists were afforded entry to the state television station's program devoted to pop music, *Aneka Ria Safari*, which served them as a platform for promotion and for gaining other, better-paying gigs. This meant that state television, which was the sole terrestrial channel in the country up until 1989, played an important role in the mediation of pop.

Long-haired male musicians, by contrast, were not allowed to appear on *Aneka Ria Safari*,[11] and this ban excluded a great many rock musicians from television broadcasts. Contrasting TVRI's exclusion of rock, later editions of *Aktuil* very much promoted the genre.[12] Above, I recounted how earlier editions of the magazine sketch pop as a continuum stretching from the masculine West to feminine Indonesia. Long-haired Western male musicians were featured in early editions, but never Indonesian men, long-haired or otherwise. Later editions, however, depict Indonesia as a masculine realm and include many images of long-haired Indonesian male musicians. In an interview with Soleh Solihun, editor Remy Sylado confessed: "Ha ha ha. We *Aktuil* editors were all *rock barat* [Western rock] propagandists" (Solihun 2004, 20).

What propaganda did *Aktuil* editors seek to espouse? Solihun avers that *Aktuil*'s appraisals of local rock bands were full of hyperbole and liberally applied the term "superstar" to local rock performers; to retain readers' interest, *Aktuil* "transformed itself into a glittering stage" (Solihun 2004, 21). But the reason for the emergence of the figure of the Indonesian male rock musician in later editions is not entirely clear. Arguably, the increase in page space devoted to Indonesian male rock musicians may be seen to reflect the maturation of the Indonesian rock scene. The sounds of Western rock were more accessible in the 1970s than they had been in the previous decade, owing to the proliferation of cassette-tape technology and the establishment of outfits like Aquarius Musikindo, which made and sold illegitimate copies of existing, copyrighted Western albums. A 2011 compilation album of progressive rock songs from the 1970s showcases a wide array of Indonesian cover bands from the 1970s.[13] It suggests that the progressive turn in rock in the late 1960s and the passage of those sounds to young Indonesians' ears via pirated (bootleg) cassettes may have inspired a wave of amateur Indonesian progressive rock bands. Certainly, advertisements in later editions of *Aktuil* are suggestive of a healthy amateur rock scene. Many of these advertisements are for stores and schools specializing in musical instruments and music instruction.

It is important to stress that *Aktuil* was not exclusively devoted to rock. Its later editions adopted the slogan "for the young and the young at heart," and this addressed youth in general, not just fans of rock and roll. In this way, *Aktuil*'s later and earlier editions resemble one another. But there are also important differences between them. Early editions address readers as a generation of consumers well positioned to reap the benefits of regime change, and later editions strive to distinguish readers as discerning consumers, critical of the regime. I see the emphasis on rock as very much facilitating this new address, rather than as a reflection of developments in the rock scene taking place elsewhere. Rock was a vital part of the magazine's ability to address middle-class youth as culturally elevated and as distinct from both the dangdut-consuming masses and from mass-produced pop Indonesia. As mentioned, both rock and pop Indonesia remained features of the magazine throughout the 1970s, but rock's increasing prominence coincided with efforts to position the magazine socially in new ways. Just as *Aktuil* began to include images of long-haired Indonesian musicians, it began to interpret these images for readers as indicators of musical quality.

In the 1970s, most rock bands performed in English, and this positioned the genre as culturally elevated.[14] *Aktuil* added to such high-culture nuances by championing rock musicians while denigrating dangdut and pop Indonesia (Weintraub 2006, 416). In 1973, for example, two published letters to the editor contrast musical quality and creative freedom with the (stifling) process of recording and the interests of recording companies (Annabella 1973, 6; Simatupang 1973, 127). In 1974, a published complaint emerges about the band AMPY's cheap publicity stunts and compares them to "selling soy sauce" (Hara-Hara 1974, 6). In a published interview earlier that year, Bens Leo invited Jopie Item to assess the quality of Indonesian pop Indonesia songs, and they both agreed that the commercially successful pop band Koes Plus did not deserve high ratings (Leo 1974, 2–3).[15] *Aktuil* readers similarly displayed an interest in conspicuously disliking pop Indonesia. In an interview with Soleh Solihun, one such reader, Aceng Abdullah, confessed that, in the 1970s, he dared not purchase a Koes Plus album, despite his secret liking for the music (Solihun 2004, 19).

Rock music's meanings as determined elsewhere almost certainly contributed to positioning the magazine as culturally elevated. Fornas avers that a globally circulating discourse of rock maintains the genre as a culturally elevated form, as distinct from mass-produced pop, and this bias clearly permeates interpretations of rock published in *Aktuil* (Fornas 1995). However, other closer-to-home developments also influenced the meanings of *Aktuil*'s rock "propaganda." Not only do later editions of the magazine deride pop and dangdut; some also protest TVRI's ban on long-haired musicians. For example, in a 1973 interview, Sugiono MP asks the pop singer Anna Manthovani for her opinion on the TVRI ban, and Manthovani replies by describing the ban as "regrettable" (Sugiono 1973, 30).

Earlier that year the magazine included the following letter, which criticized TVRI:

When Will TE-VE-ER-I Be Consistent?!?
I would like to use this space to express my humble opinion. Keep in mind, it is the opinion of a stupid person. The problem is this: I have begun to notice that in a number of respects, TVRI (I always read it as TE-VE-ER-I, but I am an amateur in matters of proper pronunciation) has adopted positions that are utterly unacceptable, even to a stupid person like myself. The policy on long hair, for example. TE-VE-ER-I has decided that no male with long hair will be allowed to perform in the recording studio. Only if a football player happens to have long hair, and that player is playing in a match that is broadcast live on TVRI, will the station be party to broadcasting images of men with long hair. This was the reason given for why Bimbo [a pop group from Bandung] was banned from TVRI. About this matter, I want to ask, in all my stupidity: "What does TE-VE-ER-I want, and why is it discriminating against men with long hair?" Nia Gantini (Gantini 1973, 6).

In its early years in the late 1960s, *Aktuil* was primarily concerned with challenging the anticolonial, revolutionary rhetoric of the former regime, partly by being seen to embrace all the West had to offer. Gantini's letter shows how, by the early 1970s, the magazine and its readers began to also set themselves apart from the new power holders. This development flags an emerging, dissenting middle-class subjectivity that manifested itself in student protests and key news outlets' waning support for the regime.[16] Its presence in *Aktuil* reveals how growing uncertainty about the regime was reflected not only in student activism and journalism but also in popular culture.

The middle-class youth that *Aktuil* addressed by no means constituted a significant political force capable of interfering with the government. *Aktuil* reached peak circulation just as the New Order regime was beginning to set down lasting roots. After a crackdown on student dissidents in 1974, hundreds of people were detained, and twelve publications were banned. Flush with revenue from oil sales after global prices rose in 1971, the government implemented an economic policy that encouraged the growth of small and medium-scale businesses, securing, according to Aspinall (2005, 26), the qualified support of the middle class: "Although the 1970s saw considerable discontent among groups with independent incomes and professional interests in a free public sphere (notably private lawyers and journalists), overall the middle class remained small, insecure and worried about unrest. . . . Most saw little point in openly challenging the state when its supremacy was so clear and while it was delivering economic growth."

Readers of *Aktuil* were among those who enjoyed the fruits of the economic growth, as evidenced by the increasingly abundant advertisements for musical instruments, fashion items, and music lessons that appeared in the magazine in the early to mid-1970s. They also enjoyed cultivating identities as discontented, critical citizens. While *Aktuil* was insignificant as a political opposition, its positioning of its readers *was* politically significant in other ways. Its emphasis on rock created distance between its readers and TVRI and mass-produced music. It also ipso facto was rock's voice in the media. Rock relied on *Aktuil* for its elaboration, and the sense of rock consumers as a public could only flow from reading *Aktuil*. Later editions, then, do not just address readers as rock consumers. They also address rock consumers as readers. Securing this link between rock and reading (which I expand on below) was crucial because it bound the notion of belonging to a social middle not only to popular culture consumption but also to critique. To understand how it did so, we need to consider the social implications of the reorganization of the press in the early days of the New Order.

THE REORGANIZATION OF THE PRESS

In the first half of the 1960s, most newspapers were linked to party politics and collectively known as *pers perjuangan* (lit., press of struggle), which Hill (1994, 14) describes thus: "The 1950s and early sixties were characterized by a vibrant, often caustically partisan press, organized along party lines. Technologically and financially impoverished but richly committed to stimulating public debate and mobilizing public opinion, even if this brought it into direct conflict with government policies." This situation changed dramatically under the New Order. Hill writes that in March of 1965, twenty-nine newspapers had been closed because of their support of *anti*communism. In the aftermath of October 1965, forty-six more newspapers were banned for *supporting* communism (1994, 34). By 1969, the number of extant newspapers and magazines had been reduced to half the 1964 level (1994, 15). Farid avers that the annihilation of the language of anti-imperialism in New Order–era public discourse was partly achieved through the speedy establishment of new systems for state control of the press (Farid 2005).

In this reorganized environment, journalists fell under a great degree of state surveillance. Moreover, news publications were no longer party organs and therefore imagined their readership in new ways. The reorganization of the press, then, gave rise not only to new kinds of journalistic writing but also forged new audiences for that writing. News publications' intended destination could no longer be the front porch of those who, by reading a particular newspaper, identified as a member of a particular political party. It had to be the front porch of those who, by choosing to read a particular newspaper, identified as a member of a social or demographic group.

As the existing body of scholarship on the New Order–era press makes clear, some of the flagship-quality publications of the period imagined their readership as a homogeneous middle class (Heryanto 2003, 31; Keane 2009, 51; Steele 2005, 165–197). The New Order state fantasized that this middle class would comprise its loyal subjects. Journalists, and intellectuals more generally, were obliged to uphold the state developmentalist mission, and this obligation was enforced by daily threats to journalists, imprisonment of prominent figures, and periodic bannings of performances and publications. Nevertheless, small spaces were found by intellectuals to summon a critical position. In these small spaces, a sense of autonomy arose. For example, Romano's study found that journalists saw themselves not as loyal defenders of the state's development program, but as agents of social and political change (Romano 2003, 55–56). Steele found that *Tempo*'s reports tended to depict the masses as victims of state development programs, rather than their beneficiaries (Steele 2005, 157).[17]

By reading across the body of work examining the press in the early New Order period, it is possible to gain a sense of a budding critical, middle-class reading public. However, one cannot gain a sense of how the emerging consumer culture may have propagated and sustained this public. *Aktuil* points to the important role played by an overlapping address—of consumers of pop Indonesia and rock, and of readers—in marking out new spaces in which a critical middle-class sensibility could grow.

Understanding the confluence of the ideologies of rock and the press in the construction of a social middle requires discussion of the idioms of class distinction, *kampungan* and *gedongan*. As discussed in the introduction, these idioms blossomed along with important dimensions of Indonesia's capitalist revolution—middle-class growth, the emergence of Jakarta as an "urban behemoth" (Hadiz 2013a, 211), the depoliticization of the masses, and the expansion of the urban poor. Print media also used and reinforced these categories and their unequal social positions: *gedongan's* refinement was intimated in colorful derisions of *kampungan's* vulgarity, in the medium of print, as illustrated by Weintraub's discussion of representations of dangdut in *Aktuil* and in the news magazine *Tempo*:

> In newspaper and magazine articles in the 1970s which most dangdut fans would never read, sandwiched between advertisements most dangdut fans would never consume—expensive alcohol, luxury hotels, air-conditioned cars, golf and high-fidelity electronic equipment—were stories about dangdut singers, concerts, recordings and fans themselves. The consumers of these magazines and newspaper articles were not the fans of the music; rather dangdut stood for the masses "out there." In these stories, readers of newspapers and magazines positioned themselves in relation to dangdut's lower class audience. The masses that constituted dangdut's audience were generally imagined in a negative light as uneducated, ignorant and irrational. They were viewed as incapable of acting together in an organised way; rather than acting they were acted upon as objects that could be read about in popular print media. When they did become active. At concerts for example, they were accused of being unruly and violent. (Weintraub 2010, 106)

Weintraub's arguments for print media's complicity in connecting dangdut to the derisive term *kampungan* reveal how *kampungan* and *gedongan* connect those who read with certain genres of popular music, and those who do not read with other genres. The argument I pursue here suggests that the term *gedongan* well captures the notion of middle-classness as a genre public. *Gedongan* accords a greater role to circulating texts than to an economic base in constituting the social middle, and it emphasizes the important role of the built environment in enabling people to "feel" the assemblies that such texts enabled them to imagine. *Gedongan* not only acknowledges the formative role of print in generating a middle-class assembly from a disparate collection of strangers, but also attends to the performative dimension of reading that made being middle class seem real.

Aktuil's foregrounding of a rhetoric of print resulted from two developments in later editions of the magazine: the switch to new spelling, and the inclusion of a feature devoted to absurdist poetry. This latter development had the effect of bringing the carnivalesque possibilities of an overlapping address of readers and rock consumers into sharp focus, and enabled the magazine to draw on distinct legacies of well-educated nationalists and wild revolutionaries to propose a composite *pemuda*. Contrary to scholars who argue that *pemuda* was banished during the New Order (see my critiques of Siegel, above) or reassigned to loyalist types (Ryter 1998), I posit that the legacy of *pemuda* as agents of progressive social change continued to thrive in the pages of *Aktuil*.

AKTUIL'S READING PUBLIC
AND THE IRREVERENT *PEMUDA*

In 1972, the government introduced a new spelling convention, referred to as "perfected spelling" (*ejaan yang disempurnakan*, or EYD, in which, for example, *tj* is exchanged for *c*; *j* for *y*; and *dj* for *j*). Herein lies another difference between early and later editions of *Aktuil*. Early editions employ the old spelling, and later editions use the new spelling.

In *Aktuil*, the introduction of EYD foregrounded readers; the switch to the new spelling prompted discussions in the magazine about how to correctly spell words. Nia Gantini's letter, cited above, for example, includes an inquiry about how to correctly render the name "TVRI" into the new spelling, and an article on Renny Constantine notes that her name must now be spelled as Konstantine. Both pieces not only display a self-consciousness about writing and spelling, but also disgruntlement, directed at the "hypocritical" power holders who continue to spell their names in the old way—e.g., Soeharto instead of Suharto—or confuse the correct way to render TVRI into the new spelling. Zt writes: "Her name is in fact Renny Constantine, and looking at her narrow nose we can be certain that she has Western ancestry. But we must spell her name in the new way—even though those who require us to do so continue to spell their own names in the old way—so we have changed it to Renny Konstantin" (Zt 1973, 19). Following her protestation of TVRI's banning long-haired performers from the studio, Gantini registers the following complaint:

> And then there is the matter of how TVRI ought to be spelt. It turns out that TVRI's use of the new spelling lacks consistency and is sometimes incorrect. The way it spells TVRI is all over the place: TI-VI-ER-I. How shameful! It should either be T-E-VE-ER-I, or TI-VI-AR-AI. Provide a proper example, why don't you, to the young, aware, and critical generation. Thank you! Nia Gantini, Jalan Mandalawangi 149/15, Ciamis (Gantini 1973, 6)

Such considerations explicitly address a reading public because they can matter only to those who read and write. Moreover, as Nia Gantini's letter suggests, the reading public addressed by *Aktuil* was not only literate, but inherently critical, and this melding of literacy and critique was similarly advanced by the irreverent and antiestablishmentarian literary content that emerged in later editions in the regular one-page poetry feature called "Puisi Mbeling" (and in which new spelling is employed). This feature was established in 1972 after editor Remy Sylado began contributing his own poems in a style he called *puisi mbeling* (*puisi* = poetry, *mbeling* = a kind of strategic naughtiness),[18] prompting readers to send in their own poems in the same *mbeling* style. Some sources claim that *Aktuil* received up to three hundred such poems every month (*Puisi Mbeling Remy Sylado* 2004, xvi). Solihun cites the following letter to the editor, which captures some of *puisi mbeling*'s appeal:

> I am really interested in the *Aktuil*'s mbeling poetry, which challenges the poetry of the Old Generation. I am a high school student, and that [Old Generation] poetry always gives me a headache. We have to memorize it in all its ridiculous detail. If you think about it, it has no quality! Thank you editor for your attention to this letter. (Letter from Soesanto Santoso, *Aktuil* 109 [1973] and cited in Solihun 2004, 16)

While the "middleness" evinced by *Aktuil* is aptly conceptualized with Indonesian idioms of class distinction, *kampungan* and *gedongan*, *puisi mbeling* also extends understandings of such idioms to be gained from existing scholarship dealing with *gedongan* as a cultural form. Browne (2000) and Weintraub (2006) position *gedongan* as an imaginary constituted by elitist derisions of the masses in print media (including *Aktuil*). But *Aktuil* reveals the layers of an emerging *gedongan* sensibility; *Aktuil's* address was not consistently elitist—it oscillated between haughty derision of the masses and ludic irreverence. Such oscillation points to the new depictions of youth as historical agents in literature tailored to young middle-class consumers in the mid-1970s.

Above I indicated that *Aktuil's* overlapping address of rock consumers and of readers created a new kind of youth ideal, in which distinct interpretations of *pemuda* associated with the 1928 generation of educated, nationalist youth and the generation who took up arms in the revolution were fused. This marriage is nowhere more evident than in the *pemuda* addressee heralded by *puisi mbeling*—he is both highly literate and obstinately wild. We have seen how the focus on rock enabled the magazine to launch attacks on dangdut as a way of establishing *Aktuil's* class position, and we have also seen how that focus marked *Aktuil* as critical, separate from mass production and state television. But *puisi mbeling* distinguishes *Aktuil's* reading public from others associated with realms of literary production. By including *puisi mbeling* in the magazine, *Aktuil* addresses readers not only as morally and socially elevated truth seekers, but also clever tricksters, as *mbeling's* carnivalesque manipulations of language not only hold the power holders to account but also poke fun at well-known literary critics of the day. For example, *mbeling* poems published in *Aktuil* consistently mocked the literary journal *Horison* and members of the literary establishment associated with it. One poem in the *mbeling* style, by Mahawan, mocked HB Jassin, the editor of *Horison*, and another, by Estam Supardi, made fun of ws Rendra, one of the first poets among those who took part in the literary renaissance of the late 1960s and early '70s to gain fame. The *mbeling* mockery of Rendra is funnier in Indonesian than its translation, since it puns on one of his well-known poems. Nevertheless, the reference to Rendra's shrunken penis retains some humor in translation, especially in light of what critic and translator Harry Aveling refers to as Rendra's poems' "excessive masculinity" (Aveling 1975, xviii).

> good evening mr. rendra
> oh, you are male aren't you sir?
> your cock,
> sir,
> has flopped

According to Seno Gumira Ajidarma, *puisi mbeling* played an important role in young people's lives in the 1970s. "We may doubt that any of this [*mbeling* writing] constitutes Indonesian literature, but the fact is that *Aktuil* was the only kind of literature that mattered to teens at that time. They had no regard at all for the much revered *Horison*" (*Puisi Mbeling Remy Sylado* 2004, xv). *Aktuil's* impact, moreover, extended beyond the realm of its readers to influence the style of a number of writers, such as Yudhistira Massardi,[19] whose works Farid describes as "highly carnivalesque" (Farid 2011).[20]

It is important not to overstate the significance of *Aktuil's* literary dimensions. Existing studies of *Aktuil* privilege written forms in assessments of the magazine's critiques and focus on the role of Remy Sylado as a key mediator of a critical youth public. Yet, while undertaking the research for this chapter, I noted readers' enthusiasm for not only reading *Aktuil*, but also *wearing* and *inhabiting* it. For them, being a rock fan was not about publicly displaying their affinity for reading and writing in the *Aktuil* style. It was, rather, about "becoming" rock by wearing flares and plastering their bedroom walls with *Aktuil* posters. These readers' testimonies reveal the way commodities enlivened ideologies of rock and the press. *Aktuil* did not just herald the composite *pemuda*, but also created space for this composite in a world full of commodities, and threw light on the performative dimension of reading that made being middle class seem real.

REAL PATHS FOR THE CIRCULATION OF DISCOURSE

On opening the cover of *Aktuil* 128, 1973, readers are greeted by a full-page image of spectacularly flared white jeans. Indeed, later editions are generously sprinkled with full-page advertisements for various fashion items, primarily flared jeans (using striking images), but also other consumer goods, such as musical instruments and music lessons. In contrast to early editions, from 1969 and 1970, which were heavily textual,[21] later editions sketched the sartorial dimensions of *pemuda*. They articulated *pemuda* not only by critiquing the state and the literary establishment, but also by celebrating the possibilities an emerging consumer culture offered for embodying youth in new ways.

The importance of materials and images to readers' experiences of reading *Aktuil* can be partly attributed to designer Maman Somantri, who implemented several changes on his appointment in 1970 (Solihun 2004, 8). As well as enlarging the magazine's format, Somantri altered the color contrast, and this had the effect of making the images appear to leap off the page. He also introduced bonuses, including stickers featuring catchy phrases (e.g., "Slow but Sure," "Don't Speed, Gas Is Costly"). Existing studies of *Aktuil* privilege written forms in assessments of the magazine and focus on the role of Remy Sylado as a key mediator of a critical youth public (Mulyadi 2009; *Puisi Mbeling Remy Sylado* 2004; Sopiann 2001b). Somantri's role as designer is somewhat neglected. But I submit that it was not only Sylado's writing, but also Maman Somantri's posters and stickers, that prompted the sudden increase in sales in the early 1970s. They certainly feature prominently in readers' recollections.

Readers' enthusiasm for these items is suggestive of their role in forging what Michael Warner refers to as "real paths for the circulation of discourse" (Warner 2000a). The magazine's advertisements afforded the rock-consuming, reading *pemuda* a dress style that allowed him to be accommodated within a world of Western-oriented consumption, and bonuses furnished readers with the materials with which to write *Aktuil* into the spaces in which they lived. Warner argues that it is not just modes of address, enabling people to imagine their membership in an assembly of strangers, that sustain publics, but rather a to-ing and fro-ing between such abstraction, on the one hand, and a concrete embodiment, on the other. Public discourse, that is, relies for its efficacy not just on the work of the imagination but also on the labor of emplacement: "From the concrete experience of a world in which available forms circulate, one projects a public . . . . Writing to a public helps to make a world, insofar as the object of address is brought into being partly by postulating and characterizing it. This performative ability depends, however, on that object's being not entirely fictitious—not postulated merely, but recognized as a real path for the circulation of discourse" (Warner 2000b, 63–64).

Real paths for the circulation of *Aktuil* discourse were forged by the materials included in the magazine. These materials enabled readers to perform their identities as rock-consuming readers in their communities, their homes, and their bedrooms—and such performances resemble what Warner refers to as bringing a "hope of transformation" into a "scene of practical possibility" (2000b, 69). As touched on above, flared jeans ("flares") loomed large in my interviewees' recollections of what it meant to be a rock fan. One informant explained to me how the James Brown cover band the Rollies was considered to be a rock band because they came from Bandung and wore flares. Flicking through the photocopied editions I had brought to the interview, he stopped at the abovementioned full-page advertisement featuring an image of white flares. "See that?" he pointed, turning the magazine toward me. "That is what we thought of as rock" (Interviews: Dek Gun, October 12, 2013; Andy F. Noya, October 9, 2009).

Moreover, it was not just flares that readers used to advertise their identities as *Aktuil* readers; possessing and displaying the magazine itself signaled membership. Sopiann cites Bandung journalist Yusran Pare's recollections of carrying a copy of *Aktuil* as he navigated Bandung's streets, and the important role the magazine played in identifying him as, in his words, a "real" youth, in eliciting in him a sense of belonging to a particularly authentic kind of youth community, members of which became connected to one another by inhabiting *Aktuil*'s real and imagined paths of circulation. In other words, in Pare's recollection, it was not enough to simply imagine one's membership in a new kind of youth assembly while reading *Aktuil* in the comfort of one's home. One had to carry the magazine as one ventured out into the public spaces of the city.[22]

As well as providing a link to an imagined community of readers, *Aktuil* furnished youth with sartorial equipment that gave them a sense of power over public space. But its social life did not end there, for *Aktuil* also contained a host of materials that could be removed from the magazine's spine and inserted into domestic or intimate spaces: stickers, iron-ons, and posters. These objects quickly became divorced from the magazine and were pasted onto walls and T-shirts in all corners of the archipelago. Two of my informants grew up in Denpasar, and another in Jayapura, and both recalled the importance of *Aktuil*'s centerfold posters in their teen years (Interviews: Dek Gun; Andy F. Noya, October 9, 2009). Dek Gun, for example, recounted how he had based his decision to part with Rp500 for a copy of *Aktuil* on the magazine's centerfold for that month. He used *Aktuil*'s centerfolds to adorn his bedroom walls, which, he confessed, had been "full rock" plastered with *Aktuil* centerfolds in the 1970s. As Warner argues, print alone is not sufficient for publication in the modern sense. "Not texts themselves create publics, but the concatenation of texts through time" (Warner 2000a, 62). Reading publics are sustained not only by writing, but by sequences of related texts that enable the readers' engagements with public discourse to be performed and felt.

Warner's insights into the multiple texts that are required for publics to sustain and endure are useful not because they offer proof that *Aktuil* readers constituted a public in accordance with scholarly definitions. They are helpful, rather, because they open space for alternative readings of the political effects of the proliferation of consumer goods that proceeded with economic growth in the 1970s. *Aktuil* shines a light on how reading critical texts was closely linked to the consumption of fashion—a link that is as salient to the analysis of contemporary politics as it is to that of the 1970s. We should not assume a direct correlation between the enjoyment of the fruits of economic growth and support for the power holders who deliver it. It is, indeed, possible that rock's critical potential was subverted by readers' consumerist urges. However, it is also possible that *Aktuil*'s unique interpretation of rock provided a frame by which youths could understand commodities as being intrinsically linked to long-standing narratives of their historical agency.

THE PRESENT: *AKTUIL*'S FUTURE

By embodying the rock-consuming reader, young middle-class men were not just hedonistically and apolitically consuming. They were piecing together an infrastructure that enabled the articulation of ideal democratic personhood in years to come. The final edition of *Aktuil* was published in 1979, and its acerbic house style was not continued in any of the pop music magazines to be established thereafter. But the figure of the quick-witted, literate, rock-loving revolutionary *pemuda* left indelible traces on contemporary politics.

On June 21, 1994, Suharto's Ministry of Information banned three news weeklies: *Tempo*, *Detik*, and *Editor*. Over the six months to follow, no fewer than 170 demonstrations protesting the bans erupted across the country. Such mobilization was unprecedented in the New Order period, and Heryanto and Keane argue that it served as an important catalyst for Suharto's eventual overthrow.[23] Notably, too, some analysts contend that both the bans and the protests indicate an increasing middle-class assertiveness and ability to mobilize en masse: "Instead of displaying its prowess, the ban indicates the regime's paranoia about the assertiveness of emerging middle-class intellectuals and their power base, the mass media. . . . The protests were a predominantly middle-class event because that was the single most important characteristic of the protesters that came to the fore, surpassing differences of ethnicity, gender, profession, religious, or ideological orientation" (Heryanto 2003, 41–42).

The widespread demonstrations protesting the bans of *Tempo*, *Detik*, and *Editor* revealed the symbolic importance the press had come to assume in middle-class political imaginaries. By the 1990s, a middle-class reading public had become a significant political force. Heryanto identifies a broader coming together of two processes to create the historical conditions conducive to building such an imagined collectivity: "The first is the long-lasting and prolific reproduction of myths about selfless and truth-seeking public intellectuals as embodied in the university student, academic, and journalist activist. The second is the expansion of capitalist industrialization under heavy militarist rule that has delivered sustained economic growth but at the expense of human rights" (Heryanto 2003, 51).

In a similar vein, I have argued that *Aktuil* reveals how, despite all attempts to depoliticize them, youth held tight to preexisting tropes of their historical agency as they navigated the new press environment and the pro-West consumer culture that the state hoped would secure their loyalty and subservience. In some respects, this argument rides the wake of Heryanto's insights into the close links between the press and middle-classness in the New Order period. However, it also extends them, by demonstrating that popular music and the broader consumer culture it inhabited were as crucial as was the press to the making of middle-classness. By embodying the rock-consuming reader, young *Aktuil* readers were not just hedonistically and apolitically consuming. They were piecing together an infrastructure that enabled the articulation of ideal democratic personhood in years to come.

Charles Hirschkind's study of cassette sermons and their roles in laying the sensory and moral foundations for Egypt's Islamic revival is usefully invoked at this point. Hirschkind argues against scholarly literature on contemporary Islam that seeks to measure the Islamic revival's democratic credentials and potential by ascertaining the extent to which it is amenable to public reason. He argues that

> cassette-recorded sermons . . . are not oriented towards politics as it is conventionally understood: their purpose is not to influence the formation of state policy or to mobilize voting blocs behind party platforms. Rather, the activities that constitute the public arena I describe as political are in a way close to the sense Hannah Arendt (1958) gives to the term: the activities of ordinary citizens who, through the exercise of their agency in contexts of public interaction, shape the conditions of their collective existence . . . . The affects and sensibilities honed through popular media practices such as listening to cassette sermons are as infrastructural to politics and public reason as are markets, associations, formal institutions, and information networks. (Hirschkind 2006, 8)

The significance Hirschkind attributes to "sensory knowledges and embodied aptitudes" in sustaining a political movement is reflected too in the concrete, lived qualities of the *gedongan* public heralded by *Aktuil*. Indeed, the very term *gedongan* denotes concretion, and it may be expected that *Aktuil*'s *gedongan* public existed not only in the abstract, as a collective endorsement of the critiques of TVRI and of *Horison*. First, as an object, it played a role in signifying metropolitan spaces and the identities that sought to find a place within them. Above, I cited Yusran Pare's recollections of holding a copy of *Aktuil* as he navigated Bandung's streets, and the important role that carrying the magazine played in identifying him as, in his words, a "real" youth, in eliciting in him a sense of belonging to a particularly authentic kind of youth community, members of whom became connected to one another by inhabiting *Aktuil*'s paths of circulation. Second, as well as by way of a mode of address inferred in a writing style, *Aktuil* also addressed readers by way of images, including advertising images, and "bonuses" such as stickers, iron-ons, and posters, which positioned ideal figures of globally connected, well-educated youth and *mbeling* youth in relation to a world full of spaces of consumption and exchange, and commodities, allowing critical middle-classness to circulate not only with words, but also with the very materials of the "capitalist revolution" (Robison 1986, vii).

TWO

Consumer Citizenship

In the 2014 Indonesian presidential elections, popular music played an important role in the campaign of the victorious candidate, Joko Widodo (Jokowi). During his campaign, Jokowi courted the rock band Slank to publicly support his candidacy. He made two much-publicized visits to Slank's headquarters in Pencil Street, Jakarta, including one in May to attend an event at which Slank announced they had officially thrown their support behind Jokowi ("Fans Slank" 2014). At this ramshackle gathering, the candidate stated that Slank epitomized the "mental revolution" that lay at the core of his campaign pitch. Jokowi also visited the band's headquarters after casting his vote on election day, to pose for a shoot with the band's members, hoping, perhaps, that the image might woo a crucial segment of undecided voters to cast their ballot for him (Kuwado 2014).

The 2014 presidential election campaign was widely considered a watershed moment in the history of post-authoritarian governance in Indonesia. It pitted Joko Widodo, a former furniture businessman with no military background, against Prabowo Subianto, a disgraced general credited with masterminding the disappearance of activists in the 1990s. Prabowo promised to return Indonesia to its pre-democratic constitution, and Jokowi sought to play up his democratic credentials, which starkly contrasted with his rival's dark past and regressive vision. As mayor of Solo and then as governor of Jakarta, Jokowi had introduced free education and health regimes for the poor, and pledged to apply that system nationwide if he were to win the presidency. Nationwide investment in public health and education would be funded out of savings to the budget achieved by scrapping fuel subsidies, which benefited the wealthy (McRae 2014; Wingo and Rued 2014).

The policy details of both campaigns have been widely discussed by other scholars. But the important role the rock band Slank played in enabling Jokowi to paint a picture of the pluralist and engaged public sphere that would blossom under his auspices has received much less attention. Slank played a part in equipping Jokowi with the ability to articulate ideas that were key to his vision of a future Indonesia. By 2014, Slank had been producing chart-toppers for near on a quarter century, and during that time the band had developed an image of itself as an advocate of youths' political participation. At several points throughout the campaign, Jokowi leaned on this image. For example, at the press conference at Slank's headquarters on May 27, 2014, when the band announced its support for the candidate, Jokowi qualified, "There are three reasons why I have come to visit Slank again. The first is that Slank has been actively encouraging people to vote. The second is that Slank have been enthusiastic anti-corruption campaigners. And the third is that Slank exemplifies the mental revolution. What's the mental revolution? It's youth being productive" (Metro hari ini 2014).

Jokowi's reliance on Slank for articulating his key campaign message points to new developments in pop celebrities' involvement in election campaigns, and their enhanced political currency. Celebrities have been performing in the service of candidates and parties since the 1971 elections, and they continued their roles in elections well into the post-authoritarian era, albeit in a more deregulated manner, as various campaign teams contracted artists to perform at electoral rallies, without necessarily eliciting these artists' endorsement (Hughes-Freeland 2007; Lindsay 2005). Whether endorsing candidates or not, idols served as contracted bards who serenaded either entire campaigns or individual rallies. But Slank's role in the 2014 presidential campaign was different and suggests the increasingly disaggregated nature of celebrity involvement in election campaigns. Increasingly, pop idols are playing roles as independent intellectuals equipped with the ability to address publics constituted by voting fans. Rather than contracting these bards to serenade campaign rallies, candidates now need to cite them to make their pitch ring through the bodies of voting fans.

In this chapter, I discuss how the celebrity politics apparent in Jokowi's pursuit of Slank arose from a background of media change, in particular the expansion of commercial television, which gave rise to the local music boom. Private television altered pop Indonesia qualitatively as well as quantitatively. First, the expansion of private television beginning in the late 1980s oversaw the blurring of genre distinctions between rock and pop Indonesia, as rock bands began to attain mainstream commercial success and official recognition. Commercial television stations provided new stages for performing pop Indonesia and rock, making local artists more visible and their trade more lucrative. A number of all-male rock bands, including Slank, achieved commercial success in this period. Music critics came to refer to them as "supergroups," conferring on them heroic qualities. Second, Slank and other acts used these new televisual stages to articulate their visions for political futures. At the same time, they were subjected to new processes for commoditizing pop Indonesia that arose from the music industry's convergence with commercial television. Narratives of change emanating from the "supergroups" were drawn into an emergent neoliberal ideology riding the wake of the consumer economy's expansion. For example, Slank's lyrics calling for political action were used to advertise products (mobile phones, instant noodles, motorbikes) that showcased neoliberal values such as flexibility, mobility, and individuality.

These developments reveal the local music boom to be much more than simply an increase in sales of local rock and pop music; it also entailed a fundamental change in the ways pop musical commodities—including images, performances, the performers' brand, their bodies—were exchanged and circulated. Therefore, to study the local music boom is not only to study the music industry but to track deeper shifts in the ways media industries generate resources for subject formation. Slank's rise as an icon of post-authoritarian citizenship highlights the increasing enmeshment of consumption and citizenship in Indonesia and reflects a broader rise of consumer citizenship in Asia. Through reference to Lukose's discussion of consumer citizenship, in which "consumer practices and discourses become an increasingly important axis of belonging for negotiating citizenship" (Lukose 2009, 7), I show how the local music boom helped to prepare post-authoritarianism for consumption, formulating post-authoritarian citizenship as *consumer* citizenship.

But the case also reveals the dynamics of continuity, as well as those of change, implicated in the formulation of post-authoritarian citizenship, and these dynamics lend credence to Ong's contention that economic globalization does not globalize citizenship, but rather causes it to mutate. In *Neoliberalism as Exception* (2006), Ong chronicles the increasing ascendance in Asia of market-driven calculations in the ways people are governed and the ways their political subjectivities evolve. She argues, however, that such ascendance does not give rise to a single "universalizing scheme for ethical subject formation." Rather, it produces "rich complexity and possibilities for multiple ethical systems at play" (22–23). Slank's model of consumer citizenship reveals the existence of such mutations. While reflecting the increasing centrality of consumerist discourses to subject formation in Asia generally (Lewis, Martin, and Sun 2017; Lukose 2009), it is also shaped in important ways by a specifically Indonesian cultural form: *pemuda*. Slank's reliance on *pemuda* to articulate its model of consumer citizenship draws attention to the very limits of neoliberal valorizations of identity malleability and self-transformation. Put forward as an icon of post-authoritarian citizenship, a proponent of a "good" post-authoritarian society, Slank retrieved and rearticulated the privileging of certain kinds of (masculine) publicness over others.

EMPATHY WITH THE MASSES

Slank formed in 1983 but did not burst onto the commercial scene in Indonesia until 1990, when the band's first album, recorded with a small label established by a graphic designer, Boedi Soesatio, *Suit Suit He He*, was released. Two of the songs from the album, "Memang" (Indeed) and "Maafkan" (Forgive me) were enormous hits, causing Slank to repeat the formula of coupling fast-paced blues/rock with gentle love ballads in several albums thereafter. This formula appeared to succeed, for Slank's first four albums won BASF awards for best-selling albums in 1990, 1992, 1993, and 1994 (Anggraini 2008).

The blues/rock compositions that featured in the band's early years betrayed their fondness for the Rolling Stones, and it was through these songs that the band fleshed out an image of an authentic, unmediated performance of simple, honest Indonesian rock. This identity was enforced by invoking the term *selengean*, meaning unkempt, and from which the band derived its name. In the 1970s, rock had also been inflected with this trope of the unkempt (male) youth, marking rock musicians as critical agents of social change. Slank's performance rearticulated these connections, but it also shifted the meaning of rock. In the 1970s, rock was conventionally aligned with metropolitan, well-to-do tastes and dominated by bands that sang in English or a flowery, poetic version of Bahasa Indonesia.[1] By positing *selengean*, Slank rendered rock as a slang, street version of its more elevated precedent, re-signifying rock as a local/national register and delinking it from the farther Western horizons from which it had hitherto been thought to derive.

After the enormous success of their first three albums, recorded with Project Q and managed by Boedi Soesatio, Slank split with the label and established Pulau Biroe (Blue Island) productions, recording their first subsequent albums with a branch of their independent production house, Piss records (later Slank records). Slank was the first band to undertake mainstream, independent pop production, and the point at which it did so coincided with the emergence of a new key term in Slank's lexicon—*biru* (blue)—which evinced autonomy and agency. As mentioned, Slank called their newly established record label Blue Island and titled their fourth, and first independent, album *Blue Generation* (*Generasi Biru*). They began to address their fans as members of a blue generation, implying that the fans were not only *selengean* unkempt rebels, but also an autonomous collectivity with particular visions and hopes for the future. According to principal composer and drummer Bimbim, the term "biru" connoted Slank's interest in imagining the host of new beginnings residing in the blue skies and blue oceans of the future tense (Sarang Slankers 2009).

> I'm no chess piece / I won't be bossed around
> Don't get in my way / I'm the blue generation
> I want to think freely / don't force me
> Because I'm the blue generation ("Generasi biru"; see Albums: Slank 1994)

The commercial success of this vision coincided with the increasing visibility of a consuming middle class and the declining importance of the notional *rakyat* (the people) in national imaginaries. As Heryanto notes, during the 1990s, a "new bourgeois hegemony" began to eclipse the dominant othering of rich people as inherently un-Indonesian. A new rich ideal emerged, which challenged negative stereotypes of the rich upheld in official versions of the national identity. "A central message in the dominant discourse about Indonesia's economy in the 1980s was that 'the rich are anything but us, Indonesians' and that 'we Indonesians are many things, but not rich.' The rich were non-Asian or non-indigenous, non-Muslim and non-*rakyat*. Since the 1990s, things have changed. The motto of the day has become 'it's cool to be rich'" (Heryanto 1999, 162). Slank's performance clearly challenged this motto and sought to reassert the moral superiority of the everyman. "Keep your money, take your Mercedes Benz away," they sang. "Get away from my Red Rose. She's mine" ("Mawar merah"; see Albums: Slank 1991).

Slank's challenge echoed an increasingly vehement and socially broadening opposition to Suharto's rule in the 1990s. There is no evidence to suggest that Slank songs operated as a voice for the student movement in a direct way, but important resonances between Slank's performance and the student movement lie in their downwardly mobile orientation. Aspinall argues that the political-economic roots of the 1990s generation of student activists lay in the considerable expansion of tertiary education throughout the 1980s, which opened university courses to lower-middle-class youth and broadened participation in campus life beyond an elite few. As the demographic makeup of university students changed, an opposition movement emerged that was much more ambitious and plural in its ideological reference points than its predecessors. Activists of the 1970s had understood their role as a corrective one—they were there to remind the regime of its moral and human rights obligations. In the 1990s, student activist groups more frequently referred to populism, the people, and the need for regime overthrow (Aspinall 2005, 116–117).

Slank's commercial success can be linked to broader quests for social alternatives in the early 1990s, but it should not be interpreted as a mere reflection of the political mood. It was also the forerunner of a broader mainstreaming of rock, which saw the genre incorporated into the fold of the pop Indonesia establishment. By the late 1990s, a number of all-male rock bands had emerged at the forefront of a pop Indonesia renaissance, signaling the melding of the two genres. As discussed in chapter 1, in the 1970s these categories were distinct, partly because rock bands, but not pop Indonesia bands, were barred from performing on the state television channel, TVRI, and partly also because *Aktuil* used rock to herald a critical middle-class public into being, aligning the genre with opposition to both the state and the pop establishment that endorsed it. By the late 1990s, rock bands *were* the pop establishment.

This mainstreaming bore important implications for rock's capacity to model an ideal post-authoritarian citizenship, for it culminated later in official recognition of rock acts as poster children of a modern cultural nationalism. By the mid-2000s, the music press no longer drew such sharp distinctions between rock and pop Indonesia, as it had in the 1970s. *Rolling Stone* Indonesia, the prime chronicle of the local music boom and its histories, included articles that documented the careers of 1970s' rock bands such as God Bless and pop bands such as Koes Plus (derided in *Aktuil*) with equal fondness ("150 Albums" 2007). The position of rock and the music press with respect to the policy makers also shifted, as rock bands emerged as icons of the new post-authoritarian administration. For example, when performing at the three-day Tuska Metal Fest in Helsinki, Finland, in 2008, the Indonesian grindcore band Noxa was warmly welcomed, assisted by staff of the Indonesian mission to Finland and Estonia. The ambassador, Harry Purwanto, reportedly made seven of his staff available to assist Noxa, several of whom attended the metal event on the day of Noxa's performance (Putranto 2008). And contrasting *Aktuil*'s sharp critiques of state policy in the 1970s, *Rolling Stone* Indonesia championed trade minister Mari

Pangestu's 2009 blueprint for the music industry and published excerpts from the blueprint over two editions in October and November 2009 (Pangestu 2009a, b).

Below, I show how this mainstreaming of rock, and the associated positioning of the all-male rock bands as icons of post-authoritarian citizenship, can be understood as a consequence of the emerging industrial forces that afforded rock with fresh circulatory routes: advertising-funded television and globalized recording. The enmeshment of these industries gave rise to cultural forms that helped prepare post-authoritarianism for consumption. The appearance of the all-male rock band at the core of the local music boom retrieved the entwined myths of rock rebellion and *pemuda*, discussed in chapter 1, and rearticulated familiar narratives of social and political change. At the same time, *pemuda* was being subject to new forms of mediation. As the local music boom played out on television, the ideal modes of belonging it proposed fused with strategies for branding consumer items, and were remade as commodities.

TELEVISION AND THE LOCAL MUSIC BOOM

As discussed in the preceding chapter, in the 1970s the market for pop music had been dominated by recordings from Europe, the US, and the UK. In the late 1960s, a number of outfits were established that recorded without permission and distributed on the Indonesian market rock albums from abroad. But this situation began to change when pressure was placed on the Indonesian government to prosecute pirates after Bob Geldof complained of Indonesians pirating copies of *Band Aid: Do They Know It's Christmas?* Faced with a new tax on locally reproduced and distributed Anglo-American albums, Indonesian recording executives began to look to the newly established festival circuit for sounds that "could be accepted by the public ear" (Sopiann 2002, n.p.). As a result of these expanded promotional avenues, higher sales figures for local rock were reached. In the last half of the 1980s, the rock band God Bless sold a record four hundred thousand copies of their *Semut Hitam* (Black ant) album (Sopiann 2002).

This new festival circuit provided a foundation for the emergence of the all-male rock band as the local music boom's primary cultural form, for those to emerge as the boom's main "supergroups" — Slank, Dewa 19, Jamrud, and Gigi — all have their roots in this period of expanded live performance opportunities for local rock musicians. In the late 1980s and early 1990s, these young rock bands gained additional opportunities to perform when a number of new, private television stations were established. In 1988, the government issued a decree that surrendered its monopoly over television, and between 1988 and 1995 four new private television stations were established (Sen and Hill 2000). Increasing numbers of people began to buy television sets to watch in their homes, and by 1997, the number of privately owned television sets had reached 20 million—a 260 percent increase on the 1990 figure of 7.6 million sets (Hendriyani et al. 2011).

The arrival of private television radically transformed the performance landscape for rock bands. For two decades, *Aneka Ria Safari*, the program devoted to pop Indonesia on the state channel TVRI, was the only televisual stage open to pop musicians, and rock musicians were barred from it. By contrast, private television stations actively sought out groups from the emerging rock scene. When the currency crisis hit in the late 1990s, television stations sought to fill airtime with music video, which was relatively cheap compared to live broadcasts of football and boxing, for example (which were cut due to financial constraints), and this furnished the bands emerging from the above-mentioned festival circuit with new promotional avenues and performative formats (Sopiann 2002).

A considerable spike in sales of local rock ensued, and by the late 1990s, a clutch of new, all-male supergroups, including Slank, Jamrud, Dewa, Gigi, and Padi, achieved unprecedented album sales of up to two million cassettes, a fourfold increase in sales of a decade earlier. As Sopiann relates, "Sheila on 7 set a new record on August 2001 when their album A Classic Story for the Future (*Kisah Klasik Untuk Masa Depan*) reached sales of 1.7 million copies. This was achieved two months before Jamrud's album Aristocrat (*Ningrat*) sold 1.85 million copies in October 2001. 'We began to sell millions of albums after 1999,' said Yan Djuhana [Artist and Repertoire director of Sony Music Indonesia]" (Sopiann 2002, 6). In this context, rock bands ceased to serve television stations as a cheap alternative to expensive sporting telecasts; they began to attract high ratings and high-paying advertisers. By 2002, when a further five free-to-air, national television stations were established, a number of channels were beginning to program live, in-studio, and other musical events,[2] and performers were being paid hefty fees for their shows on television and elsewhere. In fact, for many, their income from live and in-studio performances far exceeded income from album sales, a fact reflected in business magazine *SWA*'s listing of top singers' concert fees. In May 2004, the magazine ran a cover story titled "Boom Bisnis Musik: Mau Kaya Raya dan Populer? Gelegar Bisnis Musik Menjanjikan Banyak Peluang, Yeah . . . !" (Music business boom: Do you want to be filthy rich and popular? The music boom promises heaps of opportunities, yeah . . . !) (Djatmiko 2004; Firdanianty 2004; Hidayat 2004; Manopol 2004a, b; Palupi 2004; Rafick 2004;

Rahayu 2004; Soelaeman 2004; Sudarmadi 2004). The *SWA* issue consisted of separately authored feature articles that generally lauded the music industry's capacity to generate billions of rupiah for recording labels, producers, television stations, recording studios, musicians, music schools, songwriters, music retailers, dancers, video clip production houses, and artist management firms alike.

One such article (Djatmiko 2004) chronicles top performers' incomes from live and televised concerts, revealing such performances as far more important sources of income than royalties for album sales. For example, in 2004 Ari Lasso performed four or five live concerts a month for a fee of Rp40 million for each performance, or Rp2.4 billion in concert fees annually—forty times the amount he earned from royalties for his 2004 album, which sold a considerable six hundred thousand copies and furnished him with at least Rp600 million in royalties. Members of Jamrud claimed a concert fee twice that of Ari Lasso, which, if they performed at the same frequency he did, would have earned the band Rp4,800 million for a year's worth of concerts. Even their biggest-selling album, *Ningrat*—which according to Log Zhelebour, head of the Logiss recording label that produced it, sold two million copies—earned them less than half this amount in royalties. A final example is folksinger Iwan Fals, who fell afoul of the New Order regime for his critical compositions and large following, and whose concerts were banned in the 1980s. According to *SWA*, Fals commanded the highest concert fee of all, at Rp150 million per performance. If he performed at the same frequency as Ari Lasso, he could have earned Rp9 billion in concert fees every year. To match this figure in royalties, he would have needed to sell ninety million copies of any one album—almost fifty times the highest sales record (purported to have been) ever achieved by an Indonesian band, Jamrud, for the aforementioned *Ningrat* album (Djatmiko 2004).

In the early 2000s, commercial television expanded further. Five television stations were established between 2000 and 2002, adding to the four already established in the period between 1988 and 1995. Television set ownership continued to rise dramatically and by 2005 had reached forty million, a 100 percent increase from the 1997 figure. As Hendriyani and colleagues point out, the sharp increases in the ownership of television sets domesticated the technology, as television viewing moved from public spaces to inside the home:

> In 1962, the Indonesian government imported 10,000 TV sets and installed them in strategic locations so that people could watch Televisi Republik Indonesia, the first state-owned TV station, as an official voice of the government (Kitley,

2000). At first, watching television was an activity that mostly took place in public. The economic boom of the 1980s in Asia—including Indonesia—gave birth to a new middle class with more buying power for technological gadgets and with more leisure options (Heryanto, 1999). The 7.6 million TV sets in Indonesian families in 1990 (Gazali, 2004) increased to 40 million in 2005 (Kominfo, 2009), transforming TV watching into a typical family activity. (Hendriyani, d'Haenens, and Beentjes 2014, 323)

Unsurprisingly, as more and more people bought television sets, advertising expenditure on television increased exponentially, and television advertisments became a much more ubiquitous part of the public culture. Between 1990 and 1995, national advertising expenditure increased sixfold, and television's share of total advertising revenue increased from 8 percent to 49 percent over the same period (Sen and Hill 2010, 115–116). Between 1999 and 2007, the annual advertising spending on television increased by a further 4.6-fold (Hendriyani, d'Haenens, and Beentjes 2011).

This growth of advertising enabled new ways of commoditizing pop. Successful acts soon came to be viewed not only as products of recording labels but as advertising space for promoting other products. Pop and rock idols emerged as key product endorsers in the late 1990s and early 2000s, partly reflecting the particularly agile style of band management that emerged from the particularities of the Indonesian recording landscape at the time. As mentioned, since the early 1990s, Slank had established its own recording and distribution label, Pulau Biroe. But many of the other supergroups were signed to global recording labels by virtue of a 1993 reform package, which allowed for direct foreign investment in the Indonesian recording industry and which prompted Sony Music, Warner, EMI, BMG, and Universal to all establish offices in Jakarta between 1995 and 1997 (Sopiann 2002). Prior to the opening of the Indonesian recording industry to direct foreign investment, Indonesian professional musicians worked under a system that positioned them as contract laborers, whereby they sold their master recordings outright to recording labels. When multinational recording labels set up shop in Indonesia in the mid-1990s, Indonesian artists secured contractual deals that assigned them royalties, but these record labels were slow to institute 360-degree deals by which they recovered control over their contracted musicians' performing bodies by insisting that artists agree to be managed in-house (Interview: Feby Lubis, May 12, 2004). This meant that in many cases pop performers began to independently contract their own management teams, drawing them from their own circles of friends, and recording labels were cut out of deals musicians made with other industry actors. Music making, after all, had become much more than about making albums—in many cases, more money was to be made from live performance and endorsements.

In this context, many pop performers began to independently develop their performances as branded commodities: polished and well-rounded products that could be readily inserted as televisual content, product endorsement, or live performances by creating images of themselves and their lives that could be traded as advertising space. The pop soloist Ari Lasso provided a shining example of such self-commodification. Lasso's struggles with heroin and misconduct when he was vocalist for the band Dewa 19 were widely known in the late 1990s. By the early 2000s, a rehabilitated Lasso was enjoying a successful solo career, and he was recruited to serve as a brand ambassador for the energy drink Extra Joss, which had launched a campaign touting seven characteristics as representative of its brand image: *cinta tanah air* (love the motherland), *pantang menyerah* (never give up), *suka terobosan* (love to break through), *inovatif* (innovative), *kreatif* (creative), *berprestasi* (high achiever), and *dinamis* (dynamic). Lasso sold the public image of his suffering and subsequent triumph over heroin to Extra Joss, which sought to associate the drink with the idea of *pantang menyerah*.

CONSUMER CITIZENSHIP

It was not only stories of personal transformation that were told via commoditized narratives of musicians' lives. As pop musicians became a more visible part of the public sphere that people were struggling to imagine in new ways after the fall of the New Order, pop music also began to serve as an important site for renegotiating citizenship. This could be seen in the strong interest that emerged in producing new kinds of national history that revolved around popular music, by way of tribute albums dedicated to Indonesian pop stars past and present, for example (as will be discussed in chapter 5). As well as historical revision, other kinds of performances came to the fore, including those that fleshed out ethical and moral road maps for the reform process, or provided commentary on contemporary political problems. Moreover, a number of performers branded their performances by politicizing their speech and adopting identities as civic leaders with elaborate moral philosophies and activist agendas.

Slank was a prime exemplar of the latter kind of act. In 1998, the year the Suharto regime fell, the band released the album *Mata hati reformasi* (The eyes and heart of the reform movement) (Albums: Slank 1998). Band members also became increasingly politically active, organizing, in 2004, a long march in major cities across the archipelago to encourage people to vote in the first direct presidential elections and mounting a forceful anticorruption campaign resulting in the band's appointment, in 2006, as ambassadors for the Anti-Corruption Commission (Anggraini 2008). Also in 2004, the band released "Lo Harus Grak" (You have to act), which urged people to become politically active.

> You have to act, you have to act, O my friend you have to act
> God Willing, you will be victorious
> Advance! Advance! O my friend advance!
> Don't be afraid, don't retreat. My friend, advance!
> God willing, you will be victorious
> You may fail, but don't hesitate
> It's important to try. Come on, advance! (Albums: Slank 2004)

A number of other pop performers also emerged as leaders of protest movements in the late 2000s. Since 2012, for example, the Balinese grunge band Navicula has campaigned globally to halt the destruction of the Kalimantan rain forest. Punk musician Jerinx has been at the forefront of a grassroots movement in Bali to revoke the central government's go-ahead for a controversial resort development in the island's harbor (Moore 2013a, b), and hip hop performer Muhamad Marzuki led demonstrations in Yogyakarta in 2010 to call for retaining the region's special administrative status.

The emergence of pop idols as civic leaders draws attention to contemporary developments in celebrity politics. Three characteristics are especially notable. First is the increasing recognition of image-based idols (as opposed to the word-based intellectual) as valid subjects for articulating political authority—a point well illustrated by Jokowi's pursuit of Slank, and also instanced by the above-mentioned musician-led protest movements. Second is the emergence of a new form of associational life (the fan group) as a site for attending to that authority. Indeed, Slank's large, loyal, and well-tended fan base no doubt played a part in Jokowi's decision to approach the band to support his candidacy; and Navicula, Muhamad Marzuki, and Jerinx are all renowned for their large and active fan following. Third is the important role of affect and narratives of self-betterment (not rational-critical speech) in the forging of solidarities in and through this associational life, highlighting how neoliberal values feed this new associational life and the authoritative performances to which it orients.

This new celebrity politics bore important dynamics of continuity, as well as change. On the one hand, the celebrities to adopt identities as civic leaders were all men, and this reflects the gendered pattern of the local music boom and reveals how the prominence of all-male rock bands works to emphatically reassert the primacy of the masculine subject in the delineation of an ideal post-authoritarian citizenship. Such primacy points to historical continuity because it arises from the enduring force of the *pemuda* legacy in indexing a critical subject position. As discussed in chapter 1, the discourse of rock was shaped through recourse to this figure, who denoted an affinity for the written word. Notably, Slank retained the link between rock, a critical masculinity, and print literacy originally forged in *Aktuil*. In a spectacular demonstration of the band's eagerness to associate itself with the *pemuda* legacy, in 2004 Slank established a newspaper, meant to serve as a primary organ for communicating with fans. In it, band members pen lengthy features discussing their philosophical leanings in accordance with the "Slankissme" dictum (the band's philosophy, of which more below), in teacherly and didactic fashion. Slank endeavored to address its fans as a newspaper-reading public—a nostalgic, albeit symbolically powerful, move that papered over the material basis for Slank's rise to fame: commercial television.

While the local music boom threw up a clutch of new supergroups who posed as activists, modeling themselves on *pemuda* to propose new moral and ethical agendas, both the media forms they relied on to disseminate these agendas, and the qualities of their messages, marked them as unique political actors. Given their reliance on commercial television, it may not be surprising that pop celebrities at the turn of the century pioneered the interweaving of moral and ethical agendas fit for a post-authoritarian age with consumerist discourses advocating self-transformation. For example, around 2004, Slank began to beef up the core ideals their performance was meant to convey—a new beginning, critique, humility. The band introduced a new term meant to delineate Slank fans' ideal practice—Slankissme—which listed thirteen values to which Slank fans ought to adhere: (1) critique, (2) humanitarianism, (3) solidarity, (4) loyalty, (5) freedom, (6) simple living, (7) nature-loving, (8) humane, (9) dare to be different, (10) hold friendship in high esteem, (11) aim high, (12) be yourself, (13) open your heart and mind (Anggraini 2008). The fusion of post-authoritarian morality with consumerist discourses is evident in the Slankissme dictum. It melds long-standing civic values (such as critique and solidarity) with new ones (be yourself, dare to be different, aim high). Such melding reveals that the celebrification of politics entails not only the emergence of celebrities as political leaders but also deeper shifts in prevailing notions of civic virtue.

By melding notions of political voice with those of self-transformation in this way, Slank prepared its vision for consumption as television advertisements, which emerged as a new medium responsible for circulating such visions. Indeed, by the early 2000s, a number of political pop celebrities were circulating their agendas for change not only by singing at concerts and on CDs, but also by lending their compositions as jingles for television advertisements. For Slank and others, adopting an activist stance led to a host of lucrative endorsement deals in advertisements on television in the latter part of the decade. Iwan Fals, for example, appeared in 2008 in an advertisement for a brand of motor scooter, TVS (Suhendra 2008). And in 2008, Slank appeared in an advertisement for a brand of instant noodles accompanied by the song "You Have to Act" ("Supermie" 2008). In 2009, the same song was used as accompaniment for an ad for the telco Telkomsel (Hotline Production 2009). In the same year, Esia, a product of Bakrie Telkom that bundled network services with CDMA handsets, released a special Slank handset ("Esia" 2010). In 2014 and 2015, Slank featured in advertisements for a Yamaha scooter and a brand of snack food, So Nice ("Iklan Yamaha," 2014; PT Agung Nusantara 2015). In 2014, the band endorsed Jokowi's election campaign. After Jokowi won the election, Slank released a song titled "Indonesia WOW," citing, on their website, inspiration from the consulting firm MarkPlus In: "At heart 'Indonesia wow' was initiated by Hermawan Kartajaya, the Indonesian marketing expert and founder and CEO of MarkPlus" (Slank.com 2014).

What is also striking about these advertisements is that they all promoted products that showcased neoliberal values of flexibility, individuality, and mobility in spectacular depictions of the public sphere. In this light, rather than a rallying cry for mass mobilization, "You Have to Act" appears as a joyful annunciation of neoliberalism's very materiality and a celebration of the new paradigm governing everyday life, in which "selfhood is seen as . . . endlessly malleable" (Lewis, Martin, and Sun 2016, 4). A whole song has been disassembled, decommissioned as a vehicle for heralding democratic subjects, and stripped down to its spark plugs, firing now to drive the pistons of post-developmentalist myth making. "You Have to Act" was no longer a rallying cry but a celebration of the value of temporal flexibility and autonomous individuality that so infuse the single-use packet of instant noodles, scooter-enabled motor mobility, and the cell phone.

MUTATIONS

Several writers note the emergence of consumption-led self-realization as a key civic virtue in Asian societies, replacing old modes of national belonging, dominated by developmentalist states' agendas, with new agendas betraying the "increasing dominance of an individualist consumerist approach to everyday life in which selfhood is seen as endlessly malleable" (Lewis, Martin, and Sun 2016, 4). According to Lukose, consumer citizenship is a feature of contexts in which "consumer practices and discourses become an increasingly important axis of belonging for negotiating citizenship; in other words, for the politics of social membership, for negotiations of public life, for an understanding of politics within the nation" (Lukose 2009, 7). Both these sources contend that consumer citizenship is evident in the new ways the states are framing the modernity imperative; being modern no longer requires acquiescing to the state's developmentalist agenda. It is increasingly about consuming. For example, "in China, a good citizen is not only loyal to the party and the nation but, equally importantly, also does his or her bit to spend money and engage in consumption, which is crucial to the sustained economic growth of the nation" (Lewis, Martin, and Sun 2016, 63).

When visions for political futures are rendered and circulated as jingles for advertisements for consumer products, this surely provides a powerful illustration of the vital role consumer discourses are playing as "important axis of belonging for negotiating citizenship [and] public life" (Lukose 2009, 7). In this sense, the Slank case reveals correlations between ideological developments in Indonesia and those taking place elsewhere in the region. However, it also resonates strongly with Ong's arguments for the very multiplicity of neoliberalism's manifestations in Asia, as its interplay with other ethical regimes constrains and enables neoliberal possibilities in myriad ways. In *Neoliberalism as Exception: Mutations in Citizenship and Sovereignty* (2006), Ong describes exception as a basic principle of sovereign rule—it enables the inclusion of certain people in, and the exclusion of others from, the protection of a sovereign state. And she conceptualizes neoliberalism as more than merely an economic doctrine that seeks to reduce the scope and power of the state. Ong argues that neoliberalism can also be seen as a "technology of government" that casts governing as a technical solution to "non-political and non-ideological" sets of problems (Ong 2006, 5).

Neoliberalism as Exception explores the relationship between neoliberalism (as a technology of government) and citizenship (the inclusion of selected populations in a juridical order). This relationship, Ong argues, manifests itself as combinations of neoliberal exceptions, which "articulate citizenship elements in political spaces that may be less than the national territory, in some cases, or exceed national borders, in others" (Ong 2006, 6). "Exceptions to neoliberalism," Ong argues, "can be modes for protecting social safety nets or stripping away all forms of political protection. In Russia, for example, subsidized housing and social rights are preserved even when neo-liberal techniques are introduced in urban budgeting practices. At the same time, in South East Asia, exceptions to neoliberalism can both preserve welfare benefits for citizens and exclude non-citizens from the benefits of capitalist development" (2006, 4).

The possible combination of neoliberal exceptions and exceptions to neoliberalism are, therefore, endless, and give rise to countless neoliberal formulations of citizenship. Against Hardt and Negri's argument that economic globalization has produced a uniform global labor regime, and David Harvey's characterization of a singular "neoliberal state," Ong argues that "the dynamics and novel combinations of neo-liberal interventions and Asian political cultures challenge typological approaches based on a simple geographical North-South axis, or a typology of nation-states" (2006, 12).

Ong's observations of the ways neoliberal ideology mutates in Asian contexts echoes Appadurai's slightly earlier arguments, warning against viewing the European experience of consumerism as axiomatic of consumer revolutions globally. As mentioned in the introduction to this book, Appadurai avers that there should be a "multiplication of scenarios concerning the appearance of consumer society, in which rest of the world will not simply be seen as repeating, or imitating, the conjunctural precedents of England or France" (Appadurai 1996, 73). Indeed, the case at hand reveals several particularities of Indonesian consumerism. First, while Lewis, Martin, and Sun argue that consumerism in China has been precipitated by the state's development agenda, in Indonesia, consumerism spread at a time of regime demise and regime change and was therefore tied up with the figuring out of a new politics of belonging led largely by the media industries, including television, recording, and advertising. The formulations of consumer citizenship emanating from the local music boom, then, did not reflect a change in the ways the state was addressing people as it did in China, but rather called attention to the increasingly important role media industries were playing in providing people with the resources for subject formation during a time of political flux.

In some ways, the consumer citizenship modeled by Slank entailed novel modes of articulating and attending to political authority that incorporated neoliberal values. In other ways, it reproduced old tropes of belonging, signaling historical continuity and drawing attention to the limits of the neoliberal values that fed other dimensions of Slank's performance. Television provided a new arena for the performance of *pemuda* identity for a changing political context—an identity that assumed the form of the local rock band. Television also commodified the *pemuda* in new ways, causing citizenship to be presented as a subset of consumption. In this context, self-transformation emerged as an important element in a media-industries-led dominant framing of a good post-authoritarian society.

THREE

Hinge Occupants

In the middle years of the 2000s, a group of youths from the provincial city of Bandar Lampung in southern Sumatra (Sumatera) gathered together and began busking outside of their day jobs (as pushcart traders or construction workers), then staging more formal performances at music festivals in their hometown. By mid-2005, this group had named itself Kangen Band (Longing band) and recorded a demo CD of original compositions by guitarist Dodhy. Over the course of the rest of the year, and owing to orchestrations by band members as well as events beyond their control, Dodhy's compositions could be heard and bought in public spaces around Bandar Lampung: on the radio, on the bemo (taxi), in malls, and at sites of exchange known as the *emper-emperan*, where it joined other unofficial recordings arranged and sold on plastic sheets by the roadside, or in makeshift stalls at markets.[1] By 2006, Kangen Band's popularity manifested itself in similar form on Java.

In the same year, a former print journalist, Sujana, who had recently established an artist management company, Positif Art, discovered Kangen Band and invited its members to pioneer Positif Art's strategy for pop production. The band agreed to the remastering, repackaging, and redistribution of its debut album that had so pervaded public spaces in Bandar Lampung and across Java the previous year—a venture shared, as subsequent Kangen Band productions would be, by Positif Art and the Indonesian branch of Warner Music.

Just as it had been in unofficial format, Kangen Band proved to be commercially successful when incorporated into publishing and distribution systems of a major recording label. But once part of such official systems of musical reproduction, Kangen Band began to assume new form. Originally, the band considered their compositions to be pop Indonesia songs (Interview: Andhika, April 24, 2010). But on signing to Positif Art, Kangen Band became known as a pop Melayu band, identifying it as an outfit "from below" and easing its official production as a narrative of upward mobility. Speaking back to criticism of the band in the music press and by established pop Indonesia composers, which cast it as *kampungan*, Kangen Band's publicity machine began to make much of its humble, marginal beginnings. Narratives of the band's rags-to-riches story appeared in chain bookstores and on television. In 2007, after Kangen Band signed to Warner Music, RCTI aired a film that recounted their rise to fame, titled *Aku Memang Kampungan* (Proud to be a hick).[2] And in 2009, the band's manager published a book recounting its rise to fame, titled *Rahasia Kangen Band: Kisah inspiratif anak band* (The secret of Kangen Band: The inspirational story of a pop band) (Sujana 2009). Tukul Arwana, a successful comedian and talk show host, who plays an ugly man of humble village origins with a wicked sense of humor, is quoted on the cover: "Keep going forward, Kangen Band . . . just believe in yourself, like me" (Sujana 2009).

Kangen Band's official production as a pop Melayu band prompted a wave of commercially successful, similarly labeled bands, such as ST12 and Wali, and in this chapter I consider what the pop Melayu phenomenon can reveal of the contested forms of consumer citizenship emerging in the new technological paradigm. These contestations proceed through recourse to an old *kampungan-gedongan* dualism, and below I trace the altered media ecologies that now generate them. The chapter provides insights into the process of genre constitution. Rather than continuous with earlier Melayu forms, such as dangdut, contemporary pop Melayu should be read as a function of pop Indonesia's dispersal—its increasing availability to ordinary people in the early 2000s. This dispersal robbed dangdut of its privileged relationship to "the people" (Weintraub 2010), but it also generated new popular musical celebrations of lower-classness from within pop Indonesia.

This case involves some intricate dynamics of subaltern excorporation (evident in the way Kangen Band's first album queered pop Indonesia) and subsequent commodification (evident in the Melayu assignation given to the band). In chapter 6 I will discuss the underground media economy enabling the circulation of Kangen Band's album prior to its mainstream production; this chapter focuses on the production of Kangen Band as a Melayu act. In the chapter, I argue that the pop Melayu phenomenon reveals that the masculinist and middle-class ideals dominating the delineation of post-authoritarian citizenship are contested, but I also stress that such contestations are not always a function of lower-class resistance.

CONSTRUCTING POP MELAYU

When dangdut materialized in the 1970s, it was widely recognized as a Melayu form. Scholars commonly attribute this assignation to the genre's links to the Melayu cultural region, including Sumatra and present-day Malaysia and Singapore. According to Philip Yampolsky, dangdut was seen to evolve from a musical style that featured in scores for films made in Malaya (personal correspondence, August 21, 2009), and Weintraub attributes dangdut's Melayu associations to Rhoma Irama's forceful role in narrating the genre's history, and insisting on strong links with aesthetic forms originating in the city of Deli (currently Medan), North Sumatra (Weintraub 2010, 33).[3]

Many writers agree that in the New Order period, the terms "Melayu" and "dangdut" were invoked in publications that addressed well-to-do urban dwellers to derisively connote "the people" (Browne 2000; Mulyadi 2009; Solihun 2004; Weintraub 2006). However, such disdainful writings did not solely determine genre distinctions. It is true that dangdut was partly shaped by middle-class derisions, but this was not the only representation. In an interview with Weintraub, Irama states that he reclaimed the originally derisive term: "The name *dangdut* is actually an insulting term used by 'the haves' towards the music of the poor neighbourhoods [where it originated] . . . . They ridiculed the sound of the drum, the dominant elements in Orkes Melayu [one of dangdut's musical precursors]. Then we threw the insult right back via a song, which we named '*Dangdut*'" (Weintraub 2006, 414).

Irama's intervention renders dangdut's social constitution as a dialogic process, involving both efforts to "other" *kampungan* and efforts to reclaim it in the name of the masses. In fact, neither Irama nor the musical sound he developed originated in poor neighborhoods (Frederick 1982), so Irama's reclaiming can be seen as an instance of branding his product as one especially suited to a growing market populated by burgeoning numbers of urban poor.[4] It can also be seen as an astute manipulation of the image of poor neighborhoods in constituting dangdut as a genre. In Irama's depiction, dangdut derives value from its appeal to a distinctly poor, popular-music-consuming public infused with considerable agency, that is, endowed with the capacity to reclaim derisive descriptions of them.

Similar dynamics are implicated in the constitution of pop Melayu. On the one hand, the wave of pop Melayu bands that emerged after 2005 was heavily derided in the music press. For example, the idea that pop Melayu bands were universally lacking in quality appeared to be something of a house position among staff writers at *Rolling Stone* Indonesia whom I interviewed in 2010. For self-professed investigative music writers, they were bafflingly uncurious about this genre. In March 2009, as part of its regular profiles on the music industry, the Indonesian licensee of *Rolling Stone* ran an article titled "Inilah musik Indonesia hari ini" (This is the Indonesian music industry today). The article was derisive of pop Melayu, associating it with threats emanating from outside the metropolis (thereby invoking *kampungan*), stating that "*Pop Melayu* bands have suddenly attacked the capital and have suddenly become superstars, with their uniform music" (Putranto 2009a, 65). *Rolling Stone* Indonesia writers Ricky Siahaan and Hasief Ardiesyah separately iterated similar positions. When I asked him why pop Melayu bands whose compositions enjoyed healthy sales records rarely featured in *Rolling Stone*, Ardiesyah replied, "None of us consider their music good. . . . [It's] a quality issue" (Interview: Hasief Ardiesyah, October 8, 2009).

By contrast, after Kangen Band signed to Warner Music, Positif Art invested effort into reclaiming the *kampungan* label as a badge of pride. It oversaw the band's appearance in the above-mentioned television drama *Aku Memang Kampungan* (Proud to be a hick), which retold the story of the band's rise to fame from humble beginnings; and in 2009, Sujana published his book *Rahasia Kangen Band* (Sujana 2009). Therefore, to the extent that it serves as a sign of the *kampungan*—sometimes celebrated, sometimes derided—contemporary pop Melayu resembles dangdut.

However, unlike dangdut, the Melayu assignation bears no direct relationship to Kangen Band's original musical sound. Existing studies identify rhythm and vocal quality as distinguishing characteristics of Melayu music and dangdut respectively. According to Lono Simatupang, Melayu is a *ritme* (rhythm), achieved in Melayu Deli through use of the *rebana* (Malay tambourine) and in dangdut through use of the *gendang* (two-headed drum), and Wallach's research into the process of recording dangdut revealed that "the vocals play a . . . central, structuring role . . . . All the melodic, rhythmic and sonic features of a *dangdut* song ideally derive from a vocal melody that constitutes its most essential component" (Simatupang, n.d.; Wallach 2007, 99). Specifically, the vocal ornamentation known as *cengkok* is considered to be an important component of the dangdut style. However, nowhere on any of the songs on Kangen Band's first album, *Tentang Aku Kau dan Dia*, are any of these iconic musical elements—the *ritme* or the *cengkok*—foregrounded. Lyrically speaking, the album does recall David's insights into the predominance of despair and loneliness in dangdut songs, evincing a sense of things being beyond reach, and beyond control, in accordance with the band's name (Longing band).[5] But there is no evidence that the "sad" feel of the album was part of a conscious attempt to identify it as a pop Melayu production.

Notably, too, none of the pop Melayu musicians and fans I interviewed in 2010 mentioned dangdut musicians as important sources of inspiration and, when pressed, seemed unaware of famous dangdut composers' place in popular musical history. ST12 composer Charly van Houtten likens his music to that of Peterpan and Ari Lasso—both pop Indonesia acts that rose to fame in the early 2000s (Solihun 2010, 34). Apoy, the composer for Wali, cites influences outside pop Indonesia, but Melayu Deli is not among them. He recognizes *lagu Minang* (songs from the Minangkabau region of West Sumatra) as influencing his art (Solihun 2010, 30) and claims that vocalist Faank's skill at employing the *cengkok* ornamentation derives from the fact that he is a skilled reciter of the Qu'ran, not his love of dangdut. Indeed, Kangen Band started out covering pop Indonesia male supergroups that rose to fame during the local music boom, such as Sheila on 7, Padi, and Peterpan.

Kangen Band's beginnings point to pop Melayu's roots in pop Indonesia, rather than in dangdut, and this provenance brings to light a generic convergence and crossover quite at odds with the clear distinctions between dangdut and pop Indonesia noted by other scholars. Several observers have noted how dangdut and pop Indonesia have historically been segregated realms.[6] According to Wallach, the idea that these two genres are distinct from one another is made manifest in the arrangement and pricing of cassettes at the point of sale. Dangdut cassettes are placed lower down, and are cheaper. Nor do the two genres share recording studios, or even recording labels. When pop Indonesia musicians attempt to perform dangdut, they are often said to fail miserably (Weintraub 2006; Panen dangdut 1975; Wallach 2007). This kind of segregation draws attention to the very material, spatial, and naturalizing dimensions of a taste hierarchy. The current wave of pop Melayu bands also occupies a lowly position, like dangdut, but it is not maintained in the same way. Rather than segregated, the two genres now share producers, live and televised stages, and recording labels. Pop Melayu CDs sell for the same price as pop Indonesia CDs and are not spatially segregated in stores.

It's important to note that pop Melayu is not new—it emerges from a history of cross-fertilization that spawned the genre. The pop Indonesia bands Koes Plus, Mercy's, and D'Lloyd all developed pop Melayu repertoires in the mid-1970s. But these productions were experimental (and critically unsuccessful) forays into the genre by pop Indonesia bands.[7] Further, they were far from the lower-class nuances of the current crop of pop Melayu bands. In fact, critics' assessments of this wave yielded the term "Melayu Mentengan," the derisive connotations of which reinvoke the idea of a Melayu-Indonesia segregation:

> In the late 1960s, bands which had for a few years satisfied themselves and their limited, urban elite audiences with more or less literal translations of hits by the Everly Brothers, Elvis Presley, the Beatles, and the like—one thinks of groups like Koes Plus, Mercy's, Panbers, and Bimbo—began to make cautious innovations. Basically, they incorporated select elements of the Melayu Deli and *kroncong* traditions into their work. The effort produced a fairly slick, contemporary sound, and a number of singers, such as Hetty Koes Endang, Broery Pesolima, Titi Qadarsih, and Emilia Contessa, showed a genuine flair for it. Although pleasant to the ear, this synthesis lacked a certain spark of originality; its melodies and lyrics exuded an upper- and upper-middle-class aura. Wags soon dubbed the music "Melayu Mentengan," after the swank residential district in Jakarta, and the lukewarm public response to a "modernized" arrangement by the D'Lloyds group of the title song from the old movie Serodja seems to have made the point that one could not capture new audiences simply by recycling old hits, Western or indigenous. (Frederick 1982, 108)

In his study of the genesis of the genre in the late 1960s, Weintraub identifies pop Melayu as an early New Order phenomenon that "mediated the ambivalence and contradictions of life during a period of rapid social and cultural change" by melding the forward-looking, globally oriented pop Indonesia with Melayu's connotations of Indonesian particularity (Weintraub 2014, 165–166). Notably, in the second half of the 2000s—also a period of rapid social and cultural change—similar meldings emerged, knitting pop Indonesia's forward-looking orientation and global outreach together with (sometimes fond, sometimes parodic) renditions of Melayu-ness. For example, a 2011 Coca-Cola advertisement made for the Indonesian market featured the former MTV VJ (video jockey, aka presenter) Jamie Aditya, parodying the 1970s dangdut star A Rafiq, to the tune of one of Rafiq's hit songs, "Lirikan matamu" (Your glance). And the blockbuster Indonesian films *Laskar Pelangi* (2008) and *Sang Pemimpi* (2009) both foregrounded nostalgic interpretations of Melayu performances. In *Laskar Pelangi*, set in the 1970s, Rhoma Irama makes an important appearance in the form of a poster. He serves, it is intimated, as a proxy political leader, and also as a sartorial guide for main protagonist Ikal's first romantic foray. In *Sang Pemimpi*, an *orkes Melayu* vocalist in dazzling attire mentors one of the main teenage protagonists, Arai, in matters of the heart.

Contemporary pop Melayu sits within this broader celebration of Melayu-ness in the late 2000s. However, it is distinct for the particular ways it addresses the lower classes, and this sets it apart from both Melayu Mentengan and its later incarnations in the late 2000s. Its ability to do so rests on two developments: first, pop Indonesia's dispersal—its increasing availability to ordinary people—and second, the particular ways the lower classes attained visibility in the new technological paradigm.

POP INDONESIA'S DISPERSAL

In the 1970s, pop Indonesia addressed a predominantly middle-class audience and was associated with the regime and state television (Yampolsky 1989). It was also distinct from rock, which was barred from state television. By the 1990s, pop Indonesia was increasingly infused with rock, as the founding of commercial television expanded opportunities for rock performance. As well as infusing it with the sounds of rock, the expansion of television also dispersed pop Indonesia by making it available to the increasing numbers of people who owned television sets. This dispersing altered the genre's meaning. As pop Indonesia became more mundane, its ties to an originary Euro-America were rendered fragile.

This point is powerfully illustrated by a conversation I had with an amateur Balinese musician, seventeen-year-old Komang. Komang is a talented guitarist and vocalist and has been in a number of amateur pop bands during her teen years. She is an avid fan of the pop Indonesia acts Cokelat and Afgan, but her broad active listening crosses genre lines: she claims a deep appreciation of both the dangdut vocal style and of Kangen Band's pop Melayu tunes. This is not someone with limited musical interests or horizons. One day, as I chatted with her, a song by the band Dewa filled the air. It reminded me of a Beatles song, and I asked her if she had made the same association. Given her deep musical involvement, I was taken aback by her reply. "Who are the Beatles?" she asked me.

Ten years previously I conducted some research among Balinese men around the same age as Komang, also amateur musicians. I had found that among them, questions similar to the one I posed to Komang—comparing pop Indonesia sounds with those originating in Anglo-America—were prominent in their imaginings of the field of popular music production. Pop Indonesia composers' Anglo-American influences were important to those amateur musicians' consumptions of pop Indonesia, but in Komang's reply, we see a different way of imagining the field of pop production. Although some pop Indonesia musicians continue to cite Anglo-American acts as sources of inspiration, in the minds of many pop Indonesia consumers, the genre has nothing to do with the West. It centers on Jakarta.

Certainly, with the establishment of global music industry corporations and their recruitment of Indonesian bands, cultural forms originally thought to be derivative of the West are being rescaled as authentically local. As I will discuss in chapters 4 and 5, localness attains cultural capital as it is drawn into projects dedicated to the reassertion of middle-class cultural ascendance. Pop Indonesia, however, is no longer exclusively a middle-class project: it is increasingly available to ordinary people—that is, dispersed. Kangen Band's drawing inspiration from Sheila on 7, one of the supergroups that rose to fame in the local music boom, attests to this, and it also highlights pop Melayu's emergence from the same condition of dispersal.

The processes by which pop Melayu came to be understood as a distinct category of popular music prompt revision of existing scholarship theorizing genre construction. Weintraub contends that "music genres represent historical continuity and stability, and mark common training, aesthetics, techniques, skills and performance practices" (2010, 12). But Kangen Band's repertoire, and that of other pop Melayu bands, were devoid of such historical gestures. According to Frith, genres have an identifiable source in the production of musical sound by musicians, and are subsequently marketed to appeal to imagined audiences with imagined tastes: "A new genre world . . . is first constructed and then articulated through a complex interplay of musicians, listeners and mediating ideologues, and this process is much more confused than the marketing process that follows, as the wider industry begins to make sense of the new sounds and markets and to exploit both genre worlds and genre discourses in the orderly routines of mass marketing" (Frith 1996, 88). But the case of pop Melayu challenges Frith too, because it reveals that musicians and performers can sometimes play no determining role in genre construction. Pop Melayu emerged, after all, not from a complex interplay among musicians commonly acknowledging generic rules, but from an event: the well-publicized discovery of the provincial Kangen Band by a Jakarta-based producer, and members' thoroughly documented relocation to the capital.

Fabbri's typology, discussed in the introduction, facilitates analysis of the dynamics at play in the construction of contemporary pop Melayu. According to Fabbri, genres are constructed not only through reference to technical rules, which govern the kinds of instruments used, the ways they are used, and their relationships to one another. They emerge from broader sets of rules, the relative importance of which works to position genres socially and ideologically. As I will discuss below, technical rules came to play a role later on, but in the establishment of pop Melayu as a distinct genre, it was economic and juridical rules—"the relations of musics to record companies and the recording process and . . . the promotion process" (Frith 1996, 93)—that predominated.

For example, both the aforementioned film, *Proud to Be a Hick*, produced by the television station RCTI, and Sujana's book about the Kangen Band, establish pop Melayu's provenance not in a musical tradition but a social trajectory: the rise to metropolitan fame, via mainstream production, of provincial amateur boy bands. Such representations bear ideological consequences because they identify both pop Melayu and *kampungan* (a term included in the film's title and on the cover of Sujana's book) as a journey from provincial, unofficial realms of media production to official, metropolitan ones. Both, that is, celebrate rather than denigrate *kampungan*-Melayu, but do so in a way that reaffirms existing center-periphery relations of power.

The foregrounding of economic and juridical rules in the articulation of pop Melayu as a distinct genre highlights the developments that have taken place since the publication of Wallach's book, in which he describes Indonesian popular music genres as a "metacultural field of ideological oppositions" (2007, 68). In the book, Wallach aligns the lower-class form dangdut with collectivism and egalitarianism, and middle-class pop Indonesia with individualism. The case at hand suggests such oppositions may have all but diffused, as Melayu now articulates a narrative of upward mobility, conferring success and happiness on talented lower-class individuals, and positing their subsumption beneath a uniform consumerist umbrella of cultural forms that once voiced social alternatives. Other genres have emerged that prevent this tendency, such as dangdut *koplo*. In a 2013 article, Weintraub argues that dangdut *koplo* constructs dangdut and Melayu as sites for articulating counternarratives (Weintraub 2013). But analysis of the major label-produced albums that were first categorized as pop Melayu in the late 2000s does reveal a trajectory of pop Melayu's development that points to an effort to produce lower-classness as a variant of the masculinist, individualist, and largely secular value system once exclusively associated with *gedongan* (Albums: Kangen Band 2007, 2008; ST12 2007; Wali 2008, 2009).

Kangen Band's first album contained no trace of dangdut's *ritme* or *cengkok*, but subsequent albums included such elements, suggesting an attempt to "Melayunize" their sound. Additionally, the sad, emasculated feel of Kangen Band's first album is absent from subsequent albums. In fact, in the wave of commercially produced pop Melayu to be signed to major Jakarta-based recording labels since Kangen Band stepped up onto the national stage in 2006, the sadness and despair evident in Kangen Band's debut album never emerges again with such intensity in the pop Melayu repertoire. On Kangen Band's second album, produced under Warner's auspices, the male singer emerges as one much more in control of his relationships. This second album is more slickly produced, and more muscular, and a *cengkok* vocal ornamentation is more prominently employed. Lyrically speaking, too, the position of the man has changed. He only appears as a victim (of bitter jealousy, in this case) in "Yolanda." In the other songs, he is no longer the victim. In "Doy" (My other half), he confidently tackles relationship problems; in "Kembali Pulang" (Coming home) and "Cuma Kamu" (Only you), he declares his love, intending to sweep her off her feet; in "Dengar Dan Rasakan" (Listen and feel), "Bintang 14 Hari" (Fourteen day star), and "Dinda," he asks forgiveness for wronging his lover; in "Jangan Menangis Lagi" (Stop your crying) and "Yakinlah Aku Menjemputmu" (Be assured, I will come to meet you), he saves fallen and wronged women.

Similar to Kangen Band's second album, ST12's *P.U.S.P.A.* presents a muscular rock sound, overlaid with vocals employing *cengkok* ornamentation (Albums: ST12 2007). Many of the songs present an image of an empowered and sexually active man ("Putri Iklan"—Advertisement model), who engages in casual affairs ("Tak Dapat Apa apa"—Nothing gained), and resists being ordered around by a woman ("Cari Pacar Lagi"—Looking for another girl). In two of the twelve songs on the album ("Jangan Pernah Berobah"—Don't change; "Saat Terakhir"—At the last minute), he is abandoned and the tears fall, but it is not clear whether another man is involved. On *Cari Jodoh* (Looking for a soul mate), Wali's Melayu character comes through in many of the songs' *ritme*, in which the snare-cymbal-bass, in conversation with the bass guitar, is used to a *gendang*-like effect. This *ritme* may be found in the songs "Cari Jodoh," "Kekasih Halal" (Halal lover), "JODI," and "Yank" (Darling). The image of the philandering woman does emerge in Wali's *Cari Jodoh*, but not as overwhelmingly as in Kangen's first album. In "Cari Jodoh," "Puaskah" (Satisfied?), "JODI," "Yank," and "Adinda," the singer is abandoned, wronged or lonely, but only "Puaskah" and "Adinda" are mournful tunes. "Cari Jodoh," by contrast, is so upbeat that it presents as a parody of that quest, and all its contradictions.

Listen up! listen up!
Who can help me? Take pity on me
Please find me a soul mate
Who wants to? (Albums: Wali 2009a)[8]

Some have suggested that Wali's success is partly due to the band's adoption of Islamic themes in imagery and lyrical content. Only "Kekasih Halal" lyrically invokes Islam, but the band's name is indeed Wali (Saint), and the music video for the song "Puaskah" is set in Egypt—there are pyramids, and also urban scenes that resemble Cairo. The band released *Ingat Sholawat* (Remember to pray) in 2009. These elements signal an effort to align the band with Islam, but *Ingat Sholawat* only sold two and a half thousand albums; *Orang Bilang* (People say) sold 225,000. It was not "Kekasih Halal," but rather "Baik Baik Sayang" (Go well darling), a song devoid of religious content, that was so popular as a ringback tone (Solihun 2010), with the decidedly nonreligious lyric:

I don't want you to cry
Dry your tears
I want to know what I mean to you
Don't I take away your sadness? (Albums: Wali 2009a)[9]

An analysis of the early repertoire of contemporary pop Melayu in the late 2000s reveals its development from an appropriated version of pop Indonesia, which voiced sadness and emasculation, to a Melayunized version of pop Indonesia, revealing ping-pong dynamics of appropriation and reappropriation. The Melayunized pop Indonesia–positioned iconic Melayu elements within a basic pop Indonesia idiom, and a lyrical analysis, suggest that it served as a vehicle for extending values of individualism, upward mobility, and self-confident masculinity to pop Melayu's lower-class audience.

Below I consider the conditions from which this new form of lower-class address emerged. The end of the New Order spelled the end of the "floating masses" doctrine, by which political party activities below the district level were outlawed, in the hope of ensuring the depoliticization ("floating") of society at large. In this context, positing pop Melayu as a popular cultural celebration of the masses' newfound political rights may well seem plausible, for narratives and practices that valorize upward mobility certainly depart from the image of the *rakyat* (the people) that the floating masses doctrine implied. But the coincidence of technological advancements and political change makes interpretation of these phenomena tricky. The floating masses doctrine indeed died with the New Order, but so did other developments not directly related to post-authoritarianism ease new representations of the masses. Some aspects of post-Suharto pop musical development are only tenuously connected to regime change and reflect more strongly Indonesia's increasing global interconnectedness and technological change prompted by Suharto-era media deregulation policies.

In what follows I argue that the valorization of *kampungan* evident in the pop Melayu case arises not from the political empowerment of the masses, but from a new technological landscape that visibilized the lower classes in new ways. Such processes implicate key industry practitioners who display an interest in addressing the lower classes as a distinct group. Drawing on Mazzarella (2003), I conceptualize these practitioners as "hinge" occupants: elite cultural producers born of media globalization, who are tasked with preparing global media texts for consumption by local audiences. Identifying Sujana as one such "hinge" occupant, I argue that contemporary pop Melayu was a product of his labors to render into the vernacular global developments, including the proliferation of audience measurement regimes and of mobile phones, and a shift in media and marketing institutions globally toward what C. K. Prahalad calls the "fortune at the bottom of the pyramid" (Doron 2012, 465).

HINGE OCCUPANTS

While undertaking research in Jakarta in 2004, I was struck by the frequency with which media spotlights turned to those normally thought of as standing behind the scenes of pop music production: artist and repertoire (A and R) directors at recording labels. The staging of production I had noticed arose in part from the new ideas about how to produce music that came with the recording industry's deregulation. As mentioned in chapter 2, major global recording labels established branches in Jakarta in the late 1990s by virtue of a 1993 decree opening up the Indonesian recording industry to foreign investment. To date, most of the A and R directors of Jakarta-based transnational recording labels are those who were closely involved in the establishment of local recording labels in the 1970s.

But beneath the auspices of transnational labels, they were drawn into global marketing trends, and their task was transformed. With the transnationalization of Indonesian recording, no longer were recording labels simply a site for producing individual commodities that together make up a label's repertoire. In and of themselves the labels have become branded commodities.

In my conversations with Jakarta-based musicians in 2004, this development emerged most strikingly when the topic turned to Sony Music. For example, when I met the composer/singer Oppie Andaresta in early 2004, Universal had recently informed her that they were doing away with their entire local repertoire and that therefore her recording contract with them was no longer valid. She was seeking a new deal with a different label, and told me that Sony would be her first choice. In her view, Sony was renowned for the kind of professional management modes she favored. Of particular note were Sony's transparent reports of album sales and, therefore, their estimations of royalties due to their artists (Interview: Oppie Andaresta, March 3, 2004).

Indeed, since its founding in the late 1990s, Sony's Jakarta branch was especially concerned to develop as a patriotic venture, committed to nurturing the very best qualities of the local music boom. This can be seen in the attention the label paid to showcasing its repertoire, in the form of compilations and tribute albums, for example (I discuss this in detail in chapter 5). It can also be seen in the myths that circulated regarding the musical acumen of its senior director of A and R, Yan Djuhana. At a live-to-air concert to celebrate his band's tenth anniversary at the studio of Trans TV, for example, Gigi's vocalist Armand Maulana thanked Sony's Djuhana, whom he referred to as "Golden Ears" (si telinga emas) and whose support was apparently responsible for the group's longevity.

In chapter 1, I argued that in the New Order period, popular music genres were constituted through a ritual distinguishing in which writers (especially music critics) were key. Print journalists were valorized in ways that accorded truth value to their writings. In the post-Suharto, transnationalized popular musical environment, the task of enunciating the modern is extended to other media workers, such as A and R directors, who bring their own kind of specialist knowledge to the task. The "Golden Ears" term is often applied to such workers, mystifying them in a manner once restricted to writers, and suggestive of their role in forging a modernity that is not only spatial (as in gedongan and kampungan) but also sonic. When I first heard the term Golden Ears, it was being applied to Djuhana, but since then I have heard it applied to a range of producers, including Sujana, the manager and producer of Kangen Band who "discovered" pop Melayu. Here, the term Golden Ears suggests, are the pioneers of our sonic modernity.

The attribution of heroic nationalist qualities to these figures is testament to the increasing importance of global marketing and media institutions in the delineation of ideal post-authoritarian citizenship. In this way, it is affirming of William Mazzarella's contention that the work of such institutions is not just to oversee the global spread of a uniform set of sounds, aesthetics, and values, but rather to "move fluently between the local and the global" (Mazzarella 2003, 18). In *Shoveling Smoke*, Mazzarella argues that the global spread of such institutions opens space for new interpreters of the local—those he refers to as "hinge occupants," that is, an elite class of media workers charged with the task of anchoring global developments to local realities. According to Mazzarella, hinge occupants justify their positions by positing that global media texts require expert translation before they can address local audiences.

The term "hinge occupants" is aptly applied to those Indonesian media workers identified as being in possession of Golden Ears. Sujana's production of Kangen Band as a Melayu performance of upward mobility entailed the anchoring of transnationally circulating texts to familiar cultural forms, such as *kampungan* and Melayu. In the mid-2000s, changes were taking place across the region in the new ways media and marketing institutions were beginning to address the lower classes. In *Brand New China* (2008), Jing Wang observes that Beijing-based advertising executives consider the lower realms of Nielsen Audience Measurement scales—segment C and below—to be the most lucrative markets. And in his study of class distinctions in India's mobile phone economy, Assa Doron draws attention to an emerging genre of business and management literature that upholds the poor as the new global consumer. Doron cites C. K. Prahalad's *The Fortune at the Bottom of the Pyramid* as one of the most influential studies in this literature: "Prahalad and colleagues couch their thesis in almost messianic terms, promising a framework that would alleviate global poverty . . . . By realizing that 'the poor represent a "latent market" for goods and services,' the decision makers can help them cast off their social and economic bonds. This will turn them into liberated consumers who are even more adaptable to entering and exploiting the market economy" (Doron 2012, 465).

Kangen Band's generic reassignment from a pop Indonesia to a pop Melayu band reflected such developments, because it presented *kampungan* as a sign of upward mobility, the kind of transformation made possible when the poor are afforded the chance to participate in the consumer economy. But Kangen

Band were not the only proponents of *kampungan*'s reclaiming; this was part of broader developments in the ways lower-class people were being addressed in public discourse. In the years immediately following Suharto's fall, old notions of *kampungan* endured as they were transposed onto the scale of media consumers employed by the US firm Nielsen Audience Measurement. This firm has risen in prominence in the context of the deregulated media environment. On undertaking some research into the pop Indonesia industry in Jakarta in 2004, I found that the lower reaches of the Nielsen scale barely registered on the radar of Jakarta-based pop music institutions, all of which rushed to sell their products to urban, educated youth, denoted by the categories AB. Consequently, pop producers spoke of the masses as if they were a minority whose media consumption habits could only emulate those of the well-to-do (see chapter 4 for a more detailed discussion of this).

Since 2004, however, the way Jakarta-based media producers imagine the lower reaches of this hierarchy has changed. Jakarta-based-pop Indonesia producers now take pains to address the masses and attempt to interpellate their "specialness" as a distinct public with certain tastes and upwardly mobile life trajectories.[10] This change coincided not only with the advent of contemporary pop Melayu and related contestations over the meaning of *kampungan*, but also with the emergence of these lower reaches, the masses, as a pop music target market of undeniable importance. At a time when the business of recording was in crisis globally because of falling sales as a result of digital downloads, those Indonesian masses residing in the nation's peripheries, well beyond the metropolis, emerged as astoundingly enthusiastic consumers of pop music in a format that, in the second half of the 2000s, accounted for the greatest profits accruing to various parties in recording. This format, called ringback tones, delivered music in the form of song segments to mobile phones for a weekly or monthly fee. The work of producing music for a profit therefore to large extent required heralding those masses who, according to audience measurement regimes, bought most of it (Solihun 2010).

RINGBACK TONES

In the late 2000s, cheap mobile handsets flooded the market, and the numbers of people who owned a mobile phone increased rapidly (ITU 2019). Around the same time, mobile phones assumed new importance as a media form for circulating popular music as ringback tones—a new, astoundingly lucrative pop musical product. In the period of Kangen Band's rise to fame, the greatest profits from the exchange of music were being generated not by digital downloads of songs, live or televised performances, advertising jingles or album sales, but by ringback tones.

Ringback tones are preselected, thirty-second song segments, issued for a monthly fee, that are coded, locked, and cannot be pirated. Unlike ring tones, which is the sound emitted by a device when somebody calls it, ringback tones (more accurately known in Bahasa Indonesia as *nada sambung pribadi*—personalized connecting tones) are the sound the caller hears in lieu of a standard ringing tone. So, by purchasing a ringback tone of the Kangen Band composition "Selingkuh," subscribers ensure that callers to their number will hear the segment of the song that runs: "My darling, please understand me / the way I understand you" (Pacarku, mengertilah aku / Sperti aku ngertikan mu) (Albums: Kangen Band 2007).

Ringback tones were introduced in 2004 by Indonesia's largest telecommunications provider, Telkomsel. For Telkomsel, ringback tones provided a way to boost revenues from the sale of mobile-related products, which in large part consisted of low-revenue-producing voice calls and sms texting. Ringback tones were parasitic on voice calls; their popularity reflected people's fondness for making and receiving voice calls, and at the same time they provided precisely the kind of lucrative "value added" service so sought after by telecommunications providers. Between 2004 and 2006, they produced an estimated Rp4 trillion (approximately us$4 billion) in profit for Telkomsel (Antara News 2011; Putranto 2006).

Ringback tones did not just benefit telecommunications companies, though. They became part of a broader industrial ecology of popular music. Ringback tones are locked into the way labels promote singles, through radio play, through music video, and through live television performances. On music video and during live television performances, so-called RBT (ringback tone) codes are advertised in the form of banners, but the content of the ringback tone—that is, which part of the song has been excerpted—is not advertised. While ringback tones cannot exist without singles, and although there are no charts for them—charts are based on radio airplay—astounding sales of ringback tones are more newsworthy than chart position and therefore offer performers further promotional opportunity.

Ringback tones also advanced a tactical convergence (involving "cooperation and collaboration in areas such as content, marketing, and revenue enhancement," Mishra 2016, 103) between television, recording, and telecommunications industries. First, Telkomsel forged agreements with all the major recording labels in order to gain access to the songs (Antara 2006). Second, by 2006, in response to the high demand for the product, Telkomsel produced a variety show—*Derings 1212*—dedicated to promoting ringback tones and bought airtime on national commercial broadcaster RCTI for the weekly show.[11] In various ways, the RBT phenomenon benefited all industries involved. It served Telkomsel as a lucrative value-added service in a telecommunications providers' trade largely reliant on low-revenue SMS and voice calls. It furnished RCTI with prime advertising revenue for musical content, and it furnished recording labels with a steady source of revenue much needed in a context in which piracy was making it increasingly difficult to make money from selling CDs.[12]

As well as revealing changes in the media infrastructure, ringback tones sparked discursive shifts, for they were implicated in altering, albeit contentiously (because public discourse had not transformed, but splintered), what is "publicly sayable." RBTs were closely linked to the uptake of mobile phones among the lower classes—they were launched on the Indonesian market just as it was for the first time flooded with cheap handsets and a sharp rise in the number of mobile subscriptions.[13] Many critics expressed bewilderment at the large numbers of RBT consumers in Indonesia. After all, it was reasoned, they are quite expensive (Rp10,000, or 70 US cents per month), extremely lo-fi, and not for consumers' own listening pleasure, but for that of callers to their mobile phone. *Rolling Stone* journalist Ricky Siahaan invoked pop Melayu bands to stress the very crudeness of this new form of popular musical exchange:

> Because now the music industry is ruled by ring back tones. I mean, nobody buys CDs or cassettes any more. Everyone is downloading ring back tones. And that's where the industry makes its money, in ring back tones. Now, all those champions of the ring back tone, [pop Melayu bands] ST12, Kangen Band, Hijau Daun . . . in our opinion we are now at the lowest peak of the music industry, quality-wise. (Interview: Ricky Siahann, October 8, 2009)

Pop Melayu bands were indeed among the biggest sellers of ringback tones. In 2010, the ringback tone of Wali's song "Baik Baik Sayang" had been activated a record thirteen million times (Solihun 2010). (In comparison, the record number of officially recorded digital downloads for any one song internationally at the time was 9.8 million: Lady Gaga's "Poker Face" in 2009.) Characterizations such as Siahaan's are not particularly novel—they resemble the derogatory characterizations of dangdut in *Tempo* in the 1970s, for example, as analyzed by Weintraub (2006) and discussed in chapter 1. But what is notable are the reactions these rearticulations sparked, for derisive characterizations of ringback tones prepared a discursive ground for contesting such derisions. Debates about what constituted musical quality centering on the pop Melayu phenomenon flared up among pop Indonesia practitioners, suggesting that authoritative writings that set out to deride the masses and their preferred musics are increasingly contested, and highlighting the inextricable links between developments in media hardware and the evolution of public discourse.

Such contestation is evinced not only by Sujana's and others' reclaimings of the *kampungan*, discussed above. It can also be seen in the heated debates among pop Indonesia practitioners and intellectuals concerning the quality of Kangen Band's compositions and, more broadly, of all pop Melayu bands' compositions, suggesting that those who inhabit the middle cannot agree on the position and value of the *kampungan*. Some esteemed pop Indonesia composers even suggested that many pop Melayu compositions are musically sound. Fariz RM, a pop composer and performer whose heyday in the 1980s is was re-celebrated early in the twenty-first century with substantial support from *Rolling Stone* Indonesia, is cited as contributing the following comment to a meeting of experts to discuss the music industry, published in *Rolling Stone*: "Don't be sceptical about Kangen Band. Who says Kangen Band is not creative? . . . Don't forget they have keyed into the spirit of the people, and that is no easy task" (Putranto 2009, 68). Backstage at the AMI (Akademi Musik Indonesia, or Indonesian Music Academy) awards in April 2009, Yovie Widianto (cowinner of the Best Recording Producer category and whose band, Yovie and the Nuno, won the AMI award for the best 'Best of' Album) commented, "Pop Melayu songs are not universally lacking in quality. It's better to perform original compositions than to be a Western wannabe performing plagiarized compositions" (Sulaksono 2009, 10).

There are other defenses still, such as those that emerge as comments on the YouTube site dedicated to Kangen Band's clip of the song "Selingkuh" (Cheating) (Albums: Kangen Band 2008). Like Fariz RM, some of those who contribute their views betray their willingness to mull over, re-spin, and even explode some of the concepts (quality, the metropolis) that pop Melayu's critics reveal as key to their rehabilitation of *gedongan*'s vanguard dimensions:

> I am sure all music lovers actually like Kangen Band's songs. It's just that they are pretentious. They are just copying and echoing those who deride Kangen

Band as provincial hicks. Look at P Project's song "Bukan Superstar." Rhythmically it is practically the same as Kangen Band's song "Doy," but because it is sung by P Project, whose members are crazy and cool, everyone thinks it is cool. (wiyanataende)

Don't just protest and whinge all the time. This is precisely why Indonesia cannot advance and is still a poor country, because people can only protest all the time, instead of doing something for themselves. Were your ancestors of hundreds of years ago modern, or cool? For those Kangen Band members reading, don't take any notice of those critics. They do not deserve to be given breath by God. Go forward Kangen Band! (VAN3Z20)

MEDIA MATERIALS AND SOUGHT-AFTER LOWNESS

A number of writers have noted that the increasingly visible presence in Asian contexts of multinational corporations, in the form of media content, new technologies, or food, has "advanced middle class projects of . . . social distancing" (Doron 2012, 566; see also Liechty 2003; Lukose 2009; Mazzarella 2003; Qiu 2009; Wallis 2013; Wang 2008). Early work in this corpus focused on how the expansion of consumer capitalism in Asia has amplified the cultural power of the middle classes (Liechty 2003; Mazzarella 2003), but in later work authors began to focus on how nonelites—the poor, the information have-less, the lower classes—are engaging consumerism, throwing light on the complex and multilayered dimensions of Asian consumerisms and the multidirectional flows of capital and labor that help constitute them. Cumulatively, they paint a picture of the intricate dynamics of Asia-based forms of inclusion and exclusion at various scales of neoliberal market economies (Doron 2012; Lukose 2009; Ong 2006; Qiu 2009).

The case of contemporary pop Melayu shows how technological change is shaping similar dynamics of inclusion and exclusion in Indonesia. It also provides insights into a dimension of public life that is in need of study, for the multiscalar dimensions of cultural politics emerging from a deregulated media environment are underexamined in the Indonesian case. We know much about the consuming middle class who reside in major cities (Weintraub 2006; Heryanto 2014; Hobart 2006) but little about the cultural politics emerging as nonelites, too, engage neoliberal market economies and the consumerist ideologies that flow from them.

The specific Indonesian contours of the cultural politics implicated in the case at hand can be explored through reference to Appadurai's conception of consumerism as containing both histories and genealogies (1996, 74). One may generally observe, in the course of its journey to the center of pop production, how Kangen Band became swept up into a grand narrative meant to herald the masses, a generously imaged narrative with national reach. The masses were imagined, by virtue of global audience measurement regimes, as important target markets for new musical products. Therefore, they were depicted as avid consumers and upwardly mobile. Drawing a historical line, we might compare the use of Kangen Band's rise to address the masses (Nielsen segment C and below) with Jing Wang's observations of China, where Beijing-based advertising executives consider outlying provincial cities (segment C and below) to be the most lucrative markets (Wang 2008, 57). But a discussion oriented to genealogy might pay special attention to how the depiction of Kangen Band's upward mobility links to mythologies of metropolis and class (*kampungan* and *gedongan*) that predate the rise in Nielsen Audience Measurement's importance to the Indonesian media environment. The historical line suggests a view of the masses that is continuous with the view of all masses from the suites of advertising executives all over the world. The genealogical line suggests changes in the way *kampungan-gedongan* plays out in the realm of pop.

Accounting for such changes requires consideration not only of social conditions brought about by political change, but also of the discursive implications of changes in the material qualities of media landscapes. The pop Melayu phenomenon can be understood as a feature of the new technological paradigm, featuring the widespread domestication of television and the rapid mobile phone uptake that took place slightly later on. The expansion of commercial television availed lower-class people such as Kangen Band access to pop Indonesia. The spread of cheap mobile handsets in the late 2000s rendered lower-class people increasingly visible as enthusiastic users and avid consumers of ringback tones, enabling their address in public discourse as ideal consumer citizens, showing how media globalization does not just work to shore up middle-class claims to represent ideal citizenship, but also produces new kinds of sought-after lowness.

PART II

——

Gedongan

FOUR

Becoming Indonesia

When I first started going to Jakarta to undertake research for this project in 2004, I was struck by the number of luxury shopping malls. Malls formed an important part of my research because people usually suggested them as meeting points for conducting interviews. As well as surrounded by intrusive noise, these meetings were notable for the expense incurred for a mere bottle of water, a cup of tea, or such, at the global chains at which the interviews inevitably proceeded. In these busy, well-frequented malls, one gained no sense of an economy in crisis—only one in which a sizable group seemed increasingly capable of consuming, for such malls continue to mushroom. The cultural producers—music video producers, recording label executives, advertising executives, and musicians—who helped me conduct my fieldwork formed part of this mall-going mass. Many of them had foreign degrees; international education served as key symbolic capital that helped them secure jobs in media industries when they returned home. At the same time, while seemingly buffered from poverty, the malls exude a sense of insecurity, for vast income disparities cannot be hidden in Jakarta. Among the people who helped me by sharing their knowledge, views, and ideas, this sense of insecurity was expressed through frequent reference to *kampungan* as a trope from which they distinguished themselves.

This chapter examines the forces at play in the construction of a new *gedongan* realm in the twenty-first century. It focuses on the role of visual media in revising notions of citizenship in the context of changed media and political landscapes. In the late twentieth and early twenty-first centuries, media deregulation—particularly that of television—saturated public culture with commodity images. Popular music became a more intensely visual realm, with the advent of music video, the establishment of MTV Indonesia, and the growth of opportunities for pop musicians to appear as product endorsers in advertisements in visual media. This chapter considers how popular music's visual dimensions mediate consumerism and shape the ways it intersects with the revisions of citizenship demanded by regime change.

In chapter 2 I argued that the expansion of commercial television in the 1990s prepared post-authoritarianism for consumption, and showed how pop acts such as Slank worked within a new televisual environment to articulate and commoditize their visions of a post-authoritarian future. I argued that the *pemuda* figure remained key to those visions, advanced as they were by "supergroup" all-male rock bands seen to personify this figure—a perception that invested in the supergroups considerable political authority. This chapter continues the discussion begun in chapter 2 by focusing on the new ideals emerging in the context of heightened consumerism, and immediately following regime change, in the early twenty-first century. Such ideals, especially that of the sovereign consumer, challenged *pemuda*'s dominance.

The first part of the chapter analyzes MTV Indonesia's 2004 VJ Hunt to show how visual media associated with popular music accommodated the naturalization of the figure of the middle-class sovereign consumer—a process involving both the positing of new values and the retrieval of old tropes of class distinction. With Mazzarella, I argue that the melding of old modes of distinction (*kampungan-gedongan*) with the idealization of new values (self-transformation) can be understood as global consumerism at work. The *gedongan* sovereign consumer, that is, served as a "corporeal index" that lent credibility to transnational capitalism's abstract claims (Mazzarella 2003, 18–20).

But I also warn against viewing popular music's visual dimensions in the early twenty-first century as realms solely dedicated to the articulation of consumerist ideology. These media also harbored quests for new definitions of Indonesian-ness emerging in the context of regime change. In the second part of the chapter, I show how Indonesians' agency in the formulation of new ideals becomes discernible in an analysis that draws on Pinney's discussion of "surfacist" strategies in Indian amateur photography, and Strassler's discussion of studio portraits in Java, which marry "the possible ('this might be') to the actual ('this has been')" (Pinney 2003b, 13l; Strassler 2010, 79). The chapter analyzes images associated with two pop Indonesia acts—the female soloist Krisdayanti and the three-piece punk band Superman Is Dead. It shows how the images served as realms of surface play in which mutable, changeable bodies signaled a will to rupture with identity discourses associated with the New Order by identifying with a global realm, but also signal people's allegiances to spaces and histories established as local. They pivot around such stabilities in their quests for novel post–New Order identities.

MIDDLENESS AT MTV INDONESIA

In 1995, Indonesian audiences began to watch MTV on a newly established private television station, ANTV, which allotted between five and six hours of daily programming to the Singapore-based MTV Asia, launched in the same year.[1] The Singapore-based outfit occasionally sent production teams to Indonesia but did not program shows dedicated exclusively to the Indonesian market until 1999. In 1999, MTV established a local Indonesian studio at ANTV and began airing a daily six-hour service. In 2002, MTV Indonesia negotiated a deal with Bimantara-Citra-owned Global TV to run a twenty-four-hour service on terrestrial feed to five cities on Java (Jakarta, Surabaya, Semarang, Yogya, Bandung), as well as to Medan and North Sumatra. By 2004, in comparison to its earlier, MTV Asia incarnation, MTVI had considerably increased the volume of local product in its overall music video content.

In his book on advertising and consumerism in India, Mazzarella contends that institutions of consumer capitalism, "marketing and advertising agencies, commercial mass media, and all the auxiliary services that accompany them—are perhaps the most efficient contemporary practitioners of a skill that no-one can afford to ignore: the ability to move fluently between the local and the global" (2003, 18). Mazzarella refers to these practitioners as "hinges" and argues that their position requires them to reproduce dualisms between globalizing capital and local cultural difference. Notably, similar hinges were sought to develop an Indonesian identity for MTV. In an interview, MTVI creative director Leslie Decker stated,

> We are a global company, but we like to be local in terms of our reach .... For us it is important to be seen as local, and we are local if you look at the majority of our staff here. . . . You need to take into consideration the local, because MTV is seen sometimes as salacious and too sexy . . . . We try to tame it down. . . . Anything that is antireligious, or if it's too violent and during Ramadan, we

can't show people eating at certain times of the day, we abide by the existing rules. (Interview: Leslie Decker, May 28, 2004)

In its efforts to cultivate a locally relevant identity for the global MTV brand, MTVI devised two terms of address, which were oft repeated throughout the daily programming. In their scripted banter, VJs and guest presenters alike frequently address the viewers as *anak nongkrong*, literally, "kids hanging out." Since the noun *tongkrongan* refers to a regular hangout, naming the audience in this way conjoins young viewers (*anak*) to regularly hang out at MTVI, which affords them access to a virtual community of youths, including VJs and musicians, who also hang out there. In addition to the *anak nongkrong* term of address, MTVI airs what are referred to as "local station ids" (station identifications), which establish the channel as "gue banget!" (literally, "Very me!" or "It's so me!" employing the slang used in Jakarta). MTVI's daily programming is peppered with such station IDs in which local and international artists assure viewers that MTV is indeed "gue banget!"

In early 2004, MTVI started promoting its third VJ (video jockey) Hunt, which was to take place in eight cities (Jakarta, Surabaya, Yogyakarta, Bandung, Palembang, Medan, Semarang, and Makassar) over the month of May. Viewers between fifteen and twenty-four years old were urged to send in video applications or turn up at one of the listed locations on a corresponding date. On the specified dates, VJ hopefuls flocked to the mall in the regional center where the event was being held. The VJ Hunt was an off-air event that took place over a total of sixteen days — two days for each city. Over those two days, on the basis of their performance in a casting booth, contestants were selected to present their acts onstage before the hordes. Footage of these events, hosted by VJs Cathy and Fikri, constituted an on-air event, for it was presented as short news segments that punctuated the programming flow, and dubbed the "VJ Hunt Roadshow."

The VJ Hunt Roadshow offers a more detailed picture of how MTVI imagined the *anak nongkrong* and brings its role in naturalizing middleness into view. The Roadshow was presented as short spots from mall events in each of the eight cities and was thrown into the programming mix over the month of May. Each spot opened with VJ Cathy or VJ Fikri surrounded by a throng of fifteen- to twenty-four-year-olds milling around in the pit of the mall, awaiting their turn to audition in the casting booth. Raising their voices above the fray, VJs assure viewers that the event is *seru banget* ("really going off"). To illustrate this point, the camera pans a space packed tight with beaming youths. Cathy or Fikri then thread the way to the casting booth queue to vox-pop contestants on what they have prepared for their audition — to which practicing in the mirror, watching a whole lot of MTV, and wearing an impressive outfit were common replies.

In this way, MTV's VJ Hunt presents its audience to its audience — the homogeneous youth nation. When the camera turned on the *anak nongkrong* around the country, it showed no geographic nor linguistic variation but rather a series of malls that bound anxious VJ hopefuls who speak using Jakarta slang. The VJ Hunt's emplacement in the mall suggests that producers imagine their audience to occupy the social space of upper-middleness that malls symbolize. Certainly, documents from MTVI's research department in 2003 claimed that 78 percent of the station's viewers belong to the "Golongan ABC" (ABC group — the highest income/education segment of the population), and in the early 2000s, pop Indonesia generally addressed itself to this section of the population; when asked about their fan base, musicians most often pointed to the Golongan ABC, described as the upper-middle income segment (see below). At the same time, the imagined homogeneous middleness of MTVI's audience is moderated by idealizations of individuality throughout the programming flow. As mentioned, MTVI's tagline is "Gue banget!" and individuality is celebrated by contestants in the channel's 2004 VJ Hunt, many of whom try to persuade the panel of judges to select them by claiming as their life philosophy "Be yourself."

According to Mazzarella, commodities become desirable when they are set in "concrete" local settings, "making it look as if the world according to marketing is merely a reflection of the deepest and truest needs of the people to whom it is addressed" (Mazzarella 2003, 18). In this light, the discourses of individuality on display in MTVI's VJ Hunt may be seen to exemplify the embodying work of commodification. Certainly, the idea that sovereign consumers constitute the Indonesian citizenry has become increasingly prevalent in the post–Cold War era, contrasting the long-standing valorization of the *pemuda* figure, who symbolizes collective action associated with anticolonial struggle. MTVI's *gue banget* tagline is a good example of corporate media addressing the sovereign consumer, and a similar address peppered the Indonesian mediascape in the early 2000s. For example, a television advertisement for a cigarette called U Mild opens with an image of a short, plain-looking man with a leery grin strutting into a lively party with a beautiful and willowy woman on his arm. The image is accompanied by the following voice-over: "For some, success means having a supermodel for a girlfriend." The next set of images is a montage of still snaps of the same man in various famous European locations, accompanied by the voice-over: "For some, success means traveling overseas." We then see a good-looking, young, just-so-disheveled young man in faded jeans and T-shirt trying to push start his old Citroën down a hill, with the voice-over: "But for me, success means being able to start my classic car." The ad then concludes with the tagline (which appears in image and accompanying voice-over alike) "U are U."

Commercial television's expansion prompted an increase in the volume of media messages addressing people in this way—using the first- or second-person pronoun (*Gue banget*, U are U, Be yourself) to evince a new Indonesian "I": a sovereign consumer, an autonomous individual. Not all, however, were granted the ability to recognize themselves in this new ideal figure. Its circulation and reception was determined by taste regimes that arose as a function of media globalization. By 2004, the Nielsen Audience Measurement regime had become part of everyday discourse among industry figures, as it was widely used by radio stations, recording labels, music magazines, and MTVI to sell their audiences to potential advertisers. A. C. Nielsen categories span from "A"—the highest income earners, to "F"—the lowest. Hence, ABC, identified as "university students and above," are commonly cited by most industry players as their target audiences, and they speak of DEF (Indonesian people who do not have university degrees) as if they are a minority. In interviews, those involved in production at MTVI scarcely hesitated to express such politics of distinction. For example, in an interview, the music video director Dimas Djayadiningrat commented thus:

> The majority of Indonesian television viewers belong to the "C" group. "D" are the really stupid ones. "C" are middle to lower middle . . . . I don't know exactly, but I think of them as lower middle. "B" are Jakarta-dwelling university students. "C" are university students from other places. Maybe I don't have accurate information, but that's how I see it. The "A" group is luxurious, "A plus" is very luxurious. "D" is very underclass—those who watch the "Tuyul Mbak Yul" series; it's really bad, but people watch it and it rates highly—this never ceases to amaze me. (Interview: Dimas Djayadiningrat, May 25, 2004)

In the opening to this chapter, I described the Jakarta malls I frequented in 2004 as replete with class tension, made manifest in the eagerness with which patrons sought to disassociate themselves from the *kampungan* "hicks." Djayadiningrat's comment reveals the important role Nielsen Audience Measurement played in structuring such imaginaries. This recalls the way *kampungan* and *gedongan* were evinced in the 1970s, through the categorizing of media consumption, producing sets of associations (*gedongan* / rock / Indonesia–*kampungan* / dangdut / Melayu) that reinforced high-low, West-East, masculine-feminine binaries. However, the use of Nielsen Audience Measurement to connote *kampungan* and *gedongan* represents a significant codification of these social realms.

The expansion of commercial television and the advertising industry in the late twentieth and early twenty-first centuries not only naturalized the figure of the sovereign consumer; it also fueled an elitist cultural politics that retrieved old modes of distinction such as *kampungan-gedongan*. But visual media also served cultural producers as realms to reflect upon the kinds of true, moral, and virtuous selves that might be deemed fit for a new post-Suharto Indonesia. For example, some industry actors invoked *kampungan* as a specific kind of un-modernity, associating it with the corrupt excesses of the New Order regime. In response to my question about how he selected which music videos to air, Hendra Tanasputra, head programmer at MTV Indonesia, assured me that he did not accept bribes for programming video clips, even though some dangdut artists' managers had attempted to bribe him, and reminded me that the staff at MTVI were all educated people (Interview: Hendra Tanasputra, May 2, 2004).

Below, through a focus on images of the pop acts Krisdayanti and Superman Is Dead, I show how such identity quests proceeded by way of a to-ing and fro-ing between, on the one hand, "surfacist" strategies (Pinney 2003b, 13) that challenge notions of the Indonesian essence through celebrations of the body's mutability, and, on the other, allegiance to established ideas of home. According to Mazzarella, such to-ing and fro-ing is commodification at work. He writes: "On one level, the process of commodification requires a suppression of em-bodied idiosyncrasies and local conjunctures — the particularity of use value is in this sense subordinated to the generality of exchange value. On another level, however, commodification *needs* the concretion and tangibility of objects and people — a 'corporeal index' of sorts . . . to lend credibility and desirability to its abstract claims" (Mazzarella 2003, 20). In this light, Krisdayanti's and Superman Is Dead's images could be interpreted as mere organs for channeling global con-sumerist ideology, but I aver that by marrying self-realization to transformative desires, the images also offered themselves as spaces for experimenting with post-authoritarian subjectivities.

FLUID RACINATION

In her ethnographic study of photography, Karen Strassler describes the Java-nese visual economy as "refracted" — a term that captures her explorations of "the ways that photographic genres cultivate distinctive 'visualities' or 'ways of seeing'" (Strassler 2010, 18). Strassler argues that photographic practices can be categorized generically, and that doing so enables her to chart a course for studying the medium that wends its way between the notion that photography is an immutable technology and the idea that it "dissolve[s] entirely into its myriad social, institutional and ideological contexts" (Strassler 2010, 19). Genres work to modulate the various possibilities of photography by foregrounding certain values and backgrounding others.

By using photographic genres to structure her study, Strassler extends a comparative essay by Pinney, in which he contends that practices of photographic portraiture in India exemplify vernacular modernism, for they display a distaste for the concern with indexicality (the idea that photographs point to an essence or a truth) that has been so central to representational practices, particular to Euro-modernity (Pinney 2003a). They do so by employing "surfacism," which "stresses the texture of the surfaces of the image and the possibilities it presents for cultural reinvention." Surfacism transforms the value of the photographic image. Rather than records of what "is," photography becomes a "transformational space"; it "mobilize[s] fluid identities within a ludic idiom" (Pinney 2003a, 13).

Some of the genres Strassler studies work in this way. For example, late-colonial studio portraits allowed "people to 'put themselves in the picture' of an anticipated modernity and make contact with various desired 'elsewheres' culled from global media images" (Strassler 2010, 20). But other genres foreground a faith in photography's ability to reveal a "truth" of what "is" and what "happened." Photographs produced for identity cards are "rooted in the state's faith in the camera's powers of indexical transcription and its own ability to map appearances reliably onto identity." And students hailed photographs of demonstrations in the late 1990s (leading up to the fall of the New Order) as "witnesses" of their historical agency (2010, 20–21).

The images of Krisdayanti and Superman Is Dead discussed here are most aptly compared to the late-colonial studio portraits discussed by Strassler. She argues that the portraits show how people played with props, backdrops, and costumes to experiment with "possible selves," but they also show how these experimentations were tied to the construction of national subjects and national modernity, thereby limiting the field of possibility.

> Despite the playful, highly artificed, and theatrical modality of the studio genre, the portrait's status as an indexical trace of a particular person is not immaterial

to its efficacy. Rather, the significance of the studio portrait lies in its conjoining of fantasy and record, of projection and commemoration. Studio portraits in Java exploit photography's indexicality to serve imaginative ends, working to expand the horizons of the actual. The studio portrait's charge emerges from its marriage of the possible ("this might be") to the actual ("this has been"). Documents of the "as if" and the "not yet," studio photographs materialize desires, aspirations and experimental fantasies of becoming "other." (Strassler 2010, 79)

The images of Superman Is Dead and Krisdayanti resemble these portraits, for they too couple ludic experimentations foregrounding the fluidity of identity with notions of cultural racination. Visual representations of Superman Is Dead and Krisdayanti visibilize a desired post-authoritarian modernity by way of their subjects' playful antics, which reach beyond essentialist notions of Indonesian-ness. In this way, like the portraits Pinney analyzes, they depict identity as fluid and employ ludic idioms. Yet the discourses that accompany the circulation of these images also tether them to moral visions that identify them as local, thereby limiting the fluidity of their subjects. Images of both acts fixate on surface appearances, but these appearances are meant to point to something; they index morality and virtue, in other words, a kind of interiority—they are supposed to tell us who these people "really" are. Superman Is Dead's images are emplaced in a particular geo-cultural area—that of Kuta, Bali—and this emplacement enables the band to articulate their formulation of ideal citizenship. The images of Krisdayanti depicting her upward mobility and career success are anchored in established discourses of femininity, suggesting that, in contemporary Indonesia, the emancipatory possibilities of the "conjoining of fantasy and record, of projection and commemoration" (Strassler 2010, 79) vary according to gender.

PROVINCIAL DISCERNMENT

Superman Is Dead formed in 1996 and played a pivotal role in an emerging Balinese punk/alternative scene by establishing a regular Saturday night punk jam in Kuta. In 1997, they became the first Balinese punk band to produce independently an album of original songs. Later, the band pioneered a deal with the Jakarta-based major recording label Sony Music Entertainment Indonesia and became the first Balinese band to "go national." This they did in 2003, shortly after employing Rudolf Dethu as their manager. Dethu had recently established a clothing label, Suicide Glam, which he describes as street wear in the glam punkabilly style. Although Superman Is Dead had no formal agreement with Dethu to wear his clothes onstage, they often did, and their shiny, glossy image was most commonly understood as akin to that of Suicide Glam. In the current discussion, the punk glam scene refers to the confluence of the Suicide Glam "glam punkabilly" look with the Balinese punk scene that centered on Superman Is Dead.

In an interview, Dethu identified the band's interest in fashion—an industry that valorizes the self-transformation made possible by corporeal mutability—as simply a reflection of who they really are: "We try to stick to our beliefs: existence, individuality, being who you are," he said. "The Suicide Glam image is that you would die for being fashionable in a rock 'n roll way, you don't care what people say. We don't try to cultivate an exclusive, rock 'n' roll irreverence, it's just who we are" (Interview: Rudolf Dethu, January 20, 2005). Dethu's comment recalls Liechty's discussion of similar tensions between transformation and self-realization inherent in the Nepali magazine *Teens*. The tensions inherent to *Teens*, Liechty contends, are typical of consumer forces in "modern societies" that seek to amplify people's insecurities in the interests of nurturing desire. The to-ing and fro-ing between aspirations to self-realization and transformative desires, then, is consumerism at work: "[A theme of *Teens*] is the tension between messages that fashion is about personal style and expresses characteristics unique to the presumably unchanging essence of the individual and messages describing the constant changes in hemlines, collars, patterns, and other aspects of what it means to be young, confident and 'in'" (Liechty 2003, 221–222).

In the corpus of publicity material for Superman Is Dead, including music videos, promotional photographs, and text on the band's website, representations of the band also couple bodily mutability and mobility with claims to authenticity and geo-cultural rootedness. Both tendencies attend to surfaces because corporeal mutability manifests itself as accessories that puncture or modify skin, and mobility and geo-cultural rootedness come together when mutable bodies traverse identifiably local surfaces. For example, in the music video for "Punk Hari Ini" (Punk today), the title track from the first album to result from the band's deal with Sony, the camera frequently cuts away from shots of the band performing before a surging mosh pit, to focus on the details of various punters' and band members' bodies—their T-shirts, their earrings, their jewelry, their tattoos. In a similar vein, the music video for the song "Muka Tebal" (Thick face) opens to the sound of a buzzing tattoo gun and the scene of a parlor where drummer Jerinx is having his skin altered with the addition of yet another design, and another scene features Jerinx applying eyeliner in front of a mirror.

As the camera zooms in on bodily alterations—the wearing of a ring, the application of eyeliner and of tattoos—it draws attention to the transformational possibilities of the body, thereby mobilizing "fluid identities" (Pinney 2003a, 13). Also notable is the way both videos set these fluid identities in a "ludic idiom," because the narratives depict band members at play, or employ parody. In "Punk Hari Ini," they skateboard on the esplanade that fronts Kuta Beach, a popular tourist spot in Bali. In another, they rip up the sand with their dirt bikes. And in yet another, they ride surfboards down the face of Kuta's renowned break. The video clip for "Muka Tebal" (Thick face) narrates a hammed-up confrontation between Superman Is Dead members and a copycat band who have taken to the stage at Twice Bar, the venue owned by drummer Jerinx, and which serves as the band's home base. Band members cycle and run over Kuta's potholed backstreets as they hurry to meet at the bar.

The videos do, then, employ a kind of surfacism to "mobilise fluid identities within a ludic idiom" (Pinney 2003a, 13). However, they also plant these mobile, fluid identities in local settings, stressing geo-cultural rootedness. In both videos, band members' bodies are mobilized in scenes depicting Kuta Beach, and both feature gigs taking place at Twice Bar. Indeed, common to representations of Superman Is Dead in the band's publicity material is an association with Kuta, and specifically Twice Bar, cast as both an ideal border zone and a transnational and transethnic wonderland. In a post on the Superman Is Dead website, Dethu recovered and reassigned the national motto, "Bhineka Tunggal Ika" (Unity in diversity), to encapsulate the global-local meldings that proceed at the bar (which in 2004 also housed a Suicide Glam outlet): "Have you ever heard of the saying melting pot? That's exactly what it's like at Twice / Suicide Glam in Poppies Lane 2 where we hang out and where not only people from all over Indonesia, but people from all over the world, gather. If SID [Superman Is Dead] were Xenophobic, we couldn't possibly hang out at a place that is so 'United in Diversity'" (www.supermanisdead.net).

Dethu's post reveals how the band's idealization of Kuta, while moderating their fluidity and mobility, opens space for the formulation of new kinds of ideal citizenship. By invoking "Bhineka Tunggal Ika," Dethu aligns membership in the punk glam scene with belonging to the nation-state, casting it as a form of model citizenship. Moreover, these new ideals do not just rest on Superman Is

Dead's ethnic identities—their Balinese-ness. Kuta is idealized because it exists at a distance from Jakarta. It therefore provides a stage for the band to perform their indifference to the capital, demonstrated by their discerning navigation of the mainstream media institutions located there.

Dethu iterated the importance such indifference when he told me that "we like to be part of the mainstream, but we don't follow what happens in Jakarta" (Dethu interview). This suggests Superman Is Dead retained a sense of power over Jakarta and touches on the regimes of discernment that the band claim as evidence of their pioneering and self-determined journey through mainstream media institutions. For example, Superman Is Dead claims to be the first Balinese band to secure a major recording deal in a self-determined fashion. On their website and in interviews, the band make much of their claim to be the only Indonesian band to have negotiated a major label deal that allows them to produce albums on which most of the songs have English lyrics. Sony had originally stipulated that 70 percent of the songs to be included on their first album with the label Kuta Rock City be in Indonesian. Superman Is Dead rejected this stipulation before signing the contract and threatened to quit the negotiations. Sony then retracted the clause, and 70 percent of the album's tracks remained in English.

In the years that followed, the band developed a discerning strategy of engagement, by which they sought to avoid certain kinds of media exposure deemed not "in line with SID's artistic vision" (www.supermanisdead.net). In a contribution to the Superman Is Dead website, Dethu elaborated on this strategy:

> SID employs a kind of self-censorship to make sure we don't get overexposed. Indeed, SID is not the kind of band that really gets into the whole celebrity circus. You hardly ever see SID on tv, right? That's because we like it that way (unless the tv show happens to be in line with SID's artistic vision). Even if we had millions of offers to appear, we would still try to minimalise our exposure. It's the same with the print media. We are selective, and only want to work with certain magazines. Also with our live performance schedule. We don't want to perform live too often in one city and prefer to go and perform in areas where we have never before played a gig. All this is so that SID doesn't get overexposed. (www.supermanisdead.net)

Of further note is the way this strategy of engagement was linked to membership in the nation-state. Twice Bar was held to harbor socialities that modeled a new kind of citizenship: cosmopolitan and global, but set at a distance from

Jakarta; and Superman Is Dead's discerning journey through mainstream media institutions also enabled it to distinguish the citizenship it modeled from New Order–era modes of belonging. Above, I touched on how, in his descriptions of production processes at MTVI, Hendra Tanasputra invoked the historical past and lower classes as significant "others." Similarly conflated others — "old" Indonesia and "undiscerning" modes of media production/consumption — emerge in Superman Is Dead's authenticities. Sarah Forbes, Dethu's partner in Glam Punkabilly Inferno, the outfit that managed Superman Is Dead, claimed that the band is "picky about gossip shows because they are so Old Indonesia" (interview: Dethu and Forbes, January 20, 2005).

Superman Is Dead's coupling of fluidity and mobility with geo-cultural racination recalls Liechty's and Mazzarella's arguments that to-ing and fro-ing between abstraction and concretion, self-transformation and self-realization, is commodification at work (Liechty 2003; Mazzarella 2003). In this sense, Superman Is Dead's identity quest may be seen to reflect a context in which consumerism emerges as an increasingly dominant ideology governing subject formation. But this to-ing and fro-ing was also accommodated to a specific Indonesian context of regime change, for it opened space for formulating new ideals of citizenship in a post–New Order context. Superman Is Dead's very racination, that is, fixed the celebrated mutability of their bodies in a place, enabling them to chart a discerning course through mainstream media institutions that cast them as model post-authoritarian citizens.

Representations of Krisdayanti in the book *1001 KD* manifest a similar to-ing and fro-ing. They celebrate fluid identities and also signal allegiance to spaces established as local. However, in several respects, Krisdayanti's experimentations with citizenship deviate from Superman Is Dead's. The fluidity of her identity (the 1,001 manifestations of KD) is contained within a broader linear narrative that culminates in wealth and career success. Notably this trajectory moves her away from her hometown Batu and places her in Jakarta, unlike Superman Is Dead's narrative, which links their authenticity to their home in Bali. Additionally, also unlike that of Superman Is Dead, Krisdayanti's narrative of self-realization implicates a nondiscerning embrace of the media spotlight. The book *1001 KD* includes not only promotional images of Krisdayanti but also advertisements in which she appears. And while Superman Is Dead seek to anchor the fluidity of their identities in their geo-cultural roots, Krisdayanti does so through reference to an established discourse of femininity — an orientation that highlights the gendered qualities of a quest for ideal modes of post-authoritarian belonging, for such a discourse moderates her transformation and career achievements by casting her as "first and foremost, a wife and a mother" (Endah 2003, 40).

A THOUSAND AND ONE KRISDAYANTIS

In hardback, *1001 KD* is in a large, lavish format that consists of two hundred pages of photographs of the various styles that have characterized the singer's career; the text recounts Krisdayanti's life story as told to Alberthiene Endah (Endah 2003). The book charts Krisdayanti's course from her humble beginnings in the East Javanese village of Batu, where her divorcee mother ran a small catering business. In the early 1980s, Krisdayanti and her older sister began entering, and consistently winning, local singing competitions. On the advice of a relative, and in the interests of the girls' careers, the family moved to Jakarta in 1983, where Krisdayanti's mother got work in a salon, washing people's hair and selling homemade cakes to the clients. Both Krisdayanti and her older sister continued singing. They both joined singing groups and began participating in, and winning, competitive singing festivals. In 1989, at age fourteen, Krisdayanti secured her first recording deal. In 1991 she was a finalist in a cover-girl competition organized by a local teen magazine, *Gadis*. In 1992, she won the prestigious, Asia-wide singing competition, Asia Bagus. In 1995, she signed to Warner Music, with whom her first album, *Terserah* (Up to you), sold seven hundred thousand copies.

The *1001* KD book infers a claim that existential issues can be inscribed upon surfaces of the body. In it, Krisdayanti portrays her existence as a pleasurable and sensual bathing in images of herself, including advertising images. It contains five chapters, titled "Career and I," "Fashion and I," "Beauty and I," "Family and I," and "Myself and I." The final chapter, "Myself and I," opens with two consecutive multiple-exposure photographs that make it look as if KD is gazing into a mirror. If the autobiography as a whole suggests "I am because I am photographed," then the coming together of these mirror images with the chapter entitled "Myself and I" seems to say "I am all surface."

Superman Is Dead's videos draw attention to bodily mutability through a focus on the puncturing and adornment of skin. Krisdayanti's entire book is dedicated to a celebration of corporeal mutability; it contains dozens and dozens of photographs of her adorned in different costumes. The very ease of her self-transformation is forcefully posited by a double-page advertisement for Exoticon contact lenses, featuring Krisdayanti. For women, wearing tinted contact lenses came into fashion in the early 2000s. Staying in Jakarta at the time, I often encountered women whose appearance unsettled me for their striking blue or green eyes. This fashion stretches the notion of "surfacism" as a feature of photographic practice. According to Pinney, surfacism manifests itself as a focus on the texture of the photograph's surface, and it expands "possibilities for cultural reinvention" (Pinney 2003a, 13). Here, it is tinted lenses rather than photographs that mediate surfacism, depositing color on the eye's surface, setting up a barrier that unsettles any notion of its link to a stable interior state or inalienable cultural identity, and positing the very fluidity of identity.

The possibilities tinted lenses offer for self-reinvention are forcefully advanced by the Exoticon advertisement. It comprises a thin, wide strip of images of Krisdayanti's face that resembles a strip of photographic film. This presentation also mobilizes surfacism, because it draws attention to the photographic form that mediates Krisdayanti's changing appearances, positing photography too, like the tinted lenses the ad promotes, as a realm for cultural reinvention. In each image along the strip, Krisdayanti's eyes are a different color: sometimes blue, sometimes green, gray, or light brown. The lenses themselves are encoded with values that disarticulate appearance from notions of a stable, underlying cultural identity or inner self, but the strip photo completes this process of delinking by setting a rapid turnover of appearances on a condensed timeline. With each click of the shutter, Krisdayanti's eyes change color.

Like the Exoticon advertisement, the second set of images also sets a transforming Krisdayanti along a timeline, but it is a much longer timeline that asserts the very ephemerality of identity less vigorously. It occupies a centerfold spread in the book and pictorially documents the rags-to-riches linear narrative recounted in the body of the text. When coupled with written accounts of Krisdayanti's life, these images provide a striking contrast to the ludism apparent in Superman Is Dead's videos, which depict scenes of them riding dirt bikes and surfing. Rather than ludic, the idiom that accommodates Krisdayanti's transformation is characteristically laborious and involves a high degree of schooling. In the following excerpt, Krisdayanti recounts her high school beginnings as a poor kid whose creative acumen transformed her into a trendsetter, marking the beginning of her rags-to-riches story. The account culminates in Krisdayanti's career success and enormous wealth, conspicuously on show.

When I entered my teens, my interest in pretty clothes of course began to grow. I became aware of trends. I began to understand that if I wore clothes that were thought of as "in," people would think of me as someone with an "up to date" style. In this regard, I was lucky to have been blessed with a certain flexibility. I didn't need to have a lot of money to be able to take part in the trends. . . . When I was in senior high school, a kind of giant watch with a big face was all the rage . . . . One of its special features was its colourful band. They cost a lot of money. Only rich kids could afford to wear them. Of course, I wanted to have one too, but I didn't have enough money. After some hard thinking, I came upon an idea. I tied colourful wool around my watchband, and made it look like a really unique and interesting watch. Do you know what happened then? My style watch became the new trend at that school, and kids started turning up with colourful wool wound around their watch bands.

. . . As my career progressed, my luck began to flow. The first brand-name garment I bought was a Prada skirt. It cost nine million rupiah. And even that was a sale price, the original price was tens of millions of rupiah. How happy I was to wear that skirt for the first time! Then I started to be able to afford to buy designer clothes to wear on stage. Jean Paul Gaultier, Donna Karan and Dolce and Gabbana are some of the designers I like. Recently, I've started to collect Dior, Lanvin, Fendi, Hermes, Valentino and Versace. And of course I'm a great fan of all the top Indonesian designers. (Endah 2003, 55)

In the course of *1001 KD*, the upward trajectory recounted here is put forward repeatedly. For example, a full yellow-tinted, right-hand page in the opening chapter, "Career and I," is dedicated to the following quote, which is presented in a multicolored font of various sizes: "Often, while I am singing, I ask myself 'Is this real? Aren't I just a poor kid from Batu?'" (17). She appears to answer this question on a subsequent page in a quote that is pulled from the text, enlarged, and run across the top of the page. It reads: "Had I had a well-to-do kind of childhood, I probably wouldn't have felt the urge to better myself and become the Krisdayanti I am now" (22). This narrative links the radical mutability of Krisdayanti's body to an essence—a poor kid's beginnings—and works to attribute moral virtue to her conspicuous consumption. Krisdayanti also seems eager to tame her upward mobility specifically through reference to a discourse of femininity, which domesticates her. Such domestication appears in an image of the singer performing before a portrait of Raden Ajeng Kartini—a young Javanese woman who gained fame in colonial society at the dawn of the twentieth century for her letters to some Dutch intellectuals in which she expressed emancipatory aspirations for Javanese women; but the New Order interpretation of her legacy idealizes attention to domestic chores and skills at bodily adornment. Krisdayanti identifies herself with this New Order interpretation. Across the bottom of the page, on which she appears performing before Kartini's portrait, runs the following quote: "Adorning oneself is proof of women's power" (119).

Other references to established discourses of femininity also temper the possibilities for change that her consumerism implies, such as those to her complete and utter dedication to her fans, which emplace the attention Krisdayanti pays to her body. Her body, that is, is not expressive of individual growth nor of selfhood, but rather of selflessness, for she dresses up only to satisfy the needs of her fans. Discourses of wifehood and motherhood further constrain the freedoms she may be afforded by her immense capacity to consume, and form a central part of the book. A whole chapter is accorded to her accounts of family life and photographic evidence of her dedication to her family. The chapter opens with a full page dedicated to the following statement: "It's not easy being a woman who is the main income earner of the family. The most difficult thing is convincing others around you that there is nothing wrong with that" — but then, in the opening paragraph, she identifies herself as a "woman who obeys her husband" (150). The chapter also includes page-length testimonials of other famous people, who attest to Krisdayanti's selflessness. One such testimonial is from Rakhee Punjabee: "People assume that being a diva means you forget your family. But that's not the case with Krisdayanti . . . . She has never forgotten that over and above her position as a megastar, she will always be, first and foremost, a wife and a mother" (40).

ANCHORING MEN, ANCHORING WOMEN

This chapter has described how ideological shifts in the early twenty-first century were related to media deregulation and regime change and yielded new modes of subject formation. In place of the *pemuda*, who symbolized nationalism and collective action, a new self-determined "I" emerged as an ideal citizen. The rise to prominence of this new "I" voiced the emancipatory promise encoded in consumerist ideology. If *pemuda* was entwined with the privileging of print literacies, the new "I" inhabited a free-for-all marketplace of things, and therefore of identities. Individuality could be self-determined through diligent consumption of media texts. In theory, consumerist ideology would have leveling implications, because it posits that one can consume one's way into, and become, the other. But in practice, other forces were at play that modulated the emancipatory promise of the new Indonesian "I." First, people's ability to recognize themselves in this figure rested on their position in long-standing taste regimes, rearticulated now as Nielsen Audience Measurement but still heavily inflected with the *kampungan-gedongan* dualism. Second, in a post-Suharto context, people were not just seeking to inhabit a global marketplace as self-determined individuals. They were also interested in remaking notions of ideal Indonesian citizenship, requiring certain kinds of anchoring. The chapter argued that the qualities of this anchoring varied very much according to gender.

Such differences emerge from comparisons of the visual representations of two pop acts: the female soloist Krisdayanti and the three-piece, all-male punk band Superman Is Dead. Visual media representing both acts oscillate between a quest for transformation and one for authenticity, and I have argued that such to-ing and fro-ing can be understood as part of a question for post-authoritarian subjectivities. Both sets of images manifest surfacist strategies, which foreground the mutability of the body's surfaces, but such mutability is tempered by the way both acts seek to emplace themselves in historical and spatial certainties. These emplacements fix both cosmopolitan and patriotic politics onto the body by marrying an obsession with tactility and mutable surfaces with more stable historical and spatial contexts. In this way, Krisdayanti and Superman Is Dead's interest in tinkering with body surfaces pivots around more stable identifications. Unlike Krisdayanti's stable femininity, however, Superman Is Dead's stabilities do not condemn them to domesticity.

FIVE

Spinning Pasts

When I talked about the loss of history, I didn't mean the
disappearance of images of history, for instance, in the case of nostalgia
film. The increasing number of films about the past are no longer
historical; they are images, simulacra and pastiches of the past. They are
effectively a way of satisfying a chemical craving for historicity,
using a product that substitutes for and blocks it.

Fredric Jameson (Buchanan 2007, 61)

Can transnational capitalism be a source of discursive energy
for constructing a highly localized historical narrative
for very contextualized consumption?

Ma 2000, 133

In early 2004, while undertaking research on the music industry in Jakarta, I
received notification via sms of a press conference to take place at Sony Music
to mark the launch of an album, *Tribute to Ian Antono* (original title in English).
The album featured a lineup of performers contracted to Sony Music, who sang
rearranged versions of songs written by Ian Antono, a guitarist and a songwriter
best known for his membership in the rock band God Bless, established in 1973.
God Bless began as a Deep Purple cover band, then released its first album of
original songs in 1975. In the same year, God Bless opened for Deep Purple when
the band played in Jakarta, and went on to enjoy considerable commercial success in Indonesia up until the late 1980s.

Five years passed before I had the chance to return to my research on the music industry. When I did, in 2009, I was struck not only by the appearance of a deluge of fresh histories of Indonesian popular music, but also by the enduring prominence of God Bless in them. In April, God Bless was awarded a lifetime achievement award by the Indonesian Music Association (Asosiasi Musik Indonesia, or AMI) in a nationally televised award ceremony, and shortly thereafter released an album titled 36, a number that refers to the band's age in years. The album's launch had been preceded by a high-profile media campaign. At the beginning of the year, God Bless appeared on a popular television talk show, *Kick Andy*, and performed one of the band's hits, "Rumah Kita" (Our house)—a track penned by Ian Antono and used as the single for *Tribute*—at the country's biggest rock music festival, Soundrenaline.

In May 2009, a special edition of *Rolling Stone* Indonesia was devoted to the band. They appeared in all their aged glory on the magazine's cover, and a long feature article was devoted to the band's evolution from the early 1970s. The same article revealed plans by the celebrated film production company Miles Productions to produce a documentary film of the band. Miles Production's producer/director duo, Riri Riza and Mira Lesmana, filmed the *Rolling Stone* interview for that very purpose, and a photograph of Riza filming the interview accompanied the text published in *Rolling Stone*.

The textual layering implicated in the *Rolling Stone* article is startling. Here we have a print journalist's interview with a band, filmed by a renowned filmmaker for the purposes of a documentary film about the band—filming which was then photographed, and this photograph included as an image to accompany the print article. This layering offers a taste of the textual effervescence, the overstatement, and the hyperbole implicated in the comeback—an effervescence that reaches its pinnacle with the publication of the *Rolling Stone* piece. This chapter engages work on nostalgia to consider the impetus of such energies. It inquires into the objects of nostalgic feeling, the historical implications of fondly remembering these objects, and the institutional contexts responsible for producing such fond memories.

Pop nostalgia is not unique to Indonesia. As the chapters in Homan's collection *Access All Eras: Tribute Bands and Global Pop Culture* (2006) attest, tributes and comebacks are a global phenomenon and can be understood as a feature of the ascendancy of the image and its endless reproduction in the context of late modernity. In light of this, God Bless's comeback reveals the extent of these trends' global penetration. But representations of the past in Indonesian popular music also bear relevance to discussions among Indonesianist scholars about the challenges in the post-authoritarian era for revising the New Order's vision of modernity, and the conditions under which this vision was established and enforced (Heryanto 2014; Zurbuchen 2005). A focus on God Bless reveals the role a transnationalized popular music industry is playing in fashioning the ways people remember the New Order, and the implications of this remembering for their ability to critique its key propositions and creation myths.

NOSTALGIA

The epigraph that opens this chapter is drawn from a conversation with Anders Stephanson, in which Fredric Jameson expands on his renowned essay "Postmodernism, or the Cultural Logic of Late Capitalism" ([1984] 1991). In the essay, Jameson chronicles instances of a postmodern aesthetic that he holds to be telling of the transformed position of culture in late capitalism. There are differences, he argues, between modern and postmodern ways of understanding time, space, and images. His examples suggest a postmodern interest in depthlessness and surface play, and a loss of historicity ("a perception of the present as history . . . which is at length characterised as historical perspective") (Jameson 1991, 284).

Jameson's argument for the depthless quality of the postmodern is compellingly advanced by his comparison of the ways Vincent van Gogh and Andy Warhol depicted shoes. Van Gogh's *Peasant Shoes* intimate a deeper reality of hardship and misery, but Warhol's photographic negative, *Diamond Dust Shoes*, delights in the surface of those objects, their "glacéd Xray elegance." Jameson contends, "There is . . . in Warhol no way to complete the hermeneutic gesture and restore to these oddments that whole larger lived context of the dance hall or the ball, the world of jetset fashion or glamour magazines" (Jameson 1991, 8–9).

But the idea that the present is primarily postmodern is challenged by some of the work on nostalgia in Asia, which has been concerned with the kind of nostalgia that evokes, rather than substitutes, historicity (Ferry 2003; Ivy 1995; Iwabuchi 2002; Kelly 1986; Ma 2000). In his study of Hong Kong, for example, Ma argues, "In the discourse of postmodernism, nostalgic aesthetic is said to have contributed to the disappearance of historicity by its hybridization of styles of different historical periods and its destabilizing use of parody and intertextual references. However, this argument should be applied to the Hong Kong case with extra care. In the years before and after the handover, the upsurge of nostalgic media in Hong Kong has been characterized by a strong commitment to modernity" (Ma 2000, 137).

Ma's article studies an advertisement for Hong Kong Bank that depicted the rags-to-riches story of a Hong Kong Everyman, provoking nostalgia for Hong Kong's bygone days around the time of the handover of the territory to the People's Republic of China. He argues that this kind of nostalgic media resists the opacity and depthlessness typical of postmodernism. Rather, it asserts cultural unity by constructing a linear narrative. Ma pursues an interest in the provenance of this narrative and how transnational capital is implicated in its construction. He asks, "If there is no strong nationalism to activate an identity conferring history, where does the nostalgic desire for a historical rootedness evolve from? Does the urge derive from within the community, which has been granted a sociocultural space under non-interventive politics by both Britain and China? Can transnational capitalism be a source of discursive energy for constructing a highly localized historical narrative for very contextualized consumption?" (133).

As discussed in chapter 4, a number of studies show how multinational media conglomerates play a vital role in "producing the local" in transnationalized media environments in Asia. In his study of advertising agencies and campaigns in India, Mazzarella argues that producing the "local" is an important part of the way transnational media corporations create desire for commodities, "making it look as if the world according to marketing is merely a reflection of the deepest and truest needs of the people to whom it is addressed" (2003, 18). Others have shown how transnational media companies are implicated in the retrieval and reconstruction of local pasts. In Ferry's study of China, global media productions introduce new ideas about ideal womanhood by retrieving figures from the past, particularly the 1930s New (Chinese) Woman, that link the consuming woman to notions of progressive modernity and help to identify consumption as an ideal womanly practice in the present (Ferry 2003). Similar processes can be seen at work in Indonesia, where nostalgic productions of the local past intensify in context of the deregulated, transnationalized media environment. The God Bless comeback can be seen as part of this generalized phenomenon, whereby transnational media corporations actively produce the local (already well accounted for in the previous chapter). In this chapter, the focus shifts to the specific qualities of the production of the past in the context of Indonesia's local music boom and the opportunities it presents for historical revision. Why should nostalgia settle on the 1970s, and why memorialize rock in particular? Does the lust for local popular music histories accommodate reassessments of the preceding regime's vision of modernity, or does it commodify the past, "blocking" such reassessments?

The questions Ma poses about transnational capitalism's potential as a "source of discursive energy for constructing a . . . localized historical narrative" (2000, 133) arise from his interest in the Hong Kong case, where financial institutions were implicated in building up, from a context of "weak" nationalism, a sense of a coherent Hong Kong identity in the leadup to the handover in 1997. In Indonesia, by contrast, questions about historical narrative pertain to the possibilities for *de*constructing the forceful logics of the preceding era. In his 2014 book, Heryanto considers the challenges for this work of deconstructing, particularly for those efforts seeking redress for the victims of the 1965–1968 state-sponsored anticommunist violence. He problematizes the idea that the end of the New Order would naturally allow the victims to seek justice, thereby correcting the historical record, and setting the post-authoritarian period apart from what preceded it. This idea rests on the assumptions that all victims had been silenced during the New Order (which they hadn't) and that all of them would necessarily want to speak out after it fell (which they didn't). Moreover, attempts to open space for the victims to speak, to enable people to remember and come to terms with the violent past, often fall flat for various reasons. First, in line with the New Order metanarrative, demonization of the Indonesian Communist Party often remains a feature of such projects of remembering, suggesting its enduring force. Reviewing the documentary film *Tjidurian 19*, about members of Lekra (Lembaga Kebudayaan Rakyat, the Institute of People's Culture) who were persecuted for their links to the Indonesian Communist Party, Heryanto states that "the regime's allegations about the savagery of the communists are left unchallenged, if not reaffirmed" (2014, 113). Second, it is increasingly difficult to frame the issues in a way that is engaging to young audiences, who feel disconnected from events that took place fifty years ago. "For young Indonesians the troubled history has not been and indeed cannot be forgotten or remembered since it has never even registered in their minds" (Heryanto 2014, 116).

Through a focus on the God Bless comeback as an instance of remembering the New Order, this chapter shows how transnational capitalism may be implicated in, or provide a "source of discursive energy" (Ma 2000, 133) for overcoming, such challenges. The comeback is chosen for the variety of texts that emerged from it; those examined here include the aforementioned *Rolling Stone* article about God Bless (Denny MR 2009a), the band's appearance on the television variety show *Kick Andy* (2008), and the tribute album, *Tribute to Ian Antono*, produced by Sony Music (2004). These different texts mediate the New Order past in different ways. Some present themselves as pedagogical tools for understanding the "truth" of history; they position God Bless firmly within a historical narrative that memorializes, rather than critiques, the New Order. Others renounce historical context; narrative evaporates from their surfaces, they seem depthless, opaque, and also do little to encourage critical reassessment of the past. The chapter argues that the case of God Bless's comeback therefore affirms existing work highlighting the challenges of historical revision in the post-authoritarian era and reveals how the transnational media corporations that now play an important role in Indonesia's popular music industry contribute to the conundrum.

THE VANISHING PAST

When I arrived at Sony Music Indonesia's headquarters to attend the launch of *Tribute*, I was presented with a press release, which endeavored to establish Ian Antono's reputation as a rock legend:

> Ian Antono is an integral figure to the history of Indonesian rock music. His guitar skills get the thumbs up. The melodies he plays are so strong and full of character, it's no surprise that he has inspired so many bands and, in particular, young Indonesian guitarists. Through God Bless and Gong 2000 Ian has had a hand in the development of Indonesian rock. Ian Antono is not only a guitarist but also an arranger, composer and producer. Anggun C Sasmi and Nicky Astria are two female rockers who have found success as a consequence of his guidance.
>
> Ian, known as the "Indonesian guitar God," has now been on the scene for more than three decades. Over that time he had composed hundreds of masterpieces. It would be a pity to let his work fall by the wayside, so Sony Music decided to pioneer the production of a tribute to Ian Antono—an idea that has received enthusiastic support from a number of musicians and bands.

The press release is notable, because it presents *Tribute* as a pedagogical tool revealing of a historical truth and depth, rather than, say, purely an object of visual and sonic pleasure. Other aspects of the God Bless comeback also assert temporality very strongly, intimating a desire for historical roots. At one extreme, some texts heroize the band and leave little room for doubt or for reflection. For example, the band is referred to over and over again as "legendary," a term that points to some of the comeback's very imposing dimensions. According to the Bahasa Indonesia version of Wikipedia's entry for God Bless, "God Bless is a rock music group that has become a legend in Indonesia," and its entry for Ian Antono states that "Ian Antono . . . is a musician and composer who is also one of the guitarists for the legendary rock music group, God Bless."[1]

On the Facebook profile for *Kick Andy*, the end-of-year interview with God Bless was announced thus: "To accompany us on this last night of 2008 and welcome in the new year, Kick Andy has something special: 'GOD BLESS RETURN,' a special episode devoted to discussion with that legendary homeland band, God Bless." Reponses to the announcement on Facebook included, "They are so cool, still raging, even more so than today's bands" (Rizky Januar, at 00:01 on January 1); "I only have one comment, COOOOLLLL" (wp03sp4n, January 18); and "I just watched Kick Andy, they really went off, they are so cool and legendary" (massol507, January 16).[2]

Other instances of the comeback also assert the truth of the band's historical importance but contain less hyperbole. In his feature published in *Rolling Stone*, Denny MR opens with "God Bless' journey is a reflection of Indonesian rock history," which he must then set about demonstrating. This he does with great economy and literary skill, and the sense of a trajectory that proves God Bless's importance is aided by the accompanying images. A vertical timeline, for example, establishes the dates of album releases and changes in membership. Photographs of members in various settings stress photography's evidentiary potential. They serve here as proof of the text's truth; I might go so far as to suggest that they can *only* serve as such. The context of these photographs, their setting among the text of the feature article attesting to God Bless's important historical role, hinders alternative readings.

Other texts, though, put less stress on the band's "legendary" status and focus more on its movement away from the present. This sense of movement is evoked by emphases on the band members' advanced years, as may be seen in the titling of the comeback album (36—the band's age in years) and, most spectacularly, in the section of Andy F. Noya's interview with the band chosen for the promo of *Kick Andy*'s God Bless episode. In this promo, Noya asked each band member to state his age in turn. In his *Rolling Stone* article, Denny MR also brings God Bless's age to the forefront and cites it as evidence of the band's status as a pioneer of Indonesian rock: "At a time when many bands of their generation have dissolved, that giant, hair a-whitened, now walks alone. In its footsteps lies the pulse of Indonesian rock history" (Denny MR, 2009, 36).

These parts of the comeback, stressing movement away from the present, are reminiscent of Marilyn Ivy's characterization of nostalgia as a performance of the past's vanishing. Moreover, the coexistence of references to the band's "legendary" and "cool" status with references to its age (and distance from the present) recall Ivy's descriptions of how Japanese modernity finds itself through a double labor of longing for and distancing from past referents, a positioning that helps generate historical narrative (Ivy 1995, 242).

> To assert Japanese modernity is not an unambiguous task. Correlated with the historically-located transformations that have accompanied the rise of capitalism and nation-statehood in the 20th century, modernity implies a structure of consciousness and subjectivity with a peculiar relationship to temporality, one in which continuity (the continuity of "tradition," for example) can never be taken for granted within the upheavals of capitalist commodity relations. Traces of origin, displaced, subsist as traces of loss that infiltrate modernity's present.

If Ivy sees the task of asserting Japanese modernity as ambiguous, one wonders what her take might be on the task of asserting Indonesian modernity. Not only is there the troubling impossibility, as Ivy puts it, of remaining the same, but also the array of popular cultural choices with which Indonesians are faced in any quest for the origins of a national modernity, and the very different narratives that these different choices might intimate. So, if the God Bless comeback is to be read as a performance of the past vanishing and inviting of our longing, a part of a quest for origins that aids the construction of historical narrative, then what might that narrative be?

ROCK AUTHENTICITY: A *GEDONGAN* SENSIBILITY

In Appaduraian terms, nostalgia for God Bless is a historical phenomenon because it "links patterns of change to . . . larger universes of interaction" (1996, 74). Tributes to and comebacks of groups that found fame in the 1970s are a global phenomenon (Homan 2006), and the globalization of Indonesian popular music, evident in the establishment of branches and licensees of *Rolling Stone* and Sony Music, naturally brings with it a degree of transnational formatting in the "production of locality." We should nonetheless be able to provide some account for why nostalgia settles on certain objects, and for what these objects reveal of the genealogical forces at play in the constitution of historical narrative.

Rolling Stone, in which the comeback reaches its peak, is a case in point. The magazine's content and format are indeed heavily determined by the US principle. But in its attempts to address an Indonesian public, the magazine harks back to a familiar politics: the chronicling of culture by revered male intellectuals in the restricted but prestigious medium of print. As discussed in chapter 1, in the 1970s, rock was an important element of an elitist middle-class orientation that flourished following the left's annihilation, yet existed in ambivalent relation to the New Order rulers. Authentic consumption of rock was mediated by those empowered to chronicle its evolution; it required knowledge of a number of difficult-to-access texts (the written word, English), connoted proximity to modernity, and was reliant on the "other" of dangdut—derided as the un-modern realm of the unknowing masses—for its self-definition.

This familiar politics is indeed a tradition that *Rolling Stone* strives to uphold (for a more detailed discussion of *Rolling Stone* see Baulch 2010). In the 1970s, middle-classness was evinced in and through *Aktuil* by strategic inclusions and exclusions that served to identify rock as an expressive form and a cultural practice that could be associated with the figure of *pemuda* and, by extension, with critique of the power holders. As well as positioning rock at a distance from the state, *Aktuil* distinguished the genre from popular lower-class forms that were similarly excluded from state television broadcast: dangdut. In this way *Aktuil* positioned rock as a middle position between the militaristic state and the vulgar masses. *Rolling Stone*'s address, which heralds a discerning, male reading public (*pria dewasa*, literally adult male), is drawn directly from these styles of journalism developed in the 1970s (Interview: Adib Hidayat, October 6, 2009). By emulating this journalism, the magazine strives to call back into being the trope of the new middle-class subject whose features were considerably sharpened in the new cultural environment established by the New Order. Just as critical middle-classness was intimated in *Aktuil* through the exclusion of dangdut, so is it sketched in *Rolling Stone* through the exclusion of pop Melayu (as discussed in chapter 3). God Bless, by contrast, exudes a looming presence in *Rolling Stone*. As well as appearing in a special issue of the magazine, the band appears in a larger-than-life photograph that adorns a prominent wall in the magazine's headquarters at a posh South Jakarta address.

In this way, *Rolling Stone* relies on God Bless to posit a cultural origin for Indonesian rock, and by doing so proffers a strong sense of modernist historicity that memorializes rock's very *gedongan*-ness. Ivy argues that historical narrative is generated when nostalgia settles on preconceived notions of a premodern essence. Nostalgia for the premodern identifies "what was" as qualitatively different from "what is" and enables the charting of a history of transformation. Nostalgia for God Bless, however, identifies the band as a source of the "now," rather than something that "was." A continuous line is drawn from the birth of the band to the present-day rock modernity, as evident in the two statements that bookend Denny MR's piece: "God Bless is a reflection of Indonesian rock history" and "In its footsteps lies the pulse of Indonesian rock history" (Denny MR, 2009b, 32, 36).

The marking of God Bless's heyday as a beginning point is notable, because it shows how the New Order is being remembered as a golden age, and also a point of origin, in nostalgic renditions of Indonesian popular music. The God Bless story presents the New Order as an era of opportunity due to the new openness to Western-style popular music in the 1970s, and the resulting influx of cultural influences. Moreover, it was during this time that the foundations were laid for the emergence of rock supergroups that found fame during the local music boom of the late 1990s and early 2000s.

We may find this narrative in the shape and flow of Denny MR's feature in *Rolling Stone*, which depicts how God Bless's beginnings as a cover band afforded it the chance to realize itself as an act performing original repertoire.

On 5 . . . December, 1973, "Hard Lovin' Man," that ultra-wild Deep Purple song, was screamed from the Open Stage at Taman Ismail Marzuki. But Ian Gillan and his friends were nowhere to be seen. The song, from Deep Purple's In Rock album, was being performed by a young, afro-headed man and four rockers with similarly mad hair. They were vocalist Ahmad Albar, guitarist Ludwig Lemans, bass player Donny Fattah, keyboard player Deddy Dores, and drummer Fuad Hassan. On that night, the mostly young audience bore witness to the birth of a band called God Bless. (Denny MR, 2009b, 31)

Denny MR then goes on to provide detail of God Bless's transformation from cover band to an act performing original material. He describes how the band released their first album of originals, *God Bless*, in 1975, under the auspices of two commercial enterprises whose joint venture was dedicated to recording and marketing Indonesian acts, before ending the *Rolling Stone* piece with the image of the aging rock heroes walking off into the sunset, in their wake "the pulse of Indonesian rock history" (2009b, 36).

While the notion of the Indonesian present as post-authoritarian identifies 1998 as a point of historical rupture, no such rupture can be found in the story of Indonesian rock that the comeback strives to tell. Instead, much of the comeback intimates that the present is a culmination of the past, not its sequel; it proffers a sense of historical continuity. Moreover, by identifying God Bless as a starting point for the present, by default the comeback casts the New Order period

The mirror image of Krisdayanti that appears in the final chapter of her book.

Krisdayanti in an advertisement for Exoticon contact lenses.

1994 1997 1998 1999 2000

2001 2002 2002 2003 2003

above Krisdayanti's
life in pictures.

right Krisdayanti
as Kartini.
Credit: Barry Wi.

Berdandan adalah bukti
kekuatan perempuan....

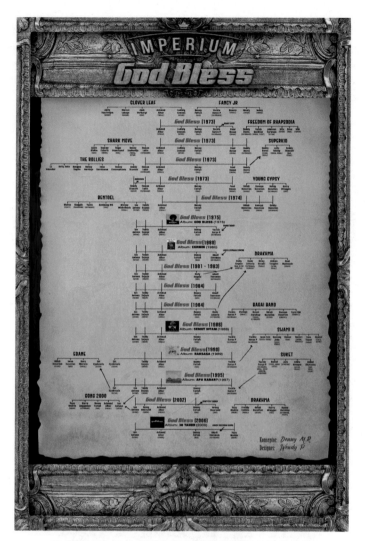

God Bless timeline exhibited at the World Music Gallery in Malang, East Java. The timeline was adapted from Denny MR's design to accompany his article about God Bless in *Rolling Stone* (Denny MR 2009a, 29). Credit, research: Denny MR; design: Wendy Purnama.

Album sleeve, *Tribute to Ian Antono* (Sony Music Indonesia 2004).
Credit: Sony Music Entertainment Indonesia.

Nanoe Biroe's President of Baduda Republic seal.
Credit: Nanoe Biroe.

as a new beginning and—unwittingly, perhaps—rearticulates the New Order's creation myth: that the regime imposed a widely sought-after order on a chaotic situation, enabling the nation to begin anew after the ideological polarization of the immediately postindependence era (Heryanto 2006).

FREE-FLOATING HISTORY

Denny MR's article about God Bless evinced a sense of the early New Order period as a new beginning, and of the present as a culmination of that new beginning. But other texts associated with God Bless's comeback sketched different narratives. For example, above I recounted my attendance at the launch of *Tribute* and the very pedagogical nature of the press release I was presented with there. This press release, I suggested, paid little heed to the album as an object of sonic or visual pleasure. But it is precisely these visual and sonic "surfaces" that other aspects of the album stress, intimating historical depthlessness and recalling the well-used Jamesonian term "pastiche."

Sony chose "Rumah Kita" (Our house) as the single to promote the album. The song was rendered in a "We Are the World"-style by a lineup of high-profile Sony artists, collectively referred to as "Indonesian Voices" (original in English). The choice of "Rumah Kita," sung by the Indonesian Voices, as the title track on a tribute album devoted to a rock hero of the 1970s may at first glance intimate a coherent "We," past and present. But although the convergence of these elements—tribute, "Rumah Kita," Indonesian Voices—reaches for the historical, it does not allow for the completion of this "hermeneutic gesture" (Jameson 1991).

Such incompleteness manifests itself in several ways. First, the album was titled in English, pointedly refraining from any Indonesian equivalent that might point listeners toward a certain history. Nor does the album sleeve do anything to recall or augment the temporality, the historical trajectory, to which a tribute would ostensibly be devoted. It does nothing to evoke Ian Antono, the legendary guitarist—there are no liner notes to signal that this is archival material; nowhere on the sleeve does one see his face or an image of him performing onstage. In this sense, *Tribute*'s sleeve is unlike the imagery accompanying Denny MR's feature article in *Rolling Stone*, which proffers evidence of God Bless's important historical role. The press release appeared to convey an interest in preservation, but only because it was penned by Denny MR, the above-cited journalist, who pitched the idea of *Tribute* to Sony, with preservation in mind. On the album sleeve, though, no liner notes appeared; the preservationist urge was pushed out of the limelight. What features most prominently is a red guitar. In place of an image of Antono himself, the names of those Sony artists who cover Antono on *Tribute* appear as watermarks over the image of the glinting red guitar.

The third way in which depthlessness becomes evident refers to the choice of "Rumah Kita" as *Tribute*'s title track, and to the mode of the song's performance on the video clip to promote the album. The song is an ode to the stereotypically simple, and timeless, rural Malay setting:

Just a bamboo shack our house
without decoration or pictures
With a roof of rice stalks and a floor of dirt
But it is ours
Indeed it's ours
Our own

The fence of our house is made of wild grasses
No carnations or jasmine
Just a wild lily in the yard
But it is ours
Indeed it's ours
Our own

It's better here
at our house
where comfort and blessings rule
everything is here . . . at our house
Must we go off to the city
which is full of question marks? (Ian Antono and Theodore KS)

Quite unlike Denny MR's feature in *Rolling Stone*, the video makes no attempt to retrieve the bygone days whence Antono apparently hails, or to emplace Sony's "Indonesian Voices" in relation to them. Antono does appear toward the end of the song, performing a guitar solo in studio, surrounded by the young Sony artists who take their turns singing lines of the song. However, the video presents no cut-aways to old footage of Antono performing, or concert crowds dressed in 1970s or 1980s fashions reveling in his musical virtuosity, as might be expected of a nostalgic production. Nor does it attempt to establish any relation between Sony's Indonesian Voices and the stereotypically simple and timeless

Malay village of which they sing. The video is shot, rather, in the "nowhere" of a studio, and the camera stays focused on individual performers as they take their turns behind the microphone.

In this sense, *Tribute* very much resembles *Diamond Dust Shoes*. Who wears these shoes? Where do they wear them? In Jameson's view, these questions cannot be answered. Who wrote these songs, under what conditions, and why? The songs are performed as if they are (Sony) originals, so these questions do not arise from listening to them. *Tribute* refuses to draw a line from present to past. "The past is there," it whispers, only to add: "But there is no 'there' there." There is no way to complete the hermeneutic gesture.

―――――

In 2004, when *Tribute* appeared, official sales of recorded music had fallen drastically because of piracy. There was still much money to be made from the exchange of music, but recordings were no longer the most valuable commodities: performers' images—their biographies, their bodies—were (see chapters 2 and 4). Further, most profits from the exchange of these valuable commodities did not, at that time, accrue to recording labels. In 2004, income from live or televised performances, as well as from product endorsement, accrued directly to the performers and their production and management teams.

Tribute appeared at a time when most of the Jakarta-based major recording labels were cooking up plans to correct this situation, by instituting in-house management stipulations for newly signed artists by which a cut of profits from all contracted artists' performances and endorsements would accrue to the label (Interview: Feby Lubis, May 12, 2004). Further, plans for instituting in-house management regimes ran concurrent with the stepping up of many labels' interest in manipulating their corporate images in order to make them more attractive to prospective artists. In this regard, Sony was most aggressive and most successful.

When *Tribute* was released, Sony Music Indonesia's Artist and Repertoire Division was beginning to display an interest in developing a corporate identity that bound its repertoire to notions of transnationalism, transparency, and new pop frontiers (chapter 3). Considering how *Tribute* was packaged with little heed to archival considerations, one may surmise that it had been designed to serve as an exhibition of the label's repertoire and of its commitment to developing "local talent" (a commitment that the choice of "Rumah Kita" as title track evinces).

Tribute, that is, exhibits Sony's cachet. "Rumah Kita" *is* Sony, Sony is homeland, hearth; at stake is not the homeland's link to history, but its link to Sony. When *Tribute* whispers "There is no 'there' there," it does so to a backbeat that sounds very much like SonySonySonySony.

In this way, *Tribute* reads as the epitome of a postmodern statement; it cannibalizes history and can only self-reference, repeatedly. It closely resembles the kind of postmodern architecture of which Jameson writes, which "randomly but without principle but with gusto cannibalizes all the architectural styles of the past and combines them in overstimulating ensembles" (Jameson 1991, 19; see also Ivy 1995, 57). *Tribute*'s links to a past are all but severed, rendering the "Rumah Kita" homeland free floating, a kind of accessory.

EMPLACED HERMENEUTICS

Jameson avers that postmodern nostalgia is categorically different from "properly modernist" nostalgia: the former does not evoke the pain of loss. In this regard, "Rumah Kita" veers away from Jameson. Above I have argued that Indonesian Voices' rendition of "Rumah Kita" exemplifies pastiche and depicts the local present as historically depthless. But as the comments section on the YouTube site for "Rumah Kita" reveals, this "depthless" present was appropriated by Indonesians living overseas to construct a personal trajectory of departure from and return to home.

creamieberry (2 years ago)
love it
sometimes I forget how much I love my country . . .

sosdestr (2 years ago)
This is so cool . . . . all of a sudden I want to cry . . . I miss indo

indojantan (2 years ago)
it's true there is no other country out there more beautiful than our country, INDONESIA

kojexo7 (1 year ago)
Indonesia!! Wait for me, I will surely return to my beloved homeland. My Indonesia, truly, your beauty will not be surpassed. This is all ours! . . . Don't let them fiddle with our peaceful Indonesian earth, Live Indonesia

semunglung (1 year ago)
love indonesia . . . . we have gone far away, to continue the struggle for
the rupiah, but we are only at peace in Indonesia.[3]

The appropriation in Sony Music's historically depthless music video to construct a personal journey recalls dynamics identified by Pinney in his study of
popular photography in India (Pinney 2003b). Pinney shows how people use
photography to escape the strictures of cultural and geographical emplacement.
Photography gives people an opportunity to put themselves in the picture of
what could be and therefore contains "transformative potentialities" (Pinney
2003a, 3). Ordinary people tap into the photographs' possibilities to deliberately
evince pastiche and historical depthlessness, but these images are by no means
beyond "the" hermeneutic gesture; they are part of an emplaced hermeneutics
and therefore challenge theories positing immutable links between images' formal qualities and their social effects:

> [That] the formal qualities of images themselves may be in large part irrelevant
> is suggested by their historical trajectories and the radical revaluations they
> undergo. If the image that appears to do a particular kind of work in one
> episteme is able to perform a radically different work in another, it appears
> inappropriate to propose inflexible links between formal qualities and effect.
> Instead, we need a more nuanced reading of the affinities between particular
> discursive formations and the image worlds that parallel them, as well as so-
> phisticated analyses of their transformative potentialities. (Pinney 2003a, 3)

The music video of "Rumah Kita" experienced a social life that endorses Pinney's arguments for the very indeterminate social effects produced by particular
kinds of images. As it circulated globally on YouTube, "Rumah Kita" flew off the
Sony axle and fell squarely into a nest of diasporic impulse. The viewers retrieve
the original pastiche and "cannibalization" evident in the video clip's depiction
of homeland as an enormous recording studio, and re-create it as the nation,
a time-space that bookends their journey. Above, I described "Rumah Kita" as
historically depthless, but the YouTube viewers' appropriation of the song cre-
ates a historical narrative by positioning "Rumah Kita" as both a "trace of loss"
and a "trace of origin" (Ivy 1995, 242) ("all of a sudden I want to cry . . . I miss
indo") and a point of return ("Indonesia!! Wait for me, I will surely return to
my beloved homeland"). The comments trace a shared personal trajectory away
from and back to the homeland.

LOCALIZED HISTORICAL NARRATIVE AND
TRANSNATIONAL CAPITALISM

In the course of the God Bless comeback, representations of history have moved back and forth in pendulum fashion, between pastiche and cannibalization of the past on the one hand and the regeneration of long-standing metanarratives of nationality on the other. Some texts associated with the comeback betray an interest in memorializing a familiar way of doing middle-class politics that flourished during the New Order period, but not necessarily the authoritarian polity as such. I have also argued that some nostalgic productions associated with God Bless are, in line with Jameson, not "properly modernist." *Tribute*, for example, is a prime example of the cannibalization of history for the purposes of a transnational multimedia corporation writing itself into the locale. It did so by assembling the artists that make up the label's repertoire around a "trace of origin" (Ivy 1995, 242), while at the same time striving to erase that trace and any connection it could be purported to have to the present. But nor did *Tribute* remain detached from historical narrative forever after. Diasporic Indonesians used the comments section of the YouTube video for the album title track, to build a shared personal trajectory, in which "Rumah Kita" signified the homeland: the beginning and end point of their journeys.

Both the appropriation of the "Rumah Kita" video by the YouTube viewers and the use of God Bless to construct a history of Indonesian rock recall Appadurai's arguments for the waning power of "megarhetorics of development," once responsible for the delineation of modernity in newly independent nation-states in the early twentieth century (Appadurai 1996, 10). In their place, "micronarratives of film, television, music and other expressive forms" are playing important roles in the ways people construct a sense of the nation. Indeed, as argued in chapter 4, via Mazzarella (2003), the production of locality is part of the work of transnational media corporations. They elicit desire for their products by "settling down" in local contexts. This "settling down" sometimes entails producing the local past, and indeed transnational media corporations — Sony Music and *Rolling Stone* — were pivotal to the production of the God Bless comeback. As we have seen, producing the past sometimes generates historical narrative, but at other times it obscures any account of "what happened."

Ma's interest in the relationship between transnational capitalism and historical narrative derives from the Hong Kong case, where global financial institutions were implicated in representing the past in ways that intimated a coherent Hong

Kong cultural identity. These representations emerged from a context of relatively weak nationalism and could be seen to equip Hong Kongers with a stronger sense of self in the leadup to the handover. But in the case of Indonesia, questions about the relationship between transnational capitalism and historical narrative center on emerging challenges for revisiting the conditions under which the New Order was established. Scholarly accounts focus on specific questions about opportunities and obstacles for public reassessment of the anticommunist violence in 1966–1968 that marked the birth of the New Order (Heryanto 2014; Zurbuchen 2005), particularly for representing the past in new ways. These obstacles do not just bear implications for the "veracity" of the historical record. They also cut to the question of whether post-authoritarianism can be said to constitute an actual mode of being in the present. In much of the scholarship on contemporary Indonesia, 1998 is cast as a point of rupture, and post-authoritarianism as something that is qualitatively new. But to what extent is this reflected in the ways people remember the New Order and how they connect it to the present?

As Heryanto argues, history cannot be neatly packaged into periods in which people are silenced and periods in which they speak out. Moreover, liberal polities no more determine that people will speak out than authoritarian polities determine their silence. Rather than an orderly distinction between authoritarian silencing and post-authoritarian speaking, he contends, the post-authoritarian present connects to the authoritarian past messily. Strong through-lines can be found in the ways young Indonesians appear to endorse past ways of doing things that analysts might expect to have been done away with once the New Order left the scene. The documentary film *Tjidurian 19* discussed by Heryanto is a case in point. The young directors were eager to expose the "truth" of what happened to the victims of New Order state violence in 1966–1968. But by doing so, they ended up rearticulating the very violence of the New Order's creation myth: that the communists were bad and that the mass killings and incarcerations were essentially about the preservation of order.

Similar through-lines can be found in the historical narrative generated by the God Bless comeback. As argued above, a project that identifies God Bless as a point of origin of rock modernity is necessarily tied up with a certain kind of remembering the New Order. Nostalgia for God Bless constructs a narrative in which the New Order is remembered as a golden age. This remembering is not specifically aimed at endorsing state violence of the late 1960s that gave birth to the New Order. Rather than memorializing the New Order state as such, it memorializes a particular cultural sensibility that emerged during the New

Order period—specifically that of *gedongan*. As discussed in chapter 1, this sensibility evinced the middle classes' separateness from the state. However, it does endorse a fundamental, state-propagated narrative of the era: that the New Order represented a sought-after new beginning, in which people's desires and aspirations would be fulfilled by a US-backed developmentalism.

This remembering problematizes the idea of post-authoritarianism as a mode of being in the present. As we have seen, the narrative sketched by parts of the God Bless comeback identifies no point of post-authoritarian rupture. Indeed, a view of Indonesian history through the lens of popular music genres, in this case rock, evinces such continuity. As discussed in the introduction, since the early New Order, Indonesia's genre system, the bedrock of its class formations, has been marked by rigidity—genre categories and their social values relative to one another have changed little over the past fifty years. Not only has the idea of *gedongan*'s cultural ascendance endured—it has been reenergized by the transnationalization of the media environment. As discussed in chapter 4, the introduction of Nielsen Audience Measurement for categorizing consumers of television, music, radio, and print prompted the retrieval of the *kampungan-gedongan* binary and the reassertion of *gedongan*'s ascendance. When viewed in this light, the present indeed appears to be a culmination of the past, with few post-authoritarian interruptions. The God Bless comeback reminds us that the New Order was not only an authoritarian polity but also a cultural system built from the state-led rearrangement of the media environment and ordered by key orienting dichotomies that strongly endure in the present. In this light, the challenges to attempts to establish a critical distance from the New Order become all too clear.

PART III

Kampungan

SIX

Television's Children

In mid-2010, I attended an on-air event for the television station SCTV in a lavish housing complex called Harapan Indah (Beautiful hope), in Bekasi, on the periphery of Jakarta. I was staying in well-established, leafy Menteng, at the city's heart. Getting to Bekasi meant a long taxi ride through the night, past the jungle of tall office buildings—the embassies, the construction and mining giants, and the multilateral aid agencies, their banks of square windows glinting like sequins. We ascended to a lonely expressway, and little could be seen but other cars speeding by.

Eventually, the toll road gave way to a familiar, harried scene. Dusty, exhaust-stained kiosks made of plywood lined the roadside: a hairdresser, a street-side dentist, a grease-smeared motorbike repair shop. Suddenly, the scene was transformed again; we turned off into the newly paved and palm-lined road to Harapan Indah. Rods of laser light could be seen in the near distance, moving crazily in haphazard arcs, exterminating any fears of rain. They signaled the location of the stage, which soon came into view. It was flanked by walls of fluorescent orange-and-yellow LED lights, advertising the sponsor. Four acts appeared on-stage that night: Maia Duo, Hijau Daun, Kahitna, and Kangen Band. Kangen Band is what I had come to see.

My interest in Kangen Band was piqued in 2009 when I undertook a study of Indonesia's *Rolling Stone* magazine (Baulch 2010). For many *Rolling Stone* writers, the matter of Kangen Band's (lack of) quality was not negotiable. Because of its appearance on television, Kangen Band also elicited criticism from several high-profile composers, who considered the band's songs to be poorly composed

(Cahyono 2009a, b).[1] However, the band's producers promoted Kangen Band's rise to fame from humble beginnings as one to be celebrated (Sujana 2009). As discussed in chapter 3, the producers hatched this narrative of upward mobility as a strategy to herald the masses, through use of old generic terms, Melayu and *kampungan*—assignations that did not reflect the ways the musicians thought of their compositions and performances. But while the narrative of upward mobility came to dominate Kangen Band's performances, it was not the only signification. First, the unofficial field in which Kangen Band initially circulated in purely sonic (not visual) form as pirate recordings and radio broadcasts predated and was untouched by the metatext of upward mobility. Second, a study of official fan practice reveals Kangen Band's performances under the auspices of Positif Art to be polysemic.

Previous chapters of the book have considered the contests over ideal forms of national belonging proceeding in the context of the new technological paradigm, and I have argued that these contests form the ideational basis for imagining post-authoritarian Indonesia. Thus far the book has focused on the elite level of professional pop musical production. In this chapter, I discuss two instances of everyday consumption: the meaning attributed to Kangen Band compositions prior to its mainstream production, and fans' errant readings of the mainstream narrative of upward mobility.

These two instances of everyday consumption draw attention to the multiple modes of consumer citizenship evolving at various loci of production and consumption within the new media ecology, highlighting its complexity. An analysis of Kangen Band's early compositions reveals how pop Indonesia's dispersal has opened up opportunities for ordinary people to perform it in new ways and alter its meanings. Members of Kangen Band used the genre to articulate an emasculated masculinity, a more common feature of dangdut than of pop Indonesia. But Kangen Band's early compositions could not be comfortably assigned to one genre or the other; the songs eluded generic certainty by traveling the back channels of the new technological paradigm. Rather than appearing at well-known stores or on television, Kangen Band's first album could only be bought at unofficial points of exchange known as *emper-emperan*: spontaneously erected or spread on plastic sheets by the roadside. In this chapter I examine the *emper-emperan* through reference to work on informal economies, with a view to understanding the cultural and political efficacies of this realm of exchange. Drawing on Sundaram (2004) and Warner (2002a, b), I argue that the unregulated networks of the *emper-emperan* render it "uncanny"—open to cultural performances that queer dominant narratives, thereby lending themselves to the elicitation of counterpublics.

I also continue the discussion begun in chapter 3 regarding the implications of Kangen Band's retrieval from the *emper-emperan* and incorporation into mainstream production processes, in the course of which it was branded as a Melayu act. This branding drew Kangen Band into an economy dominated by ringback tones, in which corporate media institutions dominated the signification of musical sounds. Nevertheless, the mainstream production of Kangen Band also opened space for different kinds of contestations, arising from readings of the band by members of its fan club, Doy Community. The establishment of the fan group can be read as the producers' efforts to enroll audiences in the celebration and promotion of Kangen Band's major label production, but it also opened up arenas for alternative readings of the narrative of upward mobility, thereby preserving Kangen Band's polysemy.

QUEERING POP INDONESIA

In the book chronicling his discovery of Kangen Band, Sujana expresses frustration at the unavailability of any images of Kangen Band that may have aided him in his quest. Kangen Band burst onto the scene in 2005 when songs from their debut album circulated as radio broadcasts, pervaded malls, and sold spectacularly at the *emper-emperan*, and despite their songs' wide circulation, the band remained invisible. It could be heard, but not seen, because no video recordings had been made of the band's performances, and by the time it gained fame, Kangen Band had disbanded when vocalist Andhika was committed to prison for a drug-related crime. The band's invisibility imbued it with a strange, uncanny quality, as indicated by popular characterizations of it as a "ghost band" (*band hantu*) (Sujana 2009).

The first way in which Kangen Band's unofficial performances were uncanny pertains to their wide circulation in purely sonic form. But a second dimension of Kangen Band's uncanniness pertains to the uncertain generic affiliations of its sound—an uncertainty accentuated, perhaps, by the absence of any visual cues. In chapter 3, I discussed how Kangen Band's composer, Dodhy, originally conceived of his compositions in the register of pop Indonesia, a genre with stereotypically metropolitan, middle-class connotations. Dodhy's compositions were certainly devoid of iconic Melayu musical features, such as *cengkok* and *ritme*. But nor did they display the lyrical proclivity for hip, metropolitan language or self-confident masculinity normally featured in this genre. In fact, the songs brazenly make use of provincially inflected slang and are markedly sad and despairing, in keeping with the band's name, which translates as "longing band." In this sense they use pop Indonesia to articulate a male emotionality typically associated with Melayu (David 2003). David argues that sad dangdut songs foreground male impotence and emasculation, and indeed, in the songs on Kangen Band's first album, the image of the philandering woman emerges strongly; either the singer has been abandoned for another man, or he is trapped in a three-way relationship. Ten out of the twelve tracks on Kangen Band's first album give voice to loneliness. In two songs, the man waits helplessly for his lover to return from afar.

> Pacarku mengertilah aku (My darling understand me)
> Seperti aku ngerti kamu (The way I understand you)
> Dan pacarku mengertilah aku (And darling understand me)
> Seperti aku ngerti kamu (The way I understand you)
> Tapi kamu kok selingkuh (But you have cheated on me — why?)
> Tapi kamu kok selingkuh (But you have cheated on me — why?)
>   (Dodhy Kangen, "Selingkuh")

These lyrics, from Kangen Band's hit song "Selingkuh" (Cheating), evidence the way their debut album, *Tentang Aku, Kau dan Dia* (About me, you and him), applies a typical Melayu sensibility to pop Indonesia musical aesthetics, thereby queering pop Indonesia. This instance of queering can be understood as a function of pop Indonesia's dispersal, making the genre more available for excorporation by subaltern youth in peripheral areas—such as Dodhy, the band's principal composer. But the album's generic uncertainty not only reflects the formal qualities of Dodhy's compositions. It can also be seen as a function of the informal economies in which the album originally circulated and was exchanged: the *emper-emperan*. In fact, the Kangen Band case highlights important dimensions of the *emper-emperan's* political efficacies. The circulation of the band's "ghostly" sounds via the *emper-emperan* point to its capacity to give voice to new musical forms that elude easy categorization, affirming Sundaram's argument that informal media economies harbor performances that are "resistant to both control as well as radical-critical strategies of intervention" (2004, 70). Moreover, the band's *emper-emperan* success had important social and political implications, for it promoted new forms of co-awareness oriented to the band's uncanny address, highlighting the role the *emper-emperan* plays in eliciting *counter*publics, and revealing that subsumption of existing forms into narratives of corporate branding is not the only work of the new technological paradigm. It also fosters uncanny circulatory routes that alter the cultural configuration of the public sphere.

INFORMAL ECONOMIES AND COUNTERPUBLICS

The trade of compact discs at the *emper-emperan* is a twenty-first-century phenomenon, which marked the end of a three-decade-old cassette age; it arose largely as a result of the spread of CD players and computers in the early 2000s, with dire consequences for performers' and recording labels' ability to eke profit from album sales. This informal realm of exchange shares many of the qualities of other kinds of informal economies, digital and otherwise, noted by scholars: elites' disdain for them; their intricate interconnections with formal economies; and their capacity to subvert dominant metanarratives and to challenge elite formulations of modernity (Doron 2012; Larkin 2004; Jain 2007; Sundaram 2004).

In his essay on "pirate culture" in India, Sundaram states that such culture "strikes at the heart of the idea of intellectual property, the mantra of current elites," sparking a range of reactionary measures, including the raid ("more of an intimidatory and theatrical act . . . than leading to any measure of legal success") and the creation of public discourse ("press stories detailing the crimes of piracy") (Sundaram 2004, 64, 69). Similarly, when trade at the *emper-emperan* began to have a marked impact on official sales at stores in Indonesia, these informal points of exchange emerged in the music press as the object of marked derision, which frequently linked piracy to pop Melayu. For example, in March 2009, as part of its regular profiles on the music industry, *Rolling Stone* Indonesia ran an article titled "Inilah Musik Indonesia Hari Ini" (This is the Indonesian music industry today). The article reported on a focus group discussion moderated by *Rolling Stone* writer Wendi Putranto and involving nine industry figures. It is derisive of pop Melayu, musical uniformity, piracy, free live concerts, and the widespread consumption of ringback tones:

> *Pop Melayu* bands have suddenly attacked the capital and have suddenly become superstars, with their uniform music.

The people are given no choice in the matter because the mass media fully supports Melayunization. [The indie band] Efek Rumah Kaca is one of the only bands to rise up in protest, with their [ironically titled] song "Nothing but Love," which became a minor hit.

But most people don't seem to care and can't be bothered debating the issue. Most of the people enjoy buying pirate CDs or pirate MP3s, or picking out their 30-second ring back tone, enjoy celebrating or rioting at free concerts. Many of them feel that cheating on their lover qualifies them to write a song. Recently, these phenomena have begun to clearly manifest in our society. (Putranto 2009a, 65)

In light of these derisions, it is important to note that the *emper-emperan* comprise a cornucopia of sounds and images, including recordings of famous preachers' sermons, Hollywood and Bollywood blockbusters, provincial garage bands, regional dance and theater troupes, and East Asian pop. They include, that is, not only pirated recordings but also those of amateur performers, such as Kangen Band, whose recordings circulate on the *emper-emperan* with the full consent of their copyright holders. Rather than an opportunity to make money, Kangen Band viewed the *emper-emperan* as a promotional tool, and the connection Putranto draws between pop Melayu and piracy is specious.

Moreover, despite the separateness of formal and informal economies suggested by the *Rolling Stone* piece, these realms are closely interconnected. As other writers have pointed out, such interconnectedness enables informal economies to serve as back channels extending to the poor opportunities to participate in the global consumer economy. Jain, for example, argues that "informality" or "porous legality" has also provided a means for wider economic participation and social mobility (Jain 2011, 152); and Doron (2012, 563) contends that "middle class ideologies are exclusive and expansive. At the same time, the poor seek to engage this economy by tapping into the unauthorized sector that responds to their demands for local participation in the global economy, while also keeping them at a certain distance from the forms and symbolic capital of this new economy." Indeed, the fact of Kangen Band welcoming the circulation of their debut album on the *emper-emperan*, because it enabled their rise to fame, is revealing of how the same formal-informal overlaps manifest themselves in Indonesia. In an interview with me, Sujana related that Kangen Band's use of the *emper-emperan* was common practice among amateur provincial-dwelling musicians, who circulate their recordings informally in the hope of generating radio requests from those who shop at the *emper-emperan* and enhancing the chance of being singled out for big-time recording contracts by talent scouts with an ear to provincial radio. Sujana himself claimed to employ this strategy, scouting provincial radio for fresh sounds from the *emper-emperan* being aired as a result of requests by listeners, highlighting the important role radio is playing as a crucial node in the path to mainstream production.

The interconnections between the formal and informal spheres is further revealed by their closely linked materialities. In chapter 2, I cited the increasing number of privately owned television sets in the late 1990s as evidence of the expansion of television and the increasing influence of this industry. By the early 2000s, television sets had become a common feature of a great majority of households in the country. A 2003 study conducted for the United Nations Global Report on Human Settlements and analyzing slum life in the Jakarta *kampung* (poor neighborhood) of Karet Tengsin cites Nielsen Audience Management figures showing that "82 percent of urban dwellers (10+ years old) watch tv at some point every day" and that "televisions are commonly switched on for upwards of 14 hours per day, even if no-one is actually watching it." As a result of television's ubiquity, the author reports, its value as a sign of prestige fell in the early 2000s and was replaced by new consumer electronics, including CD players: "In terms of endowing social prestige in the kampung, television ownership may have slipped toward the bottom of the appliance hierarchy—though it still ranks ahead of radios and electronic fans. But, it has already been surpassed by high quality cassette players / stereo tuners (58%), video CD players (18%), regular telephones (14%) and refrigerators (13%)" (McCarthy 2003, 11).

The World Bank report focuses on a specific Jakarta *kampung*, but it can be assumed that the uptake of vCD players and their status as a sign of prestige among lower-class people manifested themselves more broadly across the country in the early 2000s, providing the infrastructural basis for the expansion of the informal trade in CDs and increasing rates of piracy, which also began to become evident around the same time. The spread of CD players, then, transformed the ways people consumed music. For almost three decades, from the early 1970s, most Indonesians purchased music on cassettes, but by the early 2000s CDs were beginning to surpass cassettes as the primary mode for consuming pop music in the country. As mentioned in chapter 2, copyright transgressions had been part and parcel of mainstream pop production in the 1970s, when pirate recordings of European and North American pop acts were commonplace and sanctioned by the industry, before the entry of major international recording labels in the 1990s. Such official piracy practices ceased in the 1980s after Bob Geldof registered a complaint with the Indonesian government. The informal trade in CDs was distinct from this previously existing pirate economy in that it contained a greater proportion of amateur performances. Digital reproduction made it possible for amateurs to reproduce (or have reproduced) their recordings with great speed and in great numbers, giving consumers access to a much greater diversity of sounds, including those novel ones that could not be fitted to existing genre categories, such as Kangen Band's first album. In this way, the *emper-emperan* operated as a realm that was both alternate to and prompted changes within mainstream pop musical production (e.g., Sujana's recruitment of Kangen Band and the subsequent pop Melayu wave).

As well as having an impact on the repertoires of major recording labels, the *emper-emperan* transformed how people watched television, providing further evidence of the interconnections between formal and informal spheres. As noted above, Kangen Band and others used the *emper-emperan* to gain access to commercial radio, which then served as a back channel to mainstream production. But the social lives of the products sold at the *emper-emperan* were various. Many contained visual content that was not destined for radio broadcast and required access to a VCD player and a television set for viewing. In this way, the value and utility of VCD players, and of the informal economies that fed them, both relied on and transformed existing practices of viewing television. On the one hand, widespread use of VCD players rested on widespread ownership of television sets. On the other, they dismantled the broadcast mode that had been associated with this medium. VCD players provided the hardware that fragmented the televisual orientation, by presenting people with the vast array of screen content available at the *emper-emperan* cornucopia, including uncanny performances that exist at a tangent to generic certainty and corporate branding.

An analysis of the *emper-emperan* reveals how the new technological paradigm not only involves the tactical convergence of corporate media institutions, resulting in the incorporation of lower-class subject positions into brand narratives. It also generates informal economies that evolve in parallel with telcos, television, and major recording labels, responding to their limitations. Indeed, scholars of informal economies have shown how the modes of public participation and social membership they foster are often at odds with state and corporate narratives. Larkin shows how processes of recycling and repairing are pivotal to media piracy infrastructures in Nigeria and evince an experience of modernity as always at risk of collapsing and in need of repair, which contrasts state-led narratives of modernization (Larkin 2004). And Doron shows how repair-and-recycle economies in India enable poor people to participate in exclusive and expansive middle-class ideologies, while transforming the social life of technologies inherent to them: mobile phones. By dismantling and reconfiguring mobile phones, street-side repair workers contest both "the multinational brand's image of the consumer" in a throwaway society, and a state narrative of the digital sublime (Doron 2012, 564).

Kangen Band's treatment of pop Indonesia very much resembles the work the Indian informal repairers perform on mobile phones, as described by Doron (2012). Both dismantle materials—sounds and mobile phone hardware—direct them along paths unforeseen by global capitalism, and recraft their social lives. Following Sundaram, I contend that this work of dismantling would be wrongly described as resistance or opposition to the dominant narratives of citizenship represented by pop Indonesia. Rather, it reflects informal economies' capacity to foster performances that elude dominant formulations and opposition to them:

> Non legal domains open up new spaces of disorder and constant conflict in Indian cities that threaten the current self-perceptions of the globalizing elite. . . . However, pirate culture has no strategies of political mediation, it works through immersion and dispersal rather than representation and voice. It is resistant to both control as well as radical-critical strategies of intervention, inhabiting networks of disorder that are endemic to contemporary urbanism. This may be its greatest strength and resilience.

In line with Sundaram's characterization of "pirate culture," Kangen Band's dismantling of pop Indonesia "works through immersion and dispersal rather than representation and voice." In this sense its original uncanniness can be seen as distinct from the oppositional strategy employed by Sujana in his production of the band as a narrative of upward mobility. Rather than representing lower-classness through recourse to *kampungan*/Melayu, Kangen Band immersed itself in pop Indonesia, in order to rework it, using it to articulate something other than the self-confident, metropolitan masculinity that had so dominated the signification of the genre. As it made its way around the *emper-emperan* and radio, this act of immersion generated new forms of co-awareness oriented to Kangen Band, or "stranger sociability" (Warner 2002b, 56), suggesting the emergence of a counterpublic.

Characterizing the early enthusiasm for Kangen Band in this way, as evidence of counterpublicity, extends discussion of publics in contemporary Indonesia begun in chapter 1, which studied the role the circulation of printed texts played in marking out middle-class subject positions in the New Order period. The Kangen Band case betrays the enduring force of these middle-class imaginaries—evident in the derisive assessments of pop Melayu—but it also reveals the increasing contestedness of such imaginaries and the various ways they were being challenged. In chapter 3, I discussed the challenges to middle-class cultural ascendance issuing from the championing of *kampungan*, instanced by Sujana's production of Kangen Band. But enthusiasm for Kangen Band arising from its circulation via the *emper-emperan* points to a different kind of challenge, represented by a counterpublic (Warner 2002b): a virtual social entity evinced by modes of address that seek not to oppose or reform the dominant, but to queer it.

> In the sense of the term I am advocating here, . . . counterpublics [are such] . . . in a stronger sense than simply comprising subalterns with a reform program. A counterpublic maintains at some level, conscious or not, an awareness of its subordinate status. The cultural horizon against which it marks itself off is not just a general or wider public but a dominant one. And the conflict extends not just to ideas or policy questions but to the speech genres and modes of address that constitute the public or to the hierarchy among media. (Warner 2002b, 86)

Understanding the *emper-emperan* as an instance of counterpublicity is useful because it evokes the social effects of informal spheres, and therefore their political efficacies. The role of the *emper-emperan* extends beyond its function of forging routes for circulating texts among particular demographics. First, the status of the *emper-emperan* within a "hierarchy among media" empowers it to mark texts socially, as belonging to the low. Second, its unregulated status qualifies the *emper-emperan* as a carnivalesque haven for texts that elude established "speech genres and modes of address" constituting the "lowly" public, such as Melayu/*kampungan*, and that lend it to the elicitation of counterpublics, disrupting the established ordering of public discourse.

As already discussed in detail in chapter 3, on signing with Warner, Kangen Band's uncanniness and invisibility became a fact of their past. They began to appear in music videos and live telecast performances, much to the chagrin of a number of critics, who alleged the physical appearance of the band's personnel to be evidence of its vulgarity (Cahyono 2009a, b). The cover of Kangen Band's first album with Warner, *Yang Sempurna* (Perfection—a repackaged version of

Tentang Aku, Kau dan Dia), erased any traces of unsightliness. Nevertheless, although the album was remastered, little musical manipulation took place. This resulted in imbuing the repackaged version with a sense of underproduction. Instrumentally, the sound is tinny. The vocals are thin, off-key, and wavering. Warner's repackaging, then, entailed only a partial makeover. The band was rendered visible, but the original, unofficial sound was fully retained, and this suggests not an elimination of vulgarity, but an airbrushing and strategic use of *kampungan*.

I have interpreted this airbrushing of *kampungan* in the mainstream production of *Tentang Aku, Kau dan Dia* as an instance of a broader reclaiming of the term, and an attempt to herald the masses in new ways, using pop Melayu as a mode of address. I also argued that this use of pop Melayu may be seen as a function of the rising importance of audience measurement and the particular ways it made lower-class people visible as a lucrative market for pop music products: ringback tones. I have touched above on how Kangen Band's debut album in its unofficial form spontaneously bubbled up through the cracks in public culture, and suggested that this bubbling up sheds light on its uncanny dimensions. These qualities may be seen to emerge when cultural novelties are yet to become hinged to metanarratives. Alternatively, ringback tones offer relatively fixed narratives.

This is not to suggest, however, that Kangen Band's official meanings are irrevocably fixed. Fans attributed meanings to Kangen Band's mainstream performances that are revealing of their polysemy. In chapter 3 I discussed how these performances generated a certain metatext—a narrative of upward mobility. Below, I consider how members of Kangen Band's fan club, Doy Community, engage this narrative and bear the meanings of lower-classness that were thrust upon them.

A NEW ASSOCIATIONAL LIFE

Doy Community was but one of the many organizations of pop fans to populate the Indonesian public sphere in the early twenty-first century. In chapter 2, I discussed how the "local music boom" yielded a host of supergroups that sold an unprecedented number of albums, leading, after digitization, to rampant piracy. The groups consequently began to perform in ways that lent themselves to television shows and product endorsement, from which they quickly began to derive the bulk of their incomes. The expansion of television brought about changes in the content of pop performances, but it also resulted in shifts in the ways audiences were organized, as Indonesians increasingly began to consume pop as members of fan organizations. From the early years of the twenty-first century, the management of fan organizations had become part and parcel of pop music production.

The organizing of audiences into fan clubs and the increasing importance of television to pop performance are closely interlinked phenomena. Fan groups complement the growing importance of television and live performances to performers' livelihoods; they enhance performers' spectacularity at live and televised shows. In a context in which appearance on television was becoming ever more pivotal to performers' commercial success, such groups represented an army of fan labor that could be mobilized to perform (free of charge) as a loyal and enthusiastic audience populating the lip of the stage at televisual performances. Fan clubs serve owners of capital with convenient ways to extract value from audience members' labor.

The emergence of the fan club as a prime site for the consumption of pop music dates back to the late 1990s, with the establishment of the Slankers—the fan club of the rock band Slank, discussed in chapter 2. In 1998, the band's manager, Bunda Iffet, observed young Slank enthusiasts, discernible from their attire and the music they played, gathering in *gardu*—the bamboo or timber huts located on the street-side. She proposed formalizing these gatherings as parts of a fan organization, initially conceived of as an organ for Slank fans' social and moral betterment (Anggraini 2008). As of 2008, the club boasted seventy-five thousand members and more than one hundred branches across the country, and had become known as the most fervent of the many such clubs that had come to honeycomb the public sphere.

The Slankers' zeal is made especially evident by their preference for brandishing at concerts enormous cloth banners, which undulate lazily like flags. On the one hand, the flags operate as beacons of a rough masculine solidarity. They signal a widespread affinity for *selengean*—which denotes an unkempt style of bodily comportment and which Slank used as a term of address. In this sense, the fan group can be thought of as a vehicle enabling subalterns to assert their collective existence. On the other hand, such assemblies can be seen to aid the extraction of value from affective labor, as the Slankers' presence at televised shows significantly enhance the spectacularity of those performances, thereby feeding into *selengean*'s televisual commodification.

But more than just a promotional tool, these armies of eager volunteers also represent a new kind of associational life, mediating forms of co-awareness elicited in the process of pop consumption. Pop fan groups can be included in a broader kind of collective organizing that is beginning to coalesce not only around pop idols but also various consumer objects (such as the hijab) (Beta 2014) and practices (such as urban farming) (Ardianto, Aarons, and Burstein 2014) and is playing a vital role in delineating virtuous, ethical forms of consumption and civic life. My research among fans reveals that the opportunity to appear on television was not the only factor motivating them to join such groups. As well as televisual fame, and the thrill of getting front-row seats, many fans speak of their fandom as a moral and ethical endeavor. Moreover, fan groups often work to reterritorialize subject positions that have been commodified, such as *kampungan*. Below, I show how Doy Community harbored readings of Kangen Band that sat at a tangent to corporate narratives.

"COME ON AUNTIE, WE'RE ON!"

Earlier in the chapter, I related how music critics at the Indonesian licensee of *Rolling Stone* magazine unanimously derided Kangen Band. In their view, Kangen Band's visual presentation left much to be desired, and its provincial origins and rise to fame on the back of unofficial, unpolished recordings served as testimony of the band's inherent vulgarity. This assessment of Kangen Band and its articulation in print media is continuous with a cultural politics that favors the urban, the masculine, and the tertiary-educated, and which gained traction upon the advent of the New Order (see Baulch 2010).

The social position of the Doy Community members I encountered in 2010 may be contrasted with that of the music critics. Many in the Doy Community were female high school graduates working in various retail outlets on the fringes of the capital. They do not have the opportunity to write long articles about pop music in authoritative magazines with national circulation. In contrast to fan communities analyzed elsewhere (Jenkins 1992), their engagements with their band are not mediated by print fanzines or the World Wide Web, both comparatively rich in possibilities to contest or augment the original (official or authorized) texts. Rather, they are mediated by two other, perhaps more imposing, institutions: the band's management company, Positif Art, and television.

In Indonesia, having a fan club is part and parcel of pop music production, and all the fan clubs I have encountered have been established, and are super-vised and funded, by the band's management team, which may or may not be a department within the band's recording label. In fact, this corporatized style of fandom is not unique to Indonesia but may be thought of as one facet of a universally manifesting media convergence: the blurring of production and consumption. In an interview with Matt Hills, Henry Jenkins contends that the World Wide Web facilitates direct dialogues between producers and fans, blur-ring the distinctions between them (Hills 2001). Deuze and Banks characterize this particular aspect of media convergence as the rise of co-creative labor, in which "practices of user-created content and user-led innovation are now sig-nificant sources of both economic and cultural value" (Deuze and Banks 2009, 419). Emerging co-creative relations, they contend, prompt new queries about agency and identity.

It is true that the corporatized dimensions of the Doy Community may be understood in context of this "historical" (i.e., transnationally manifesting) phenomenon, co-creative labor. But the forms that mediate these relations, the structures in which they proceed, vary from place to place. In such structures, some "genealogical" features of consumerism may be found: features that more powerfully shape questions of agency and identity than the generalized fact of co-creation itself. As mentioned above, fanzines and the World Wide Web played little or no role in Doy members' relationship with Kangen Band and Positif Art. Rather, that relationship proceeded primarily through the medium of television, and its contours can be related through an account of the show at Harapan Indah.

I arrived in a taxi at Harapan Indah to commence my research into Kangen Band. The taxi dropped me off as soon as the stage became visible in the distance. I had to plow through a thick crowd before reaching an opening in a cyclone fence, guarded by the usual meager-framed bouncers. They allowed me to pass, and soon I found myself in the Kangen Band tent, backstage. A couple of band members were seated before brightly lit mirrors having their makeup done. Andhika, the vocalist, was standing in the middle of the tent, surrounded by personnel from an infotainment show. One of them was interviewing him, and the others were involved in filming. "Pendidikan akhir sampai mana?" (What level did you reach at school?), she asked him, to which Ankhika replied, "SMP" (Sekolah Menengah Pertuma; Junior high).

The show that night was a relay of single-song performances by the different acts, so Kangen Band was ascending to and descending from the stage in four-act intervals. This was no place to conduct an interview, I quickly realized, and trudged off to watch Kangen Band's first song performance from the side of the stage, just inside the cyclone fencing. The weight of a dense crowd pressed young boys' cheeks hard against the fence's metal patterning. Periodically, giant water jets appeared from somewhere on high, and the crowd was sternly hosed down. Overhead, television cameras on booms rooted to trusses, like prehistoric creatures with impossibly long necks, swooped down on the stage and crowd, hunting for shots. There were quite a lot of people on my side of the cyclone fence, too, but not enough to force the same suffocating proximity. These people, I soon realized, were the members of the fan clubs of those acts performing that night.

When I encountered the members of Doy Community at the lip of the stage, I was struck by the number of women fans. It is surprising that this struck me, because I had so frequently seen the wildly gesticulating, grinning female pop consumers on the morning television shows devoted to live-to-air pop performances. In the flesh, though, the very public presence of these young women seemed more compelling. Perhaps, being at the show, I was taken back to my researches in the late 1990s among underground musicians and audiences, who were overwhelmingly male. By contrast, women played important roles as authority figures in Kangen Band's fan culture. The group of fans I met at Harapan Indah had been led there by the head of Doy's Kerawang chapter, a minuscule young working woman called Uci.

While Kangen Band's many performances in third-tier regional cities are not likely to be televised, for Doy members of the Jakarta region at least, performances of exuberance at televised shows are precisely what Positif Art hopes of them (Interview: Sujana, April 27, 2010). Doy members' compliance with this hope is therefore of note and may be thought of as an illustration of successful disciplining. Moreover, if Uci's way of inviting me to participate is any indication, Doy members do more than simply comply. They view these moments of performing exuberance for television cameras as central to the practice of fandom. When Kangen Band struck up and the cameras dipped and dived overhead, Uci beckoned to me and shouted: "Ayo tante, kita harus eksis!" (Come on, Auntie, we're on!).

The part television cameras play in this process of performing fandom is notable for three reasons. First, it distinguishes Doy from the more ghostly contours of Kangen Band's unofficial circulation and consumption prior to its rise to fame, by turning Kangen Band into something spectacular. Second, it points to how Kangen Band's shift to spectacularity generates new kinds of subjectivities among fan viewers, to whom a sense of being witnessed, and not just witnessing, is key ("Kita harus eksis!"). Further, it reminds us of the laboriousness of fandom: Doy members are not allowed to just take pleasure in the spectacle; spectacularity is expected of them too. It is through television, in other words, that co-creative labor, which suggests complicity and consensus, is achieved. Television incorporates and intertwines Positif Arts' expectation of the fans with the fans' self-perceptions. Therefore, it goes some way to uncovering the implications of this co-creative labor for identity. It does not, however, directly address the question of agency. What does Doy members' co-creative laboring for spectacularity mean to the fans? What does it suggest of their relationship to the metatext we have been discussing?

Whenever I asked them what had initially appealed to them about Kangen Band, Doy members simply reiterated the narrative of upward mobility: "Mereka dari bawah" (They came from below). The fans' repetition of the metatext seems strange when we consider that most fans encountered Kangen Band prior to its repackaging under the auspices of Warner Music and Positif Art and therefore only became aware of the narrative of upward mobility after the fact. It could not really have been the reason for their initial attraction to Kangen Band. Had they become so identified with Positif Art that they not only labored for Kangen Band's televisual spectacularity but also trotted out at will the tag line it had devised for the band? What does this instance of co-creative labor suggest of agency?

This question may be considered through a discussion of some other dimensions of Kangen Band fandom, which extend beyond the televisual spectacular. Upon our meeting at Harapan Indah, Doy members immediately invited me to come the next day to their base camp at Andhika's home in Cibubur. The fact of this base camp's existence was raised with regularity when, over the days that followed the event at Harapan Indah, I asked fans what had prompted them to join Doy. One day, Uci sent me a text message to inform me of a Kangen Band performance on *DeRings*, one of the many live-to-air morning television shows that feature pop performances, and suggested I might like to attend. When I replied that I could not, she seemed especially keen for me to join the fans after the show in the trek to Andhika's house at Cibubur.

This territorial aspect of Kangen Band fandom is intriguing because it takes place outside the official structure of fandom that privileges televisual spectacularity. Of further interest is the link Doy members draw between this territorial aspect and Andhika's good moral character. Uci attempted to relate this good moral character to me by referring to the fact that he sits on the floor and shares meals with the fans who hang around his house. She cited it as one of the prime reasons prompting her to resign from the Peterpan (a pop Indonesia band) fan group, whose fans rarely came into contact with band members, and join up instead with Doy. Of particular note is the way in which she contrasted her descriptions of Andhika as *baik* (good) with the aesthetic values attributed by media structures that privilege the spectacular. Above, I have briefly discussed how Doy members are inextricably entwined with these structures. And yet, Uci offered the following comparison: "I used to be a member of Peterpan and Ungu fan clubs, but we could never get to meet the band members! Kangen Band are more humble and closer to their fans. They invite us to eat with them, invite us to their house. So when we hear people saying awful things about Andhika, that he is ugly, we respond that at least he is a good person, and humble" (interview: Uci, April 28, 2010).

The stress Doy members place on Andhika's good moral character resists two powerful narratives. First, it directly rejects the authoritative critics' derision of Kangen Band. Second, it also exists at a tangent to the narrative of upward mobility, and this emerges in the different perspectives on what constitutes Kangen Band's origins. In a conversation with me, Kangen Band's manager, Sujana, complained that Dodhy, the band's composer, was beginning to hawk willy-nilly his compositions to upcoming bands without asking Sujana's permission first. Sujana explained Dodhy's antics as a case of "kacang lupa kulitnya" (a peanut forgetting its skin) (Sujana interview). In order to stress Andhika's good moral character as evident in the fact of his socializing with fans, fans employed the same metaphor, but in the negative: Andhika is like a "kacang tidak lupa sama kulitnya" (peanut who had not forgotten its skin). These two very different conceptions of what constitutes the peanut's skin infer quite distinct interpretations of the narrative of upward mobility. In Sujana's view, he himself is key to Kangen Band's rise. In the Doy members' view, Sujana does not feature at all. It is they who provide the protective womb.

The idea that in fandom we find a political impetus that exists at a tangent to the corporate structures that discipline the fan is affirmed by what Uci shared with me of her tasks as organizer of the Kerawang chapter of Doy. In her descriptions, the gathering up of members to attend live shows as instructed by Positif Art of course featured, as did the need to perform audiencehood for television cameras. But I was especially curious about how she used the word *berantem* (to fight) to describe her dealings with the security guards who staff the entrance to the area right before the stage, often separated from the mass of the crowd by cyclone fencing. Surely she did not mean to say that she came to blows with these guards, but her use of the term is suggestive of an aggressive physicality, which she described as one of her most pressing responsibilities. At live shows, it is her job to ensure that all the Kangen Band fan club members are allowed to advance to the lip of the stage. She must represent their interests and ensure that they are not disappointed. It is these interests that so often brought her into confrontation with the guards, a rubbing up against authority that Uci recounted with glee.

EMOTIONAL CONNECTIONS THAT DISRUPT ACCUMULATION

This chapter has examined how distinct forms of circulation bear distinct modes of belonging, with distinct political implications. In the early part of the chapter, I endeavored to distinguish people's affinities for *Tentang Aku, Kau dan Dia* in its earliest "informal" form from the enthusiasm for Warner and Positif Art's production. The former responded to Kangen Band's uncanniness—its invisibility and generic uncertainty—circulation of which was enabled by an informal CD economy giving rise to a counterpublic, a form of stranger sociability forming up around a text that queered dominant narratives of pop Indonesia. This draws attention to how the new technological paradigm not only commodifies preexisting cultural forms. It also generated novel forms of circulation (*emper-emperan*) that exist at a tangent to but not separate from dominant ones (television).

As discussed in chapter 3, this novel cultural form was considerably reworked in the course of its mainstream production. Kangen Band's reassignment as an upwardly mobile Melayu act associated the band with long-standing notions of lower-class belonging—*kampungan*. And while Sujana's reworking certainly challenged middle-class delineations of ideal post-authoritarian citizenship, such challenges were articulated in terms of corporate branding.

Above I have argued that the publics that formed up around these branded challenges—that is, around the production of Kangen Band as a narrative of upward mobility—were organized in ways that eased the extraction of value from fans' free labor. The Doy Community, for example, harbored intimate connections among those commonly oriented to Kangen Band. It oversaw the enfolding of this narrative of upward mobility into fans' everyday lives, making it appear to reflect their deepest desires and true selves. In this way, fan organizations perform the embodying and territorializing work that is needed to make commodities appear desirable. As Mazzarella points out, commodities are seductive not just because they suppress "embodied idiosyncrasies." Commodification needs the "tangibility of objects and people . . . to lend credibility to its abstract claims" (2003, 20).

But while fan groups create the "conditions of consciousness in which buying can occur," they also bear disruptive potentials. As Clare Hemmings argues, "while affective labour is the hidden centre of capitalist accumulation, since it remains unremunerated yet is what bestows value, it also produces emotional connections that threaten to disrupt that accumulation" (2005, 550). Fan clubs serve owners of capital with convenient ways to extract value from audience members' labor. Indeed, Doy community harbored moral and ethical endeavors that sat at a tangent to "visions of the good" inherent to the corporate branding of Kangen Band. The fan group, that is, spawned solidarities that contested dominant narratives, affirming Warner's argument that the composition of a public is open-ended, because a text's reception and circulation is unpredictable and cannot be determined in advance.

SEVEN

Provincial Cosmopolitanism

In the early years of the twenty-first century, a strange word erupted on the streets of Denpasar and settled like leaves of ash on people's backs. The word, *baduda* (dung beetle), refers to fans of the Balinese pop singer Nanoe Biroe, who sings in low Balinese, and it circulates the streets in the form of T-shirts they wear while riding their motorbikes around the city. This belonging, and the performance of it, holds a special political potency. It emerges in context of the revival of ethnic Balinese-ness in which the pure and the high are formally privileged. *Baduda*, by contrast, suggests a fondness for dirt, the low and the impure.

The T-shirts the Baduda like to wear around Denpasar are designed by Nanoe Biroe himself and available from his merchandise store, which, as well as a space of exchange, serves as a center for noncommercial Baduda activity, especially Saturday-night drinking sessions. In early Baduda appearances, by far the most ubiquitous design featured a black-and-white, meme-like image of Nanoe Biroe's head, very much resembling the iconic Che Guevara meme, haloed by a series of beams and surrounded by the words "President of Baduda Republic" (in English).

At first glance, Nanoe Biroe appears to provide a fairly good example of the increasing interplay between pop culture commodities and activist politics (de Luca and Peeples 2002). Scholars of Indonesia have also noted the increasing enmeshment of banal pop culture commodities with the figure of the activist, conventionally positioned as an elevated, heroic, and unsullied guardian of truth. Doreen Lee (2011), for example, contends that consumer culture is playing an increasingly important role in the ways Indonesian student activists seek to make themselves visible, and Alexandra Crosby (2013) discusses Javanese environmental activists' adoption of punk aesthetics and their tactical remixing of political images with consumer objects.

In light of this work, it's important to stress that the case presented here is not one of activist politics. Nanoe Biroe makes little attempt to call to account, in activist mode, the excesses of power, and the linguistic and historical reference points that mark activists as extraordinary social actors are absent from his address. Rather, Nanoe Biroe points demonstrably to another important historical force: rock. As discussed in chapter 2, in the 1990s, Slank's compositions accentuated the links between rock music and a lower-class, masculine urban street life by using key idioms (e.g., *kampungan*) that signified such life, thereby allowing people to understand rock as an Indonesian form that poor people could enjoy; previously it had been identified closely with the West and the well-to-do. By aligning himself with Slank, Nanoe Biroe identifies his roots in these shifts, which, as I also argued in chapter 2, can be understood as a consequence of television's expanded role in pop's mediation in the 1990s. In this chapter, I consider how the case of Nanoe Biroe and the Baduda draw attention to subsequent developments, including post-authoritarian administrative decentralization and the popularization of mobile phones, are also playing a part in shaping notions of the local. The chapter explores how Nanoe Biroe's Slank-inspired speech circulates via motorbikes, T-shirts, and mobile phones, showing how these technologies channel Nanoe Biroe's address through and around the streets of Denpasar, prompting new kinds of speech, connection, and assembly.

One of this book's central arguments has been that delineation of the "local" proceeds in a context of considerable flux and implicates heightened experimentations with key dualisms such as *kampungan-gedongan* and East-West. In chapter 3, I examined an example of such experimentations, specifically efforts to commodify *kampungan* by producing Kangen Band in such a way as to accentuate *kampungan*'s allure. In chapter 6, I discussed new forms of associational life resulting from such high-end production of a sought-after lowness, and showed how this commodifying opened new spaces for lower-class women to exercise organizational prowess, as fan club leaders and coordinators.

In this chapter, I focus on an instance of lower-class performance and fandom emerging at the provincial level. This context brings my discussion of the manipulations of the *kampungan* taking place in the realm of popular music more closely to bear upon a post-authoritarian context, because Nanoe Biroe and the Badudas' language play is strongly influenced by a shift in language ideologies resulting from post-authoritarian administrative decentralization. While the previous chapter studies the lower-class organizational life emerging from television's expanded role in the mediation and circulation of pop, this chapter places lower-classness in the context of a more complex juncture. It aims to provide a glimpse of how the new technological paradigm, while founded on the New Order–era expansion of television, has also been profoundly shaped by post-authoritarian cultural shifts forged by administrative decentralization. The case of Nanoe Biroe and the Baduda offers insights into how this juncture is equipping people to use popular music as a resource for composing and articulating social alternatives—alternative, that is, to dominant delineations of locality emerging in context of administrative decentralization and the expansion of consumerism.

In keeping with the book's central theme, the chapter pays attention not only to how Nanoe Biroe articulated lower-classness as something new and desirable, but also to the technologies that mediate and circulate this address. The chapter includes discussion of everyday uses of mobile phones by Nanoe Biroe fans, but I endeavor to locate mobile phones in a broader "circulatory matrix . . . through which new discursive forms, practices and artifacts carry out their routine ideological labour of constituting subjects who can be summoned in the name of a public or a people" (Gaonkar and Povinelli 2003, 386). Considering Nanoe Biroe as part of a "culture of circulation," I aim to evince the new technological paradigm not as a set of impactful machines (e.g., television and mobile phones) but as a circulatory field inhabited by popular music, among a number of other public forms. For, as Gaonkar and Povinelli remind us, "In a given culture of circulation, it is more important to track the proliferating co-presence of varied textual/cultural forms in all their mobility and mutability than to attempt a delineation of their fragile autonomy and specificity . . . . It is more important . . . as Michel Foucault long ago suggested, . . . to move between the sparkle of the "thing" and the quiet work of the generative matrix—the diagram" (Gaonkar and Povinelli 2003, 391).

This approach proves useful to an attempt to flesh out the new technological paradigm through reference to specific cases, such as that of Nanoe Biroe and the Baduda. According to Gaonkar and Povinelli, conceptualizing the present as a series of unruly systems of interlocking circuits, containing both various scales of recognizability and various kinds of captivating effects, rather than as a map of incommensurable regimes of meaning, can advance the ongoing recognition of the plural nature of modernity and its palpable and affective, as well as textual and rational, dimensions. The public forms that travel this circuitry are transfigured, rather than translated, into various scales of recognition. Translation suggests erasure and writing out, while transfiguration preserves and even foregrounds the trace of the circulatory path, like the palimpsest or the overdub, heralding new publics and forging new circulatory tributaries through supplementarity, rather than erasure. In my discussion of Nanoe Biroe and the Baduda, various dynamics of transfiguration are at play: that of Indonesian pop, that of iconic imagery that depicts popular voice, of low Balinese, and of Denpasar's urban space, through play with surfaces and edges of urban space, rather than through the staging of "insurgencies" such as political demonstrations.

The chapter examines how the word *baduda* and the image of Nanoe Biroe transfigure Balinese-ness, and this unearths the various transnational flows implicated in locality production. I am interested in how words and images move around, but I am also interested in what people do with them and how they are taken up in the making of new solidarities and the remolding of urban space. In the second part of the chapter, I examine how mobile phones and motorbikes fashion the ways Baduda move and gather, thereby gaining purchase on new moorings in a context of post–Cold War flux and fluidity. Following Abdoumaliq Simone, the chapter investigates how this mooring exemplifies an "infrastructural" as opposed to a "territorial" mode of locality production that involves the transfiguration of texts, as well as Nanoe Biroe and the Baduda's "extraterritorial" operations and affective encounters with the surface, edges, and borders of urban space. According to Simone, territories are political technologies that regulate the scope of urban life, and infrastructures exist in tension with this regulating. Infrastructure, too, contains political technologies, "not simply in the materials and energies it avails, but also the way it attracts people, draws them in, coalesces and expends their capacities" (Simone 2013, 243). As a study of the Baduda shows, motorbikes and mobile phones not only regulate the scope of urban life, but also make available new resources for solidarity making.

THE INVOLUTION OF INDONESIAN ROCK

Nanoe Biroe began his career as a pop musician with Biroe band, whose name he later adopted as his own on beginning his solo career. With Biroe band, Nanoe Biroe won first place in the East Indonesia division for the Surabaya rock contest and went on to record an album with renowned producer Log Zhelebour. It was not long, however, before Nanoe Biroe left Biroe band and struck out as a solo artist in 2005. His first solo album, *Suba Kadung Metulis* (It's written now), was produced by the Balinese label Jayagiri Production and sold handsomely. Within two months, ten thousand cassettes had been sold. To date, forty-eight thousand copies of the album have sold (Muhajir 2014).

After the success of his first album, Nanoe Biroe went on to record three more albums with Jayagiri Productions—*Matunangan Ajak Dewa* (Married to the Gods) in 2007, *M3tamorforia* in 2009, and *+POsitif* in 2010—although sales fell sharply over this period with the rise of digital piracy and file sharing. Following in Slank's footsteps, Nanoe Biroe established an independent label, Baduda Productions, to record his fifth and sixth albums, *Matur 5uksma* (Thankyou) in 2011 and *Timpal Sujati* (True friend) in 2012.

What these albums trace is not just a trajectory of sales figures and Nanoe Biroe's shifting position in the industry, but also his attempts to use song texts and album titles to delineate a moral philosophy. The enthusiasm for his songs was generated out of Nanoe Biroe's success as a live, as well as a recording, artist. As he began playing around the island after the release of his debut album, Nanoe Biroe quickly became known for his easy and charismatic stage style. At shows, he intersperses his songs with a flowing banter, lightened with a liberal dose of wisecracks and puns but firmly tethered to his assessments of contemporary social ills and his suggested remedies for them. He affects a gentle, priestly style, but one packed full with a sense of fun, and this unusual combination has the effect of drawing his audience in and making them feel as if they want to get close to his words.

Nanoe Biroe's moral message makes specific linguistic interventions into Bali's ethno-religious revival through his playful use of low Balinese. In songs like "Menyama" (Togetherness) and "Timpal Sujati" (True friend), Nanoe Biroe preaches the value of togetherness and friendship in a tone hotly scornful of conspicuous consumption and material wealth. The prominent place these words assumed in youth culture in the 2000s reflects a general filling up of Balinese public culture with uses of Balinese language around the turn of the century. This can be understood as a direct consequence of the post-authoritarian decentralization agenda, including the issuing of licenses for provincial television stations, and the holding of gubernatorial elections from 2004, increasing the need to address newly localized voting publics, often in regional languages. From this general filling up flourished an array of meanings attached to being part of a Balinese public. No longer was it simply about performing peace and happiness on the cultural tourism stage that the authoritarian New Order regime had erected

(Picard 1996; Vickers 1989). It was also now about being part of a democratic polis and about performing modernity and advancement in the realm of youth culture, including that of popular music.

Language ideologies, then, had been transformed. During the New Order, regional languages had been positioned as indices of backwardness, but now they begin to adopt the mantle of modernity. The political implications of this transformation is well illustrated by the Nanoe Biroe case: it points to how the new valorization of provincial languages opens opportunities for language play, because it expands the field in which youth can convivially consume in their mother tongues. Nanoe Biroe rose to fame in Bali in the middle part of the first decade of the twenty-first century amid a clutch of new Balinese pop performers who emerged in the context of the establishment of the island's first television station, Bali TV. This new group of pop Bali performers, including acts such as Lolot, xxx, Ubud Band, and Joni Agung (Fushiki 2013), associated singing Balinese pop songs with an emerging hip, metropolitan, rock-and-roll-inflected culture, and drew Balinese pop away from its overwhelmingly Mandarin pop style and rural nuances.[1]

In developing contemporary performance styles, many Balinese pop artists have looked to nationally renowned pop bands for guidance and inspiration, and, as mentioned above, Nanoe Biroe also stands out for his unashamed borrowing from the Jakarta-based blues/rock band Slank. In fact, in several ways, Nanoe Biroe announces his indebtedness to Slank, which, as already discussed in chapter 2, found fame in the early 1990s with their hit "Mawar Merah" (Red rose), in which the band sings the virtues of the raggedy (*selengean*) dress styles of urban lower-class males. By appropriating the term *baduda* to describe his fans, Nanoe Biroe clearly draws on Slank's celebration of the ordinary man's moral elevation. Moreover, Nanoe Biroe's stage name also draws from the title of Slank's fourth album, *Generasi Biru* (Blue generation)—intended, according to principal composer Bimbim, to assign to youth the task of forging progressive social and political change by shaping the blue skies and blue oceans of tomorrow (see chapter 2).

By identifying with Slank in this way, Nanoe Biroe positions himself in the path of new flows of pop music resulting from the expansion of Asian music industries, including Indonesia's, after the end of the Cold War. However, it is not just Asian pop, but cultural flows from various directions that converge on the figure of Nanoe Biroe and the associational life he inspires. The above-mentioned T-shirt design, featuring a Che-like Nanoe Biroe, well reveals the complex web of flows that feed Nanoe Biroe and the Baduda. While Nanoe Biroe's stage name clearly nods to Slank, the band is not really present in this design, which instead bears traces of more globally recognized icons, such as Che Guevara, Bob Marley, and Barack Obama.

Indeed, this image of Nanoe Biroe converses most insistently with the well-known image of Che Guevara, which it closely resembles. In another image, on a poster celebrating the eighth anniversary of the Baduda fan club, for example, the same "photocopied" image of Nanoe Biroe dons a beret bearing a star—a direct reference to the Guevara image. Nanoe Biroe's transfiguration of the Che image to depict himself positions him as a member of a pantheon of icons indexing a global "the people" and enframes him as a member of a global "the people."

Public representations of Nanoe Biroe flicker unsteadily between the photocopy-like image of his face and that of Guevara. The "President of Baduda Republic" image delights in its status as a copy and is therefore remedial in that it "at once plays up the pleasure of reproduction while making light of the status of source or original" (Cartwright and Mandiberg 2009). It presents itself first and foremost as a media object disinterested in revelatory claims, and it does so in two ways. First, set against a black background, Nanoe Biroe's face appears out of nowhere, or bathes in a nowhere; the source is completely emptied out. Second, by depicting Nanoe Biroe's face as an amalgam of light and shadows, the image draws the viewers' attention to the labor of copying: as his face here resembles a poor photocopy, Nanoe Biroe teases the viewer with his resemblance to other such decontextualized icons—the face of Barack Obama, the face of Che Guevara. Rather than truth, what is offered up is the image's captivating surface and the pleasures of reproducibility that the foregrounding of such surfaces make possible.

In their discussion of the various ways in which images are enframed, Spyer and Steedly offer a typology that is useful to understanding how certain kinds of images are equipped to induce such pleasures. Using the various reworkings of Alberto Korda's photograph of Che Guevara as an example, they argue that while some images stake claims to represent "real life . . . something more important happening elsewhere," others seem to celebrate their status as media objects and "relish re-enframement." By cropping the photograph in particular ways, they aver, "showing Che abstracted from any historical and political context," Korda prepared the image for widespread proliferation, enabling it to "breed like rabbits," spawning the hybrid, bleached-out, and silkscreened-like version, which "turned it into a statement, a brand, or an uncluttered icon more than anything else" (Spyer and Steedly 2013, 21).

The role these hybrid versions play in orienting Nanoe Biroe's identity politics demonstrates their enduring capacity to captivate, and the social lives they continue to enjoy as a result of those captivating qualities. Two overlapping but separate bodies of work help explain these qualities and their ability to sustain. The first advances arguments for the importance in democratic public cultures of the iconic and the spectacular, as "visual illustrations for citizenship" (Smith 2009, 73; Hariman and Lucaites 2007). Rather than fundamentally unmodern, scholars like Hariman and Lucaites argue, the rhetorical features of icons play important roles in the budding of stranger sociability based on modern notions of civility. Monologue, images, and affect are as crucial to actually existing democracy as are dialogue, printed words, and rational critical talk about them. Indeed, some scholars have pointed to the crucial role of images in shaping the national political order in Indonesia. According to Strassler, for example, the Indonesian national political order is one in which, since the establishment of state television in the late 1960s, "visibility and circulation via the image form a privileged means of recognition for all political agencies and events" (Strassler 2014, 100).

The second body of literature that can help account for the endurance of the Che image and its transfiguration as Nanoe Biroe pertains to ordinary people's heightened capacity to manipulate and publish images as a result of the proliferation of interactive screen technologies. In particular, work discussing how such technologies expand ordinary people's capacities to explore the possibilities of image making and the kind of work images can do is especially relevant to understanding Nanoe Biroe's Che image. As Bolter and Grusin (1996) remind us, fascination with both hypermediation and with realizing immediacy has a long history of at least several centuries, but these contrasting urges tug ever more urgently upon one another in computer-mediated society. Hypermediation, which Nanoe Biroe's Che image fervently embraces, is no longer reserved for an elite few—multinational tech and media companies, guardians of high art and the like—but extends to ordinary people, who display not only the pleasure they derive from experiencing copies without strict recourse to an original, but also an ability to manipulate copies, by assigning to them what Kajri Jain refers to as "auratic objecthood" (2007, 18).

Jain argues that auratic objecthood does not always derive from authorial originality; it can also stem from "performative practices in the realm of circulation and reception" (in Jain 2007, 18). Indeed, it is precisely the lack of authorial originality that makes Nanoe Biroe's image auratic and enables it to elicit veneration as something that inhabits, or interrupts perhaps, realms of circulation and reception known to Balinese youth. Bolter and Grusin contend that copies attain aura through remediation, by which they masquerade as authentic originals rather than translations, erasing any trace of their source. But something slightly different is happening here. Nanoe Biroe's hypermediated image eschews immediacy and any notion of originality; it holds tight to the original copy of Che, transfiguring rather than remediating it, thereby turning an ordinary lowly Balinese face into an object of veneration, imbuing it with aura, rendering it iconic. As we shall see, Nanoe Biroe's eschewal of immediacy is nevertheless significant to the immediate political context insofar as it reveals the arbitrary nature of stereotypical images of Balinese-ness, makes new kinds of archival knowledge possible, and calls into questions the validity of iconic images held to constitute the national political order.

REWORKING LOCALITY THROUGH IMAGE PLAY

Several scholars have documented the deep material, spatial, and political impacts of the tourist gaze and its long-standing role in shaping ideal ways of being that construct Balinese-ness as unique, peaceful, and unchanging. Vickers (1989) has discussed in detail how iconic representations associated with the tourist gaze reduce Balinese-ness to a handful of gestures, poses, and occupations: the topless beauty, the dancer, the woodcarver, the painter, and the ceremonial procession, for example. And Picard argues that Balinese adopted these icons as true reflections of their cultural identity (Picard 1996).

In the 1990s, new ideas about the relativity of the Balinese context arrived with new technologies of interactivity—cartoons in the local paper—producing a new sense of social immediacy. Warren (1998) has chronicled how land conflicts resulting from large-scale tourism developments were represented in cartoons in the local press as conflicts between big-capital suits from Jakarta and hard labor by bare-chested, saronged Balinese rice farmers. In these cartoons social immediacy was expressed as a condition of relativity to Jakarta.

In the last decade or so, this repertoire of images has expanded further. The visual field constituting Balinese-ness has become much messier, partly as a result of cheap technologies for producing and sharing images, and partly as a result of administrative decentralization and associated changes to ways of speaking and ways of seeing Balinese-ness. In addition to those presenting Balinese-ness to the tourist outsider, we now see the blossoming of images more opaque to the tourist gaze and which address, rather, a newly constituted Balinese public, which since 2004 has been a voting public and since the 2002 Bali bombings has had a growing sense of itself as a minority religious group under threat. The images that both feed and articulate this public include those of the warrior/vigilante gang leaders, whose images line major thoroughfares, the *omkara* symbol (the word "om" in Balinese script), and the temple silhouette.

Among this new assemblage of images, the image of Nanoe Biroe that portrays him as a copy stands out, for it strives to evoke Balinese-ness without reference to any of the stereotypical symbols of Hindu observance—the *omkara*, the sarong, the *udeng* (Balinese male headdress), or the temple silhouette. Nanoe Biroe hovers to the left of this repertoire and calls upon young people to venerate a Balinese-ness that is being pulled in new directions. The proposition that Balinese-ness is a copy of Che is politically significant because it reveals the arbitrary nature of the stereotype. Arguably, the Nanoe-Biroe-as-Che image could be seen to step off onto other, possible alternative images of Balinese-ness—Bali as a mass grave, Bali as the face of a domestic violence victim, Bali as an empty global brand.

This image play can be understood in context of Strassler's observation about the paramount role images play in defining the "national political order," as cited above. It gains particular significance in view of the images of presidential authority in enclosed public places. Nanoe Biroe's Che image, enframed as it is by the word "President," cheekily offers an alternative presidential representation, drawing this object of veneration off public walls and animating it by transposing it onto T-shirts and mobile bodies. In this way, Nanoe Biroe proposes himself as an alternative president, who instead of looking down gloomily and stuffily from a high wall is mobile and nudges softly against people's bodies.

At the same time, Nanoe Biroe's image is the kind that, to quote Spyer and Steedly, "relishes re-enframement" (2013, 21). Enframed by the word "President," Nanoe Biroe proposes an alternative kind of political authority that is mobile and affective; but set in another context, he shifts the significance of this image beyond questions around the seat of the Indonesian presidency to a more global realm, depicted as a range of uncluttered icons. The back of his merchandise shop is covered with a wallpaper that Nanoe Biroe designed and had made, featuring the Che-like image of himself among similar images of Mick Jagger, Marilyn Monroe, Michael Jackson, and Kurt Cobain. Positioned among these figures, Nanoe Biroe identifies himself as a member of the global masculine popular, but what is also interesting about the wall is that it also depicts a range of Indonesian figures, both political heroes and pop culture icons: first president Sukarno, murdered human rights activist Munir, early twentieth-century dissident Kartini, comic Benyamin S, folksinger Iwan Fals.

This wallpaper represents an intriguing kind of archive, and composing it requires an epistemological leap of faith with deep political consequences. "There is not political power without control of the archive, if not memory. Effective democratization can always be measured by this essential criterion: the participation in and access to the archive, its constitution and interpretation" (Derrida 1995, 4). Here, reconstitution and reinterpretation are taking place across a couple of vectors. First, we see how the representation of Nanoe-Biroe-as-Che image allows him to write himself into a history of global popular culture in which East-West divisions are completely done away with. Nanoe Biroe proposes that he too, like Michael Jackson, Mick Jagger, and Kurt Cobain, can be an uncluttered icon or, as Man Danoe (Nanoe Biroe's brother and manager) offered when I asked him what properties these figures shared—"a legend." The wall rejects the idea that Nanoe Biroe is derivative simply because he sings in a regional language and addresses a regional audience. It renders visible something that has been happening gradually and quietly for around a decade: the overturning of prevailing ideas about Indonesian pop as a lesser copy of performances staged at a US source.

The second thing the wall achieves is a blurring of the boundaries between the popular and the political. What we see here is not only Nanoe Biroe and other Indonesian pop figures being written into global pop history, but also the insertion of political figures into this global history. Nanoe Biroe sits alongside not only Kurt Cobain but also murdered human rights activist Munir and independence hero and first president Sukarno. This mélange of the popular and the political both upsets existing epistemologies that clearly distinguish the two, and posits new forms of political authority. By positioning himself on this wall, Nanoe Biroe stakes claims to a kind of authority that starkly contrasts that evinced by the public, sullen, and immutable display of power inherent in the traditional presidential portraits.

Nanoe Biroe's wallpaper typifies an emerging digital sensibility featuring an affinity for decentering, fragmentation, and embracing copies. This emerging sensibility can be seen in the way digital texts are arranged in informal economies by the roadside in willy-nilly fashion, mixing Hollywood and Bollywood blockbusters with local theater performances, for example, with little attempt to distinguish and categorize these forms. It can also be seen in the emerging field of Indonesian DIY fashion, documented by Luvaas (2013a). He discusses how young Indonesian fashion designers based in Bandung seek to defuse the aura of international brands, such as Mastercard and Starbucks, by ludically reworking them into T-shirt designs.

Indeed, when I asked Man Danoe about the source of the images featuring in the wallpaper, he replied that Nanoe Biroe had obtained them from the internet. The fact that the internet—Google image archives, perhaps—as a source of these images gave me cause to pause to reconsider what the wallpaper may suggest of Nanoe Biroe's agency. On the one hand, the wallpaper reveals the claims he adeptly stakes to political and cultural authority, a radical proposal for the global political validity of a rock performance hailing from the margins of an ex-colony. On the other, it also exemplifies the kind of participation in image making that Jodi Dean observes to drive communicative capitalism (Dean 2008). As Robert Gehl points out (2009), new kinds of archiving via data storage that relies on people not shutting up defines the dominant order.

When people's access to and participation in the archive is enabled by forces not of their own making, the extent to which such participation exemplifies agency remains uncertain. But where agency does reveal itself more clearly is in the work of interpreting the archive, in this case for a geographically delineated public, as revealing of hidden dimensions of what Appadurai calls "social immediacy" (1996, 179)—that is, in producing new definitions of locality and establishing a dialogue around what it means to be of a place. In the Nanoe Biroe-as-Che-as-President-of-Baduda design, this work of interpreting is largely performed by the word "Baduda." Above, I discussed how the image of Nanoe Biroe as a copy of Che stretches Balinese-ness beyond existing image repertoires that constitute locality. I have also discussed how the word "President" enframes Nanoe Biroe as an alternative political authority. And thirdly, I have argued that the inclusion of Nanoe Biroe's image in the wallpaper evinces a digital sensibility that empowers postcolonial provincial subjects like Nanoe Biroe to challenge epistemologies identifying them as peripheral and derivative, by writing themselves into the center of a global, masculine, popular realm.

What the word "Baduda" does here is enable the image of Nanoe Biroe's glance to boomerang back, to shine a light on what inclusion in this masculine global popular realm means for Balinese subjectivities, that is, those constituted in and through use of the Balinese language. Unlike the image of Nanoe Biroe as Che, which not only relishes re-enframement, but the meaning of which is relatively transparent to all and sundry, the word "Baduda" strongly resists re-enframement and is opaque to anyone who doesn't speak Balinese. Baduda renders the Nanoe-Biroe-as-Che image auratic because it introduces the image to a realm of circulation—Balinese—that makes objects appear to pertain to the socially immediate. "Baduda" suggests that the Nanoe Biroe Che image reveals hidden dimensions of social immediacy. Let me now detail precisely the kind of dialogue about locality that this word sets up.

Above, I argued that the prominent place the word "Baduda" occupied in Denpasar's cityscape in the mid-2000s reflected the filling up of Balinese public culture with uses of regional language as a result of administrative decentralization. Language ideologies were transformed; what it meant to be Balinese had shifted. No longer was it just about performing tradition on a tourism stage, but now it was also about being part of a modern democratic polis, and composing hip articulations of the regional language in rock-and-roll performances.

But the consequences of changes to what it meant to be part of a Balinese public were diffuse. Roughly coincident with the emergence of a new hip kind of Balinese pop, following the 2002 nightclub bombings, which caused hundreds of fatalities and resulted in a downturn in the Balinese tourism industry, including widespread layoffs, the growing push for a return to fundamental Balinese values could be seen in the rising use of he term *ajeg* (stable) in public discourses of Balinese-ness. According to Allen and Palermo (2003), the notion of *ajeg Bali* can be glossed as generally connoting a desire to return to village (agrarian) values and a concern with the declining Hindu population on the island, manifesting themselves in the increasingly visible display of symbols of ethno-religious identity. Its key mediators were various kinds of high culture, such as, first, modern intellectuals with university links who convened and participated in seminars dedicated to defining *ajeg Bali*; second, the high form of the Balinese language, which increased its role in public discourse as it began to articulate as radio, print, and television news; and third, the regional newspaper, the *Bali Post*, which frequently devoted considerable page space to papers presented at the above-mentioned university seminars.

Ajeg Bali serves as backdrop to Nanoe Biroe's performance, providing him with a frame of Balinese-ness to problematize and transgress. If *ajeg Bali* redrew the contours of a Balinese high culture by articulating it in high Balinese, mediated by universities and the press, Nanoe Biroe pioneered fresh terrain for fleshing out a new kind of Balinese low, expressed as a form of DIY consumer culture. Nanoe Biroe's performance intuits a cosmopolitan, horizontal orientation, forged through his proclivity for dirt and the low—his instinct for its material forms and for heralding it into being. During an interview with Anton Muhajir (2014), for example, he proudly showed his Nokia clone phone with a cracked screen—the antithesis, perhaps, to the technological sublime. His preferred mode of transport is that icon of mobile patina, a grubby, beaten-up Vespa. And his speech is largely articulated in low Balinese and mediated by T-shirts, upon which Nanoe Biroe's provocative words appear, in large letters (as if they were being yelled): "YOU'RE SO UP YOURSELF!" announces one. "WHETHER YOU'RE RICH OR POOR, YOUR SHIT STINKS JUST THE SAME!" proclaims another.

CIRCULATION AND RECEPTION

Several scholars of Indonesia argue that image and wordplay, which serve as means for people to engage questions about political authority and the ideal polity, have heightened, as the media forms on which such playful inquiry and critique can become inscribed have proliferated (Crosby 2013; Strassler 2009). Strassler, for example, discusses how, in the early reform era, Indonesian banknotes were taken out of circulation and reentered into circulation in new forms (as ubiquitous stickers, as art, as photocopies), and with new meanings (as a medium that inspired reflection and critique). This "remediation" had the effect of bringing state power down to earth and opened space for people to creatively ponder Indonesia's post-authoritarian political future, as well as comment on contemporary political and economic ills.

Nanoe Biroe also practices remediation, and to similar effect. Inspired by Slank's language play set to rock music, Nanoe Biroe takes low Balinese out of circulation as an exclusively oral medium and recirculates it as a written one, primarily in the form of T-shirt-borne messages. By doing so, he reveals the contingent nature of power and its reliance on the organization of language. By shifting the organization of Balinese, he is able to critique dominant discourses of the locale and propose alternative visions of Balinese-ness. This is what Simone calls "operat[ing] extraterritorially—in other words, where an expanded notion of political technologies entails putting things into relationship so as to make contingent the use to which they have been put in the past, to open up spaces of contestation and experimentation" (2013, 244).

But there is more at stake here than just remediation, than low Balinese withdrawal from and reinsertion into circulation, than the opportunities for critique and reflection that emerge as a result of this. There is also the matter of how the Baduda assemble around Nanoe Biroe's low Balinese and write themselves into it, essentially producing new organizational forms allowing infrastructure to "draw them in, coalesce and expand their capacities" (Simone 2013, 243). These organizational forms expand the field of contestation over what constitutes Balinese-ness and therefore draw attention to some of the novelties and intricacies of political communication in post-authoritarian Indonesia.

Interestingly, it is not online social media but fashion items that play the most important role in affording fans access to Nanoe Biroe's moral philosophy. In my interviews with Baduda, T-shirts emerged as objects of prime importance. Fans shared that they rated buying T-shirts at Nanoe Biroe's merchandise store as a preferred mode of support for their idol, above purchasing albums or attending concerts. The great value these objects held for fans results partly from Nanoe Biroe's art school background and his talent for composing eye-catching T-shirt designs, which he sells from his merchandise outlet and which have been circulating in public spaces in Denpasar for around a decade now. However, fans' high regard for the T-shirts also reflects a more generalized trend in DIY fashion unfolding at national scale (Luvaas 2013a). In Luvaas's study, designers in the provincial capital of Bandung index "a push to express, engage, be part of an active youth movement, . . . [to participate] in cultural production in one's own right." These plays, he argues, represent "a rather typical example of the reach and influence of digital culture, global capitalism and the new 'creative economy.'"

Luvaas's argument is of interest because it draws attention to the broader offline manifestations of digital cultures. The explosion of DIY fashion constitutes digitally mediated speech not because it is present online but rather because it is crucially informed by discourses of web use, which empower people to play with globally circulating linguistic resources, including images. In Luvaas's account, designers effect a home-grown consumerism by using a vulgar, visceral humor to bring the multinational sublime down to earth. (A T-shirt I saw in Bali exemplifies this humor. It apologizes for its wearer, in words rendered into the instantly recognizable Sony Ericsson font [Digital Sans EF]: "Sorry, Erection"). And Crosby (2013) writes of how environmental activists in Central Java use internet memes of Latin American freedom fighters to stake out preferred positions in the public sphere. The most powerful illustration of Nanoe Biroe's T-shirts' place in digital culture is the important role they play in circulating memes. As already discussed, Nanoe Biroe's image circulates locally as a flattened image of his dread-haloed face, citing the image of Guevara and enabling him to mark out a position largely at odds with *ajeg Bali*.

DIY fashion, then, does not just shape the content of Nanoe Biroe's speech, but also the manner of its circulation. This is important, because it highlights some unusual features of the digitally equipped circulation of celebrities whose political currency is geographically delimited, such as Nanoe Biroe's. Baduda T-shirts, that is, do not just circulate Nanoe Biroe's speech, but also animate it, revealing its reliance not just on digital communication but also on fans' mobile bodies.

MOBILIZING

In interviews, fans identified wearing T-shirts as their preferred way of participating in Baduda fandom (focus group discussion 2013). Indeed, most of the profits for the Nanoe Biroe brand come from the sale of T-shirts from his merchandise store in South Denpasar, U-Rock, and not album sales or concerts. Using T-shirts to attach his speech to fans' bodies, he animates it, sends it buzzing around the streets of Denpasar. Of particular interest here are the machines responsible for mobilizing Nanoe Biroe's speech. As it happens, the word "Baduda" burst quite spectacularly onto the streets of Denpasar around 2005, around the same time that there was a sudden explosion of young scooter riders in the city, due to the introduction of cheap credit regimes for purchasing Japanese scooters. Private ownership of transportation skyrocketed.[2] Where previously there had been one scooter per family, now there were three or four. This altered the ways in which people moved their bodies in urban space and opened new possibilities for the circulation of politically potent signs and messages.

As other writers observe, the increase in numbers of motorbikes on the road in the twenty-first century is not just a Balinese, but a generalized Southeast Asian phenomenon (D. Lee 2015; Truitt 2008). As Doreen Lee argues, in Indonesia their popularization has advanced a break with linear narratives of state-led modernity. People now dart into alleyways, navigate unconventional routes, thread dangerously around trucks, play cat-and-mouse with police—all at great risk. "Moto-mobility" also sees the forging of new ethical codes, rules, proper gendered conduct, and kinds of assembly as moto-humans become increasingly immobile, stuck in traffic (D. Lee 2015, 238, 245). Motorbikes also provide new opportunities for visibility and display—modification of these machines plays an important role in youth cultures revolving around them. Nanoe Biroe is well aware of new opportunities for display afforded by moto-mobility. Nanoe Biroe's social media communications strategy may be poorly conceived (Muhajir 2013), but his use of T-shirts to communicate lays bare his astute use of motorbikes—he very much capitalizes on a new generation of mobile men and women. As mentioned, many of his T-shirts bear enormous words so to be visible on the road. Merchandise, in other words, affords Nanoe Biroe's speech moto-circulation, highlighting the political affordances inherent in people's increasing embeddedness in technologies of mobility.

"When people inhabit a city, they situate themselves and are situated through the intersections of infrastructure and technical systems," writes Simone. "People figure themselves out through figuring arrangements of materials" (2013, 243). In seeking to convey how people both inhabit and are inhabited by the city, Simone explores the dynamics of territory ("a bundle of political technologies for measuring, administering and regulating the scope of what it is possible to do in the city" [243]) and extraterritorial operations ("where an expanded notion of political technologies entails putting things into relationship so as to make contingent the use to which they have been put in the past, to open up spaces of contestation and experimentation" [244]).

Nanoe Biroe's marrying merchandise to moto-mobility provides a good example of such extraterritorial operations. Two political technologies are being employed extraterritorially in this case: merchandise and motorbikes. While merchandise is an increasingly common way for musicians to generate profit in an age of rampant piracy, Nanoe Biroe extends this use of merchandise by using it to circulate bold messages in the cityscape. Motorbikes, as argued above, can be read as a manifestation of the increasing value attached to individual autonomy. They help normalize the neoliberal condition. Here, however, we see them employed as communicative machines, as sandwich boards for Nanoe Biroe's speech.

Digital technologies, however, are by no means absent from this scene. Facebook in particular is an important medium for display and connection among fans, especially female fans, the Badudawati. As it happens, the Badudawati celebrate their embeddedness in motorbikes, and this is evident in the ways they fashion their profiles on Facebook. In the remainder of the chapter, I want to turn to a discussion of digitally mediated Baduda assemblies, and to consider what role they suggest mobile phones are playing in forms of lower-class associational life emerging in the context of an evolving neoliberalism.

MENYAMA

When I asked the Baduda what it means to them to be a Nanoe Biroe fan, they immediately invoked togetherness: "Menyama," they consistently replied (Focus group discussion 2013). "Menyama" is the title song from Nanoe Biroe's seventh album, *Timpal Sujati* (True friend). The appeal of *menyama* as a key word points to the Baduda's strong attraction to song texts, seen to delineate their communal identities and moral aspirations. When I asked them how they realize *menyama* in the course of their fan practice, they referred me to two time/spaces of Baduda coalescing, revealing how quickly their moral aspirations are translated into spatial practice. Both gatherings are, as we shall see, telling of how a new infrastructural matrix is prompting emergent forms of belonging and associational life.

The first of these gatherings took the form of a ritual Saturday night get-together, which the fans cheekily referred to as a seminar, an acronym for *semeton minum arak*—palm-wine drinking community. Twenty years ago, I observed similar gatherings, which took place in various spaces of the city—somebody's house, on the street side, in a cassette store, or in a community radio station. Invariably, such gatherings were overwhelmingly masculine. Attendance at them required little capital outlay, and rather than being centered on those with money, they centered on those with musical and rhetorical abilities, and relegated others to a kind of onlooker status referred to as *bengong*: staring emptily into space.

Observing the seminar, it became clear to me that while musical and rhetorical performances remain an important part of the gathering, being *bengong* is a thing if the past. So was the overwhelmingly masculine character of the Saturday-night drinking session. It is true that female fans, the Badudawati, remain on the peripheries of the seminar, but their presence there still suggests changes to the genderedness of key time/spaces at which national or provincial identity is being redrawn. Those on the peripheries of the seminar—mostly women—are not silent and staring emptily into space but busy and preoccupied with their phones. When I asked the women what they were doing on their phones, they claimed to be issuing shout-outs to peers not in attendance, or uploading photos of the gathering to Facebook. In this way, smartphones can be seen to decenter the gathering, introduce spatial complexity, and open it to various modes of Baduda performativity. Armed with their phones, the women are able to be present at both the overtly masculine seminar and the more feminized Badudasphere on Facebook, affirming Lim's arguments that online performances and interactions do not transcend time/space power relations but fragment them, producing new kinds of spatially bounded power contests (Lim 2014).

When we turn our attention to the women's performances on Facebook, we find that the plot of spatial complexity thickens considerably. Above, I referred to Facebook as a feminized Badudasphere, and indeed, when I connected with some of these women on Facebook, I discovered that they took their careers as Badudawati very seriously, adopting the word "Baduda" or Nanoe Biroe album titles as their profile names, clearly taking pride in their visibility as Baduda. Gektusukma, for example, presents a stable Baduda identity, consistently wearing an array of backward baseball caps and an assortment of black T-shirts. So, although Nanoe Biroe's social media strategy may be poorly conceived,[3] Facebook is an important medium for display and connection among fans, especially female fans. The Badudawati may be marginal to the core Baduda ritual, the seminar, but on Facebook they appear front and center, frequently wearing T-shirts bearing the word "Seminar," as if to reclaim this time/space as their own. In one post, Putu Tomboyz leads a phalanx of Badudawati dressed in various Nanoe Biroe designs—Gektu's "seminar" T-shirt stands out. On Facebook, these women cannot be overlooked or silenced. They demand attention.

But it's not just by enabling a to-ing and fro-ing between the masculine offline and feminized online spaces that smartphones afford temporal and spatial complexity. The Badudawati's uses of Facebook also display a dialogic relationship with other new mobile communications technologies and this particular form of mobile media. Facebook is being used as a forum to experiment with representations of mobile bodies, for the Baduda very much celebrate their embeddedness in motorbikes. This is clear from the ways in which the Badudawati interweave themselves with motorbikes in their bodily fashionings on Facebook. In several posts, Gektusukma dons the kind of face mask people wear to reduce fume inhalation while on their bikes. In several others, she wears a motorbike helmet, or has it positioned close by. Similarly, Putu Tomboyz poses as a mobile moto-human in her profile pic, on a seriously modified machine. Gektu also shares news posts about lost and found motorbike licenses, and items informing people how to change the name on their motorbike registration. These posts afford a sense of the material forms implicated in the administration of a motorbike-riding public, and how these material forms are drawn into people's everyday life, including their social media profiles.

Another dimension of Baduda fandom involves mass gatherings devoted to improving urban spaces, and this reveals important dimensions of Nanoe Biroe's and the Baduda's shared civic vision, in particular their orientation toward infrastructural repair, especially at the city's margins and borders. At one event, the Baduda pooled their energies to paint degraded footpaths in the city square, and on another occasion fans were called to a concert in the Badung River aimed at bringing authorities' attention to the need to have the river cleaned up.[4]

In interviews, fans recounted their attendance at these events, especially the river concert, as seminal experiences in their careers as Baduda. The concert was recalled as a scene of *becoming* Baduda; being in the river, getting wet, and splashing around had altered people in significant ways. Also of note is the media form used to call this transformational assembly into being. When asked how they came to know of the concert, fans said they had received an SMS broadcast from Nanoe Biroe's management team informing them of when and where the concert was to take place. Nanoe Biroe's brother and manager of his U-Rock store in Denpasar affirmed this (Interview: Man Danoe, December 14, 2015). He showed me how U-Rock customers' mobile phone numbers are diligently recorded in an exercise book by the cashier, then transferred to a database, whence they are called forth, in the form of SMS, to mobilize shoppers at intervals to spectacular events that transform them as Baduda.

While not unique to Nanoe Biroe, this mode of addressing consumers is significant to Nanoe Biroe's endeavor to distinguish himself and his followers as belonging to the low. When I asked Man Danoe why the management team preferred SMS over, say, Twitter or WhatsApp, as a way of heralding fans, he replied that Twitter was "too confusing" and that SMS was simpler, more direct, and easier to use, indicating patterns of antipathy to and affinity for particular media forms. I contend that these antipathies and affinities are shaped not by the technical capacities of each application but rather by the discourses that shape them as distinct cultural forms. In contemporary Indonesia, SMS is infused with a decidedly lowly flavor—as the realm of the rough, the vulgar, the direct. Ferdiansyah Thajib writes of how subalterns use SMS to code their speech, and this causes urban elites to reinvoke class distinctions in relegating such coded speech, and the medium that affords it, to the realm of the uncivilized (Thajib 2011). SMS is a consistent theme in dangdut songs, and readers of the *Bali Post* send their messages to the editor, for publication in a special section titled "SMS," in rough, critical tones reminiscent of Nanoe Biroe's speech.

Man Danoe's use of SMS to publicize Nanoe Biroe's river concert reminds us of the important role being played by media forms, not only in the elicitation of publics, but also in marking them with particular social qualities. Media technologies are not value-free instruments for disseminating texts, but possess signifying power; by shaping the meanings of the contents they circulate, technologies exert a cultural force. As discussed in chapter 1, in the 1970s print media attained meaning as a socially elevated and critical media form, which enabled its use for eliciting a *gedongan* public. In the 2000s, SMS came to be recognized as a lowly cultural form, in contradistinction to the more refined modes of messaging via Blackberry Messenger and Twitter. But as Nanoe Biroe's use of SMS to herald a lowly public shows, SMS does not just disempower users by marking them as low. It also serves as an important resource for the elicitation of counterpublics.

CULTURES OF CIRCULATION

This chapter has sought to reveal some of the processes by which locality is produced at a complex historical juncture at which rising consumerism coincides with digital uptake and the significant cultural changes wrought by the sudden decentralization of administrative authority in Indonesia in 2004. Of all the chapters in this book, this final chapter probably does most to evince the various cultural flows and circulatory routes that populate and shape the new technological paradigm. The role cultural flows and circulatory routes play in enabling people to imagine their membership in localities at national and subnational scales has long been recognized (Anderson 1983). But in an increasingly globalized world, this imagining requires far greater effort. In the context of the new technological paradigm, producing locality entails a labor of piecing together a here and now from seemingly disparate cultural forms that follow and cut various circulatory paths. "Local subjects" inhabit ever more layered spaghetti-junction circuits that inform and produce them.

This chapter examined locality production through recourse to Gaonkar and Povinelli's (2003) "cultures of circulation"—a concept that enables recognition of the important role of nonelectronic media (such as motorbikes and T-shirts) in place making. In the chapter, I explored the cultures of circulation that Nanoe Biroe and the Baduda inhabit through a focus on two dimensions of locality production. First, I examined the transfiguring of both the Che image and the world "Baduda" when they were enframed together in such a way that pulled Che into Balinese worlds and pushed low Balinese into a global commons. Such enframing transfigured Balinese-ness by associating it with a copy (the Che-like image of Nanoe Biroe). Nanoe Biroe's transfiguring of the Che image, that is, proposed a new conception of Balinese-ness in which its place in a global circulatory route was very much foregrounded. Second, despite the marked absence of "authorial originality" (Jain 2007) in the Nanoe-Biroe-as-Che image—the fact that it delighted in its status as a copy—the image nonetheless attained aura. In the chapter, and following Strassler (2014) and Jain (2007), I argued that this aura can be understood as a function of the reception and circulation of the image, rather than authorial originality. Exploring Nanoe Biroe's reception and circulation, I unearthed the new associational life that grew up around his performances, and the relationships that members of the assemblies enjoyed with communication technologies, widely defined: not only mobile phones, but also T-shirts and motorbikes. Each of these technologies not only circulates Nanoe Biroe's novel conception of Balinese-ness but also extends the possibilities of its reception and articulation.

Conclusion

This book has examined the role media change plays in reshaping modes of social organization and tropes of citizenship. It has done so through a focus on the local music boom, inquiring into the processes implicated in producing "the local" in the context of the boom. The book has argued that belonging and citizenship are forcefully shaped by flows of ideas—both "genealogical" uniquely Indonesian ones and "historical" ones that circulate transnationally (Appadurai 1996, 74)—attached to media contents *and* technologies. By foregrounding ideational developments it offers an alternative to accounts of twenty-first-century Indonesia that rest on political-economic approaches.

In order to attend to the roles media contents and media technologies play in forging tropes of citizenship, *Genre Publics* has engaged theories of publics. In chapter 1 especially, I have cited Warner intensively, but Benedict Anderson's 1983 classic is aptly invoked here. In *Imagined Communities*, Anderson explores how the mass circulation of printed texts (beginning in Europe's early industrial era) enabled readers to get a sense of themselves as part of an unstratified "mass," that is, as those who acted collectively by inhabiting printed texts' paths of circulation. Two features of printed text allowed readers to imagine themselves as members of such a horizontally connected mass. The first pertains to the way they advanced a standardized use of language, and the second pertains to the way they marked calendrical time and located readers in it, affording them a sense of being together in the present.

Both these features can be found in the way *Aktuil* heralded a middle-class public into being in the 1970s. As discussed in chapter 1, the new spelling introduced in 1972 played an important role in shaping *Aktuil*'s "stranger sociability" (Warner 2002b, 56), and the magazine's title, which means "now," alluded to its very contemporaneity. In this sense, the book has commenced by bringing some of the questions that preoccupied Anderson to bear upon the context of contemporary capitalism's development in the country. How is Indonesian-ness being imagined in the late twentieth and early twenty-first century? It has been concerned with two important changes that took place in this period and identifies two technological paradigms: first, the ideological about-face in the late 1960s, including the establishment of the pro-US military New Order regime, its top-down developmentalist agenda, and the radical reorganization of print and popular music in line with its counterrevolutionary ideology; second, the privatization and globalization of key media industries in the 1990s, in which citizenship became increasingly bound up with consumption, and in which processes commonly associated with the neoliberal—the ethicalization of everyday life and the valorization of mobility, individuality, and flexibility—flourished. The book has studied the changes and continuities in locality production across these two periods of Indonesia's capitalist development. Following Appadurai, who advocates that the plural nature of consumerism can be discerned by distinguishing the histories of consumerist ideologies from their genealogies—where "history leads you outward, to link patterns of change to increasingly larger universes of interaction; and genealogy leads you inward, towards cultural dispositions and styles that might be stubbornly embedded in both local institutions and the history of the local habitus" (1996, 74)—I have examined the historical and genealogical roots of the local music boom.

I have argued that the processes of locality production inherent to the local music boom rest on genealogical modes that rely on specifically Indonesian tropes. They are dialectical in nature and contested along class lines, where class is understood as a form of publicness fundamentally shaped by pop music genres. This dialectical process of producing locality in the early New Order period distinguished it from the kinds of national imaginaries discussed by Anderson. According to Anderson, the use of secular Malay in print in the late nineteenth century evinced the kind of awareness of shared social positioning that gave rise to nationalism. In the New Order period, a reorganized print media industry, featuring new spelling and addressing now a readership that was no longer aligned to political parties (as it had been in the immediate postindependence period), also gave rise to a new form of stranger sociability, but one that marked itself as distinct from the *kampungan* masses not actively engaged in the production of written language, thereby intimating itself into a social position indexed by the term *gedongan*. In chapter 1, I argued that rock and print intertwined in ways that heralded a middle class into being, making it appear as an actually existing social entity, pointing to the role that circulating texts play in producing class structures, and revealing these structures to be forms of publicness—that is, imagined.

The middle-class public that emerged from the New Order's reorganization of the media environment did more than simply strive to establish a taste regime that qualified *gedongan* as culturally ascendant. As argued in chapter 1, *Aktuil* shaped rock in ways that associated it not only with an elevated middle-classness, but also with critique of the state. This position of rock's separateness from the state was achieved in *Aktuil* through recourse to the *pemuda* legacy—another genealogical trope that evinced youths' historical agency by harking back to their role in the revolution and earlier nationalist period. Drawing on the *pemuda* legacy, *Aktuil* addressed reading rock consumers as political and historical agents. The political implications of this heralding became apparent later, in mass demonstrations protesting the banning of three news weeklies in 1993, and later again in Joko Widodo's pursuit of the rock band Slank's endorsement for his 2014 presidential election campaign.

The book has traced the evolution of these genealogical tropes in order to identify changes and continuities in the contested production of locality across both technological paradigms. In the context of the new technological paradigm from the late 1980s, both the *kampungan-gedongan* binary and the *pemuda* legacy endure as features of the local music boom, but they relied on new circulatory paths that changed their meanings. For example, in chapter 2, I discussed how the expansion of television pushed all-male rock bands to the center of public life, blurring the distinction between pop and rock and drawing the *pemuda* figure into the mainstream of pop production. Through a focus on the case of Slank, I argue that the all-male rock band sketched an ideal form of publicness by drawing on the *pemuda* legacy and inflecting it with new values associated with neoliberalism. In chapter 3 I posited the mainstream production of Kangen Band as an example of *kampungan*'s reclaiming and the increasing contestedness of middle-class cultural ascendance in dominant modes of post-authoritarian citizenship.

These changes to the power dynamics implicated in the *kampungan-gedongan* binary and to the social positioning of the rock-consuming *pemuda* describe a history (as opposed to genealogy) of technological and ideological change not unique to Indonesia. To study the local music boom is not only to study a peculiarly Indonesian post-authoritarian cultural nationalism. It is also to explore post-developmental consumerism: a generalized Asian phenomenon entailing the expansion of commercial television, the rise of Asian sites of global cultural production, the associated recalibration of East-West dichotomies formerly current in such sites, and the increasing importance of consumption and narratives of self-betterment to the delineation of civic virtue (e.g., Fuhr 2016; Lewis, Martin, and Sun 2016; Wang 2008).

All these developments are manifest in the Indonesian case described in the book. In it, I have attributed the increase in sales of Indonesian pop artists in the late 1990s and early 2000s to the expansion of television, particularly commercial television, which opened new opportunities for pop artists to perform, enhancing ordinary people's exposure to them. I have also discussed how rock, once associated with the West, was remodeled as an authentically local music form, partly as a result of the way Slank's performance valorized lower-class street life (chapter 2), and partly from the ways in which newly established global recording companies presented their Indonesian repertoires as representative of local authenticity (chapter 5). Both instances provide evidence of the recalibration of East-West dichotomies. I have also discussed how the local music boom oversaw the commodification of rock and the *pemuda* figure that helped position the genre in an Indonesian history, thereby tying notions of civic virtue that *pemuda* represented to consumption. The *pemuda*'s historical agency was reworked as rock acts were drawn into narratives of self-realization, expressed as TV ads for products endorsed by such acts, such as mobile phones, motorbikes, and instant noodles—all of which happen to materialize prime neoliberal values of flexibility, mobility, and individuality. In this perspective, the local music boom can be seen as a genealogical manifestation (i.e., featuring the manipulation of *kampungan-gedongan* and *pemuda*) of historical change (the rise of "consumerist Asianism" [Fuhr 2016, 8], of which more below).

This is an important point to make, because it helps to establish the contribution of this study of Indonesia to a broader body of work attending to the post–Cold war shifting toward Asia of the center of gravity of global pop cultural production. In his 2016 book, Michael Fuhr studies such shifts in detail, using K-pop to understand the cultural effects of post–Cold War globalization. Responding to the rise of globalization as a buzzword in international trade discourse in the 1990s, the South Korean government promulgated its own globalization policy, and the Korean entertainment industry began to adopt globalization strategies, of which K-pop is exemplary. As well as policy change in media industries, the 1990s also witnessed the development of new markets and new media technologies, prompting the diversification of styles of pop and enabling the market for Korean-made pop to grow larger than that for Western pop in Korea. Fuhr describes K-pop as a soundtrack for twenty-first-century Korean modernity and is at pains to argue that its Korean-ness cannot be understood in culturally essentialist terms. K-pop deterritorializes and then reterritorializes Korean-ness, and acts as a window through which to view both Korean conceptions of the global and reconfigurations of the national. In his book, Fuhr uses K-pop to lay bare the mechanics of this mutual globalizing and localizing, placing these processes against a backdrop of a "reshuffling of . . . Asian modernity" (2016, 8), in which intensified inter-Asia flows are enhancing a sense of Asians' cultural proximity to one another and an emerging "consumerist Asianism" that at the same time decentralizes global flows, by orienting them away from a Euro-American "core."

Like the Korean pop industry that Fuhr discusses, the expansion of Indonesian pop examined in this book emerged from a context of post–Cold War deregulation of media industries. Therefore, the two cases share common historical roots, in a political-economic sense. As I discuss in the book, such commonalities underscore the pan-Asian implications of post–Cold War trade liberalization; comparison of the Indonesian local music boom with Fuhr's discussion of developments in K-pop help locate the Indonesian boom as part of parallel developments in Asian media industries—the reorienting of global cultural traffic and reinvigorated articulations of the local/national as cultural borders shift.

However, there are also important differences between the Korean and Indonesian cases that make "consumerist Asianism" an ill-fitting descriptor of the local music boom. In Indonesia, the pop performances that assumed a dominant position in the delineation of the new nationality were positioned at a distance from "Asia." Fuhr argues that K-pop can be read as an example of the periphery speaking back to the core, but in the Indonesian case, globalization of the recording industry reinforced the cultural ascendance of the West-oriented, masculinist middle-class pop-rock culture. It did not give rise to cultural forms with both a high degree of global translatability and a distinctive Asian flavor, as in the Korean case.

As Fuhr insightfully points out, the branding of national pop (e.g., K-pop, the local music boom) works in two ways: it both draws the horizons of global pop in, closer to home, and identifies the national as somehow distinctive within the global arena. A study of K-pop is a study of the new ways in which global citizenship is scaled in the context of post–Cold War consumer capitalism. K-pop locates Korea in a new global modern tapestry—it serves as a resource by which

Korean youth can both locate themselves in a new global order and experiment with ideas about the national character. In *Genre Publics*, the local music boom, like K-pop, serves to elevate Indonesia on a global stage of twenty-first-century consumer capitalism. However, it also filters the global through various scales at the national level. The local music boom opens up new contestations between mass and middle-class cultural forms, denoted respectively by the terms "Melayu" and "Indonesia." In context of the boom, these cultural forms compete to delineate new national ideals, and this reveals the contested and unsettled character of locality production.

But the book not only chronicles the genealogical features of the post–Cold War development of Indonesian pop. It also highlights the place of Southeast Asian centers in the shift in the center of gravity of global pop cultural production toward Asia. In the last decade or so, a body of scholarship has emerged that considers, broadly, how these new Asian hubs of global media provide tools for reconfiguring Asian histories, communities, and selves, and in which Fuhr's book can be positioned. Indeed, a body of work with a wide scope has quickly emerged from the inter-Asia pop music society grouping, established in 2005, and includes studies of Asian pop stars (Benson 2013; Shin 2009), television franchises (Fung 2013b; Yang 2009), social movements (Manabe 2015; Mōri 2005), and industries (J. Lee 2009). But much of the scholarship about the expansion of Asian pop industries has focused on East Asian hubs for the production of content with regional transborder currency. When work on Southeast Asia appears, it often refers to how Southeast Asians are consuming Japanese, Korean, Taiwanese pop culture. Southeast Asia appears as a net importer of cultural content from the North. This skews the picture of Southeast Asian pop culture industries more broadly and also of the cultural diets of Southeast Asian audiences. While it is true that, in the twenty-first century, Indonesian audiences consume Asian pop in ever greater numbers (Heryanto 2014; Jung and Shim 2014), it is also true that in the same period the Indonesian pop industry has expanded considerably. As Fung notes, geographies of global pop culture production are shifting, but this book has demonstrated that they are doing so at various scales, the cultural and political implications of which cannot be grasped through a sole focus on East Asian pop industries and their cultivation of regional markets.

Indeed, one of the book's central arguments is that media deregulation, and the local music boom to which it gave rise, bore political consequences that manifested themselves as part of the specific context of Indonesia's emerging democracy in the early 2000s. It prompted changes to the identities of those invested with political authority, and the modes of its articulation and reception, but also featured the stubborn endurance of long-standing cultural forms, namely the critical male subject denoted by the term *pemuda*. On the one hand, at a time of political transformation and media globalization, moral and ethical visions were entrusted to celebrities, such as members of Slank and other all-male rock bands that emerged as the local music boom's principal proponents. They not only performed the *pemuda* role but also played a vital part in linking it to consumer brands. In this sense, the consumer citizenship advanced by the local music boom did not just promise personal transformation and self-realization for all and sundry. It idealized certain kinds of consumer subjects who circumscribed proper ways of belonging to the transformed nation. The local music boom's rock bands sent long-standing cultural forms on new circulatory routes, using the routes to reassert the primacy of the middle-class, masculine subject in the new technological paradigm (chapter 4 and 5).

On the other hand, rock idols' assumption of the *pemuda* role also indexed important shifts in the identities of those thought to legitimately embody political authority, and the ways their visions were received and enacted. As moral and ethical visions were entrusted to celebrities, especially male rock idols, such idols began to assume roles previously reserved for campus-based intellectuals. They developed moral philosophies and activist agendas in a manner well illustrated by the Slank case, and this reveals the political impact of image-rich media such as television, which provided the foundation for political celebrities' commercial success, as discussed in chapter 2.

It is not just modes of articulating authority that have changed, though, but also the socialities emerging from people's common orientation to authoritative texts. As discussed in chapter 6, the increasingly important role television played in the mediation of pop prompted the organizing of pop consumers into fan groups—a new kind of associational life harboring multiple kinds of co-awareness structured by rock idols' political address—such as Nanoe Biroe's call to cultivate a low Balinese subject position, or Kangen Band's queering of *pop Indonesia*. By examining elements of this new associational life in chapters 6 and 7, the book shows how the local music boom bore political implications that extend beyond mere changes to media content, and it also presents new perspectives on political change afforded by a focus on popular culture.

In this sense, the book augments existing work on contemporary Indonesian popular culture. In his 2014 book, for example, Heryanto uses a focus on screen culture (film, television, and social media) to trace developments in cultural politics in the post-authoritarian period in Indonesia. Popular culture, he argues, reveals the experimentations with national identity that took place in the context of the power vacuum that developed after the New Order's fall. Such experiments reveal three broad trends, all of which have been largely overlooked in Indonesianist scholarship in the post-authoritarian era.

First, an exuberance and optimism about the possibilities of democracy, which mirrors the optimism of early independence: in both periods, people of diverse cultural backgrounds and political persuasions came together in the face of a common enemy. In and of itself, this coming together produced new and creative ideas in political and cultural spheres. Heryanto seeks to illuminate the histories of ideas that come to the fore in the post-authoritarian period in order to create a distance between his own account and those that overestimate the cultural change that arrived with regime change. Many twenty-first-century cultural novelties, he posits, have their roots in developments that took place in the New Order period. A focus on popular culture adds historical complexity to the picture of political change. Second, rather than considered critique and reflection on the nation's history, hyper-nationalism played an influential role in experiments with identity emerging in the context of the post-authoritarian "power vacuum." Third, Heryanto interprets this hyper-nationalism as a function of "historical amnesia" in relation to the mass killings of leftists in 1965–1966, and the subsequent suppression of leftist ideas. Historical amnesia and hyper-nationalism, Heryanto avers, go hand in hand.

Genre Publics shares many of Heryanto's concerns. For example, I am also keen to highlight the disjunctive relationship between regime change and cultural change. An examination of the local music boom suggests that the hyper-nationalism Heryanto refers to (and of which the local music boom serves as an exemplar) is a feature of trade liberalization (specifically, the globalization of Indonesian's recording industry and the privatization of television in the mid-1990s), rather than a distinctly post-authoritarian phenomenon. I also aim to use popular culture (in this case popular music) as a lens through which to view unnoticed dimensions of the archipelago's political history. Specifically, I show how pop music genres elicited new, classed publics that both enabled people to imagine their place as citizens and served as resources that people manipulated in efforts to shape ideal tropes following the capitalist revolution in the late 1960s, thereby challenging the predominant idea that the Indonesian middle class was a child of economic growth coupled with prevailing anticommunism.

But *Genre Publics* differs from Heryanto's *Identity and Pleasure* in a couple of respects. Its focus is popular music, so readers not only gain a sense of the important role popular culture plays in shaping publics, but also learn of the *longue durée* of Indonesian popular music's development, the historical forces responsible for its organization into genres, and the social and cultural implications of such genres' significations. Therefore, it speaks directly to themes that have been pivotal to popular music scholarship for some time. Furthermore, *Genre Publics* studies the links between developments in popular culture and emerging ideological contours of public life not only by examining narratives of ideal citizenship that circulate as media content but also by exploring new technological affordances by which pop consumers navigate the everyday. For example, as discussed in chapter 2, as commercial television played an increasingly important role in the mediation of pop and in the public culture in general, it pushed rock to the forefront of public life, enabling rock performers to present themselves as moral visionaries, whose visions were circulated as television ads, thereby preparing post-authoritarian citizenship for consumption. In this perspective, television plays a vital role in the cultural shifts that both make possible and are necessitated by regime change. I have argued that the new technological paradigm ushered in by media deregulation in the 1990s was primarily a televisual one, but I have also attended to the array of technological affordances that are being made available by the ever-changing media ecologies through which pop consumers navigate the everyday. I have considered how such affordances enable new kinds of movement and assembly by which people stretch metanarratives of the "local" (chapters 6 and 7) issuing from big media institutions such as Sony Music Indonesia, MTV Indonesia, and *Rolling Stone* Indonesia (chapters 4 and 5), and ask: what happens when the televisual present is thickly overlaid with intricate hives of personal devices—both those capable of communicating at a distance with publics, such as mobile phones and compact disc players, and those that intervene in and reshape urban crowds, such as T-shirts and motorbikes? What new senses of localness result from this ever deeper layering of media machineries?

Above, I argued that attending to technological change affords an understanding of the political implications of media change and therefore extends accounts of Indonesia's political history; but an understanding of the new technological paradigm as composed of rich layers of media machineries also extends theories of the digital present. Drawing on Castells, I have presented a history of Indonesian capitalism constituted by technological paradigms; but the Indonesian case challenges the importance that Castells accords to digital technologies in contemporary modes of social organization. Digital technologies certainly play a role in affording political celebrities the ability to mobilize their fans, but these figures and the structures they address are ill-described as children of a digital generation. The reality is much more complicated. As argued in the introduction to the book, producing the "local" of the local music boom is not only highly contested. It also takes place at a complex historical juncture featuring regime change, administrative decentralization, and media change on a number of fronts.

As discussed in chapters 6 and 7, such media change not only implicates mobile phones and television, but also a host of other new communicative devices, such as "informal" compact discs, DIY fashion, and motorbikes. These other new media technologies are as important as mobile phones in mediating the forms of co-awareness arising from fans' common orientation to their idols' address. For example, in chapter 7 DIY fandom and motorbikes expand communicative opportunities for young Balinese women. The Badudawati discussed in this chapter gained access to these technologies concurrently, and together they formed a symbiotic ecology that enhanced young women's public presence and political voice. In chapter 6, Kangen Band fans originally came together as a counterpublic through their common orientation to informally circulating CDs, and their status as such relied on the dominant status of televisually mediated publics. These examples highlight the ways digital media intertwine with other new media forms in the new technological paradigm.

As Lewis, Martin, and Sun (2016) assert in their book on televisually mediated modernity, in much of Asia television is a new medium, and not a legacy form, and this fact has a crucial bearing of the significance of television as a cultural form in Asian contexts. I posit it also has a crucial bearing on the contours of digital change in Asia: if commercial television is a new medium and not a legacy form, this calls for fresh theories of digital change. In this book, I have aimed to present a picture of digital uptake as riding the wake of a historical rupture forged by the (slightly earlier) popularization of commercial television. I have also aimed to show how the contours of new communicative practices ushered in by digital technologies are significantly blurred by the fact of their concurrence with change on a number of fronts, including political change and linguistic change, but also the emergence of other new analog communicative devices, which, like digital, enable people to articulate and circulate ideas in new ways.

ACKNOWLEDGMENTS

The research for this book was undertaken over the course of three postdoctoral appointments from 2004 to 2017. Over that time, I also had a baby and raised her. The greatest thanks go to my mum, Robin Lucas. In my daughter's early years, my mother devoted months to living in Bali to help me with parenting as I struggled with successive precarious jobs and a slow and painful marriage breakdown. When my daughter reached primary school, Mum took on school holiday care. Mum's partner, Bob Northey, whom my daughter wryly calls "my so-called grandfather," provided her with loving guidance and took her to see lots of movies. My siblings, Lib, Kate, and Michael, and their families had them all over for meals and sleepovers. In early 2017, I opted to defer the start of a new job in Kuala Lumpur so I could finish the first draft of this book. Mum came to live with us. She took the bus to do the shopping and lugged the groceries home to cook up a storm for our evening meal so I could focus on writing. Then she helped us pack up our lives and make another transnational move, the fourth in five years.

My husband's family in Bali shared a lot of the burden too, especially my sister in-law, Henny Laulang. In the interstices of caring for her ailing mother and working the night shift as a security guard, she would pile my daughter and her two cousins, Miki and Erik, onto her motorbike and take them off on one of her famous adventures, which typically involved *bakso*. My daughter also spent quite a bit of time at her cousins' house, cared for by their mother, Kadek. First Mbok Mang (Rizki) and then Mbok Ana took on weekday care.

Completing a piece of writing takes persistence and focus. These are skills we learn by ourselves and impose on ourselves. We learn how to boss ourselves into sitting at the desk and putting words on paper. We learn about our own tricks of procrastination and how to speak sternly to them, too. But support networks help clear the space and time needed to get to the desk, and ground us in ways that nurture our authentic voice. Thanks to dear friends Liz Gunn, Jude Addison, Tamz Rasmussen, and Ariadna Matamoros-Fernandez for keeping me in touch with the deeper "me" beyond the ravenous whirlwind of academia. Thanks to Mei for all the joy that your pop culture obsessions, sass, and thoughtfulness bring.

This book began in 2003 when I took up a postdoctoral position at Leiden University's Institute of Cultural Anthropology and Development Sociology in the Netherlands. The two-year position was part of a project called Indonesian Mediations, funded by the Dutch agency KNAW and led by Professors Patricia Spyer and Ben Arps. In Leiden I undertook the research for, and wrote drafts of, chapters 4 and 5. A version of chapter 4 was published as a book chapter titled "Cosmopatriotism in Indonesian Pop Music Imagings" in Jeroen de Kloet's and Edwin Jurriëns's edited volume *Cosmopatriots: Globalization, Patriotism, Cosmopolitanism in Contemporary Asian Culture/s* (2007). A version of chapter 5 was published as "God Bless Come Back: New Experiments with Nostalgia in Indonesian Pop," in *Perfect Beat* in 2011.

The Leiden postdoc was career defining for me. I had written my PhD in meek isolation, spending three years getting to work at 7 a.m. and powering through the chapters. I didn't teach, and I didn't socialize much. At Leiden I quickly found myself part of the "Indonesian Mediations" gang—a collective Wiwik Sushartami likes to call the "Leiden mafia." Many of its members have shaped this book through their friendship, ideas, works, and cooking. My friendship with Wiwik Sushartami began with a series of lunches and dinners during the wintry months at our respective abodes. I relied on Wiwik for her analysis of Indonesian female pop artists, and it was she who advised me to take a close look at Krisdayanti (chapter 4). Sharing an office with Bart Barendregt provided the world's greatest rationale for procrastinating, so vast is this man's knowledge and so mesmerizing his stories. Through Bart, I was personally introduced to a number of the US-based ethnomusicologists whose work is heavily cited in the book: Jeremy Wallach, Philip Yampolsky, and Andrew Weintraub. Ratih and Julian Millie—also frequent dinner party companions—never ceased to entertain with their commentary of the Leiden scene. Edwin Jurriëns was also a postdoc with Indonesian Mediations. His work on talk-back radio in Bali first got me thinking about the role old media forms were playing in Indonesian democratization. Patsy Spyer's flair for resisting the allure of hiding in one's academic identity provided me with an early model of how to "be" an academic, for which I remain very grateful. My time with the Leiden mafia has been a touchstone for my academic practice ever since. Fifteen years on, I am still collaborating with all of them.

In July 2005, six months pregnant, I left Leiden to go and live in Bali. I took an unpaid twelve-month break, then in July 2006 I accepted a two-year job as a research associate with a project called Finding a Voice, funded by the Australian Research Council and led by Professor Jo Tacchi. Jo has been a supportive referee on my many job applications since that time. In 2009, I commenced a three-year postdoctoral fellowship also funded by the Australian Research Council and led by Professor Ariel Heryanto, titled "Middle Classes, New Media and Indie Networks in Post-Authoritarian Indonesia." The research for chapters 3 and 6 was undertaken during this period. A version of chapter 3 was published as a book chapter titled "Pop Melayu vs. Pop Indonesia: Marketeers, Producers and New Interpretations of a Genre into the 2000s," in *Sonic Modernities in Southeast Asia*, edited by Bart Barendregt (2014). A version of chapter 6 was published as "Longing Band Play at Beautiful Hope" in a special issue edited by Julian Millie and myself titled "Media/Politics in Indonesia," in the *International Journal of Cultural Studies*. In 2012 I commenced work on another Australian Research Council–funded project, "Mobile Indonesians: Social Differentiation and Digital Literacies in the 21st Century," a collaboration with Associate Professor Jerry Watkins and Professor Heryanto.

During the period of the ARC fellowship and the early fieldwork for "Mobile Indonesians" I continued to live and work in Bali. Neither project could have been completed without the intellectual contributions of our Bali-based research assistants, Gde Putra, Roro Sawita, and Anton Muhajir, all cultural activists and writers involved in the founding of the key Balinese cultural organizations Sloka Institute, Taman 65, and Bale Bengong. This book is peppered with their ideas, experiences, and networks. Putra undertook a thorough review of the editions of *Aktuil* magazine I had procured, which served as the foundation for the discussion presented in chapter 1. Roro alerted me to how the different features of mobile phones—sms/voice calls and data use—were being classed and gendered in distinct ways, and started me thinking about how the social characteristics of media forms were evolving. It was Anton's idea to do a study of Nanoe Biroe and his followers, the Baduda. With his compatriots at Sloka Institute, Intan Paramitha and Gus Tulang, he organized a daylong focus group discussion with the Baduda.

Many others helped me along the way in the research process. The music journalist Denny MR went out of his way to connect me to pop artists in Jakarta.

Many of my interviews with managers, artists, and record label executives would have been impossible without Denny's help. Denny also helped me procure some copies of *Aktuil*, as did the writer Theodore KS, and I could not have written chapter 1 without these resources. I am also grateful to the many musicians, managers, record label executives, music writers, and fans who participated in interviews: Roy and Ivan Boomerang, Feby Lubis, Rudolf Dethu, Log Zhelebour, Armand Maulana, members of Rocket Rocker, Pak Yan Djuhana, Pak Iin Aquarius, Pak Handi Musika, Mishal Varma, members of Pas, Makki Ungu, Oppie Andaresta, Audy, Lesley Decker, members of Jadugar, Piyu Padi, members of 7 Kurcaci, Dhani Dewa, Rizal Mantovani, Amel Affandi, members of Superman Is Dead, Sarah Forbes, Ade Putri, Yudhis Sony, Dimas Djayadiningrat, Azis MS, Harlan Boer, Indra Ameng, David Karto, Tagore Dwisapta, Soleh Solihun, Adib Hidayat, Ricky Siahaan, Wening Gitomartoyo, Hasief Ardiesyah, Wendi Putranto, members of the Trees and the Wild, Fariz RM, Eka Brandals, members of Nymphea, members of Mocca, Edward Sova, members of Burgerkill, Oka, Andhika Kangen Band, Sujana, Nanoe Biroe, Gektusukma, Nyoman Agus Swanjaya, Ivan Januar, Putu Billy Indrawan, Wayan Ariawan, Nyoman Widarta, Wayan Sugiyaksa, Man Agus, Agus Parliawan, Ni Putu Dewi Suyastini, Ni Luh Made Indah Widyasari, and the members of Doy Jabotabek.

People who live precariously become hyperaware of the value of support networks but in their desperation risk overburdening them. In two between-jobs periods, in early 2012 and early 2014, I left Bali and went to live in Canberra to teach at the Australian National University's School of Culture, History and Language. I thank Ariel Heryanto for this opportunity. My aunt Jessica Lucas and her husband, Ali Kayaya, kindly let us stay in their very comfortable backyard bungalow in Queanbeyan, a short walk from the local school. Colleagues at the ANU provided references and reviews as I frantically scribbled job applications and grant proposals. I am grateful to Edward Aspinall, Ariel Heryanto, Ross Tapsell, and the able team at the ANU College of Asia and the Pacific Research Office for this. I am grateful to Jerry Watkins for expertly structuring our successful grant proposal for "Mobile Indonesians" and for his mentorship and friendship thereon. And I am also grateful to Julian Millie and Amrih Widodo, who agreed to work with me on the "Voices in Post-authoritarian Indonesia" symposium at the National Film and Sound Archive in Canberra in 2013, where a version of chapter 6 was first presented.

In 2014 I landed a three-year Vice Chancellor's Senior Research Fellowship at

Queensland University's Creative Industry faculty. In June of that year, we packed all our belongings into my Suzuki Swift and drove three days from Canberra to Brisbane. Mum came along to lend moral support.

I took my ARC-funded project, "Mobile Indonesians," to QUT and worked on it there. In the first year of my fellowship, the Digital Media Research Centre was established, and my research took place under the auspices of this body. At QUT, I worked on chapters 1, 2, and 7. A version of chapter 1 was published as "Genre Publics: *Aktuil* Magazine and Its Role in Shaping Critical Middle Class Youth in 1970s Indonesia" in the journal *Indonesia* (2016), and much of the discussion in chapters 2 and 7 appears in a 2017 article in the journal *Cultural Politics* titled "The Everyman and the Dung Beetle: New Media Infrastructures for Lower Class Cultural Politics."

The QUT job marked my first foray into hard-core media and communications territory, and I would like to thank Professors Mandy Thomas and Jean Burgess for accepting me into this space. Professor Terry Flew worked with me on a series of events related to Digital Asia, as did Associate Professor Adrian Athique and Dr. Luzhou Li, both of the University of Queensland. Thanks also to Ariadna Matamoros-Fernandez, Angela Daly, Fiona Suwana, Wilfred Wang, Meg Zeng, Brenda Moon, and Jiajie Lu for hanging out with me in Brisbane. After my fellowship ended, Jean and Terry kindly granted me an adjunct position and a desk at the Digital Media Research Centre, where I spent several months putting together the first draft of this manuscript in early 2018.

In July 2018 I moved to Kuala Lumpur to take up an (ongoing!) position at Monash University Malaysia's School of Arts and Social Sciences. It was here that I completed a second draft of the manuscript in early and mid-2019. I would like to thank our head of school, Professor Helen Nesadurai, for keeping our teaching duties reasonably light and giving us plenty of time for research in between semesters. Thanks to new buddies Susan Leong, Koh Sin Yee, Ana Grgic, and Ting-Fai Yu for making the settling-in process all the more enjoyable. And thanks to Mei for being so amenable to all this relocation!

Finally, I thank those who suggested ways to improve the chapters in their previous iterations in journals and edited books, the anonymous readers who reviewed the first draft, and the team at Wesleyan UP—Suzanna Tamminen, Jeremy Wallach, Debra Wong, Jackie Wilson, and Sherrie Tucker—along with freelancers Christi Stanforth, Jessica Freeman, and Glen Novak, for being so patient with this monograph, which has taken much longer than expected.

NOTES

Introduction

1. In Indonesia, a sizable underground scene, comprising a nationwide network of punk and metal bands, 'zines, and shows, emerged in the 1990s, in the wake of the promulgation of media deregulation policies. Underground bands were distinctive not only for the sound of their music but also for their distaste for mainstream commercial modes of production, involving television and major labels. In the 2000s, a number of underground bands (including Superman Is Dead, discussed in chapter 4) were signed to major labels and played important roles in the mainstreaming of punk and metal and the official acceptance of these genres as representative of a desired modernity. On underground music see Baulch 2007b, Moore 2015, and Wallach 2007.

ONE Establishing Class

1. My research suggests readers were a mix of children of petite bourgeoisie, high-ranking military officers, and low-ranking civil servants, including university lecturers and village heads. Denny Sabrie, the founder of *Aktuil*, was the son of a high-ranking civil servant (and presumably a military man). Graphic stories in *Aktuil* depict the ideal middle-class domestic environment as a high-ranking officer's home in a military complex, and some of the letters to the editor published in the magazine suggest that some readers lived in such homes. But not all readers were people of means, or from military families. Sabrie came from a family of considerable means, but two of my informants had been left fatherless after the mass killings of leftists in 1965–1966, and they were not from rich families. One of them put himself through school by selling cakes in the schoolyard.

2. Habermas, too, draws attention to the importance of coffee, the press, and the proliferation of places to consume these in seventeenth-century Europe in the beginnings of an ideal public sphere that "compelled public authority to legitimate itself before public opinion" (Habermas 1991, 25)

3. Other writers have drawn attention to the importance of *pemuda* in the development of student activism during the New Order; see, for example, Aspinall 2005 and D. Lee 2011. But *Aktuil*'s power lay in its ability to draw this trope into the everyday of pop culture consumption: to address not just activists, but middle-class youth in general.

4. Frederick (1982) attributes the bannings to the influence of the leftist cultural organization Lekra (Lembaga Kebudajaan Rakjat, Institute for the People's Culture). In a 2014 book chapter, Weintraub argues that "emphasising the Old Order's hostility to Western pop tends to obscure the diverse activities of musicians, producers, recording companies, and fans of popular music" (Weintraub 2014, 169). Sen and Weintraub both note how student-run pirate radio stations flouted the ban, and Weintraub stresses the important role of commercial pop from the United States and Europe in influencing Indonesian composers and performers during this time (Sen 2003; Weintraub 2010). Mulyadi avers that the rules of these prohibitions were neither clear-cut nor consistently applied. Sometimes musicians performing the forbidden styles appeared as guest stars at state-sponsored live events, or as contestants in the national public radio song contest (Mulyadi 2009). Budi Setiyono's piece documents the arrest of Koes Bersaudara members (Setiyono 2001).

5. Letters to the editor and the life stories of those former readers I interviewed for this essay (one grew up in Jayapura and another in Denpasar) show that *Aktuil*'s circulation was not limited to Java; it extended across the archipelago.

6. Sopiann cites editor Remy Sylado, who surmises that the reason for waning sales was that the editors' tastes had aged beyond what appealed to the sixteen-to-seventeen-year-old readership.

7. Indeed, *Aktuil* was by no means isolated from military circles. Denny Sabrie's father was presumably a military man and may have been responsible for securing the publishing license for the magazine. Sopiann notes that *Aktuil*'s publishing license was issued by the West Java Regional War Authority (Penguasa Perang Daerah Jawa Barat), "a very powerful military organization" (Sopiann 2001b).

8. Private correspondence with Manunggal K. Wardaya, November 23, 2015. Wardaya has researched in detail and written at length about the 1960s all-female band Dara Puspita, including their success in Europe and Indonesia.

9. Dramatizations of filial defiance extended beyond *Aktuil* and endured in other artistic productions well into the 1970s. In pop composer Zakaria's songs from the 1970s, which consist of dialogues between lovers, or between fathers and daughters, women are also portrayed as pioneers of cultural critique. As Weintraub notes, in Zakaria's compositions, women exist as public beings who make plain their desire to venture beyond the home. Young girls want to have careers, and married women want to have affairs (Weintraub 2014, 179). Like *Aktuil*'s portrayals of women's thoughts and feelings, Zakaria's sharply contrast with those apparent in "Camouflage-Shirted Guy," sung from the perspective of

a woman gazing adoringly at a soldier. One of Zakaria's songs, "Don't Sit in Front of the Door," proceeds thus (Weintraub 2014, 179, trans. Andrew Weintraub):

FATHER: Don't sit in front of the door / Listen to your father's words / When will I be able to marry you off?

DAUGHTER: You're good at talking / Hearing you makes me embarrassed / Because I want to go to school / And other things [i.e., marriage] have to wait.

FATHER: Good, but listen to me / A young girl does not need to be smart / As long as she can write and read / Even if she achieves a good education / In the end she still works in the kitchen.

DAUGHTER: Father don't say that / Girls nowadays have to move forward / If I can become a doctor / I can take care of children and grandkids.

10. Sopiann contends that Sylado's appointment was connected to the fact that the authority responsible for *Aktuil*'s publishing license shifted from the West Java Regional War Authority to the Department of Information in 1970 (Sopiann 2001b).

11. Mulyadi affirms as much on page 55 of his book, but on page 27 he elaborates that although the proscription on long hair was the reason TVRI provided for banning Rhoma Irama from television broadcast, the excuse was considered dubious by many people. Mulyadi points out that long-haired males, including the rock musicians Ahmad Albar and Ucok AKA, appeared on advertisements shown on TVRI. Mulyadi suggests that the real reason for banning Bimbo and Irama was political, as Bimbo's song "Tante Soen" was thought to depict the president's wife in unflattering light, and Irama had aligned himself with the PPP (Partai Persatuan Pembangunan, United Development Party). Nevertheless, the sense that rock existed outside of television broadcast persisted in *Aktuil* (Mulyadi 2009, 55).

12. Such foregrounding coincided with the appointment of Remy Sylado as editor and Maman Somtanri as designer in 1970 (Sopiann 2001b).

13. The three-LP set, *Those Shaking, Shocking Days: Indonesian Hard, Psychedelic, Progressive Rock and Funk: 1970–1978*, was released by the San Francisco–based label Now-Again Records. See Taufiqurrahman 2011.

14. Arguably, foregrounding reading also advanced *Aktuil*'s elitist agenda because it allowed the magazine to launch unanswerable attacks on dangdut, which was not represented in print (Weintraub 2006, 211). The fact that no print media dedicated to celebrating dangdut existed until the appearance of *Tabloid Dangdut* in 1996 is testimony to the cultural force of rock and print's proximity in the pages of *Aktuil* (Solihun 2004, 69).

15. This is not to suggest that Leo and Item did not recognize Koes Plus's achievements and talent. In private correspondence with me, Weintraub stated that Leo is a fan of Koes Plus and was one of the first to write about the band in *Aktuil*. Said Item, "Commerically, Koes Plus rules. But their songs are trash. They have none of this [points to chest].

Commercially, they are successful but the songs have no feeling" (Leo 1974, 72; translation by the author).

16. In 1972, Gunawan Mohamad wrote an article in *Tempo* titled "Serving, with Criticism," expressing the avoidance of direct attack that was in vogue among supporters-turned-critics in the early 1970s. In it he posed the question, "What kind of criticism is wished for and permitted by the authorities?" and concluded with the advice: "Anyone who doesn't want to have his head split needs to choose wisdom over audacity" (Steele 2005, 58). On supporters-turned-critics' avoidance of direct attack see Aspinall 2005, 24.

17. People's faith in the value and existence of this critical news-reading public only came to light in retrospect, when widespread demonstrations erupted following the banning in 1994 of three news magazines — *Tempo, Editor,* and *Detik.* See Heryanto 2003, 42, and Keane 2009, 52.

18. Wawancara Remy Sylado, May 19, 2004. In Javanese, *mbeling* means naughty or rebellious. Unlike *urakan,* which implies rudeness and willfulness, *mbeling* carries overtones of cunning and strategy. See *Puisi Mbeling Remy Sylado* 2004, xi (the foreword, "Sekapur Sirih").

19. Seno Gumira Ajidarma, Abdul Hadi WM, the three Massardis (Noorca, Yudhistira, and Adi), Efix Mulyadi, Kurniawan Junaedi, and Edy Herwanto are cited as writers who were supportive of Remy's *mbeling* poetry (Sylado 2004, xvi).

20. See also Anderson 1990, Sylado 2004; Scherer 1981.

21. The early editions included only one text advertisement, and that was for a bus company.

22. Sopiann writes, "In a short space of time, *Aktuil*'s attributes found their way into all corners of the city of Bandung, and *Aktuil* quickly became an important status symbol for Bandung youth. 'It felt like you weren't a proper teen if you didn't have your copy of *Aktuil* with you,' said Yusran Pare [a Bandung journalist], who, as a boy in the 1970s, would beg his father to buy him a copy of *Aktuil*" (Sopiann 2001b).

23. "The *Tempo* demonstrations were some of the first serious open challenges to the regime's legitimacy, and some later observers considered them to have played a significant role in the loss of authority that helped precipitate President Soeharto's eventual fall from power in 1998" (Keane 2009, 53). See also Heryanto 2003, 41–42.

TWO *Consumer Citizenship*

1. This is not to suggest that bands identified as pop Indonesia acts never composed or played rock songs. The organizing of cultural forms into categories will never prevent border crossing, but isolated instances of category blurring are not always forceful enough to undermine the coherence of a genre. For example, Koes Plus was a pop Indonesia band popular among the lower classes which also composed and played rock songs.

However, this does not mean that the existence of Koes Plus undermined the dominant meanings of rock.

2. Trans TV seemed particularly active in this regard, and over the month of May 2004 contracted Iwan Fals for a month of weekly, live-to-air, in-studio concerts. Also in May, SCTV hosted the SCTV Music Awards, heavily promoted on the channel in preceding weeks.

THREE *Hinge Occupants*

1. Kangen Band members drew no financial reward from such airplay and roadside exchanges. But, in contrast to the official condemnations of piracy, which paint this practice as undermining musicians' interests, Kangen Band members recall this time with great enthusiasm; it led to their well-documented rise to national prominence (Sujana 2009). I prefer the terms "official" and "unofficial" over "legal" and "pirated." "Pirated" implies theft, but members of Kangen Band did not take issue with the widespread reproduction and exchange of their performances at the level of the *emper-emperan*.

2. See *blogbandindo.blogspot.com/2009/07/kangen-band.html* for a discussion of the film.

3. In Weintraub's book, the view of dangdut as strongly grounded in Melayu is not consensual. Weintraub quotes Elvi Sukaesih as refuting any stylistic similarities between Melayu music and dangdut (2010, 34).

4. Farid argues that the New Order's "Green Revolution," a program by which farmers were compelled to plant high-yielding varieties of rice to advance the country's drive for self-sufficiency, increased inequality in rural areas and pushed many farm laborers out of agriculture and into manufacturing. As a result, the urban working class grew in the 1970s (Farid 2005).

5. Ten out of the twelve tracks on *Tentang Aku Kau dan Dia* give voice to the male vocalists' loneliness. The image of the philandering woman emerges strongly; either the singer is trapped in a three-way relationship ("Penantian Yang Tertunda," "Selingkuh," "Tentang Bintang," "Tentang Aku," "Kau dan Dia") or has been abandoned for another man ("Karma," "Jika," "Adakah Jawabnya"). In two other songs, he waits helplessly for his lover to return from afar ("Menunggu," "Petualangan Cinta").

6. But it's important not to overstate this segregation, for dangdut and pop cohabited at recording label Remaco (Aribowo 2002; Panen dangdut 1975; Sakrie 2008a and b, 2009).

7. More successful was Malaysian Search Band's later foray into this genre. Dressed and coiffed like a heavy metal band, Search Band enjoyed a hit in Indonesia with "Isabella," a song described in *Tempo* as a "scene of sadness" (*berlatar sendu*). "Isabella" was at the top of the Indonesian charts for some months in 1989 (Cholid, Suseno, and Atamimi 1989). This song made a comeback on *Indonesian Idol*, where it was sung by one contestant,

Widya, whose proficiency at "Melayu-style" singing earned him a place in the following round. It was also included on a repackaged version of ST12's second album, *P.U.S.P.A.*

8. Pengumuman, Pengumuman / Siapa yang mau bantu tolong aku, kasihani Aku / Tolong carikan diriku kekasih hatiku / Siapa yang mau?

9. Aku tak ingin kau menangis bersedih / Sudahi airmata darimu / Yang aku ingin arti hadir diriku / Kan menghapus dukamu sayang'.

10. One of the memorable ways this optimism forces its ways into domestic space is in the form of multilevel marketing, founded on the very promise of upward mobility. In my own ethnically and socially diverse neighborhood in Denpasar, growing numbers of my neighbors spent more and more of their time at multilevel marketing meetings, or urging other neighbors to either buy their wares or join their meetings. Another example of the prevalence of narratives of upward mobility is provided by the trilogy of novels based on the novelist Andrea Hirata's childhood in a family in provincial Belitung; despite her family's scant financial and minimal educational resources, she went on to win a scholarship to the Sorbonne. These novels, which have been made into the aforementioned films, *Laskar Pelangi* (2007) and *Sang Pemimpi* (2009), to enormous critical and commercial acclaim, proved to be a very powerful explication of the idea that economic hardship allows the possibility for advance.

11. The show featured interviews with and performances by high-selling acts, fitted around host Nirina Zubir's presentation of RBT charts (www.scribd.com/doc/86084799/Certa-Sedih-Di-Balik-Semarak-Nada-Sambung-Pribadi-Telkomsel).

12. In 2006, sales of pirate CDs outnumbered official sales by fourteen-fold, and in 2007 sales of pirate CDs were twenty-seven times higher than sales of official CDs (Jayanti, Djamaludin, and Latifah 2011).

13. Mobile subscriptions per hundred inhabitants doubled every two years between 2003 (10) and 2005 (20), and again between 2005 and 2007 (40), and yet again between 2007 and 2009 (80). See ITU 2019.

FOUR *Becoming Indonesia*

1. In 1995, MTV had already established separate feeds for India and for the Mandarin-speaking world. Both MTV India and MTV Mandarin, produced in Taiwan and serving Singaporean, Hong Kong, and Taiwanese audiences, were uplinked from Singapore, as was MTV Asia, which fed the Indonesian, Philippine, Malaysian, and Thai markets. Each of these "markets," as MTV executives refer to them, now boasts its own, locally produced MTV.

FIVE *Spinning Pasts*

1. "God Bless," http://id.wikipedia.org/wiki/God_Bless, accessed June 13, 2009; "Ian Antonio," http://id.wikipedia.org/wiki/Ian_Antono, accessed June 13, 2009.

2. http://engb.facebook.com/note.php?note_id=53561658915&id=30362238746&index =4, accessed June 13, 2009.

3. "Rumah Kita," Indonesian Voices, https://www.youtube.com/watch?v=doXixfVbhFA, uploaded May 13, 2013.

SIX *Television's Children*

1. Among those who publicly denounced Kangen Band were composer Erwin Gutawa and musician Ridho Hafiedz of Slank (Cahyono 2009a, b), musicians Giring Ganesha, vocalist of Nidji, and David Bayu Danangjaya, vocalist of Naif (http://music.detikhot.com). Among elite critics, such denunciations were controversial. Composer Yovie Widianto (Sulaksono 2009) and former Superman Is Dead manager Rudolf Dethu judged Kangen Band's original compositions superior to other pop Indonesia bands' plagiarisms (Suicide Glam mailing list, June 19, 2008).

SEVEN *Provincial Cosmopolitanism*

1. In several publications, Fushiki has analyzed pop Bali, which she sometimes refers to as pop Bali alternative (Fushiki 2013, 2010, 2009, 2008), but she does not mention Nanoe Biroe. Others to have written about contemporary Balinese popular music, but not the pop Bali scene, include Dethu (2011), Harnish (2005), McIntosh (2010), and Moore (2015, 2013a, b). Some pop Bali acts (Lolot, Joni Agung) had close connections with the indie acts studied by Moore (2015), but most indie acts sang in English or Indonesian, and pop Bali is defined by its Balinese-language repertoire. Dethu's edited volume, *Blantika Linimasa*, includes some contributions about pop Bali musicians.

2. In 2000, total annual motorcycle sales in Indonesia amounted to 864,144 units. By 2011 the figure was approximately 8.05 million. Between 2002 and 2005 sales increased by more than 100 percent (2002: 2.29 million; 2005: 5.07 million) (http://www.aisi.or.id /statistic/). In a 2016 *Financial Times* article, Lockett cites Indonesia as "one of the world's largest markets for motorbikes" and states that "in 2015 Indonesia accounted for 70 per cent of all motorcycle and scooter sales among the five nations tracked by the [Asean Automotive] federation (excluding Vietnam, another major market)" (Lockett 2016). The five nations tracked by the federation included Indonesia, Philippines, Singapore, Thailand, and Malaysia.

3. As a research assistant on this project, Anton Muhajir undertook a study of Baduda's social media uses over a two-week period in October 2013. Based on a combination of Baduda's self-reporting he found that Baduda favored Facebook above all other social media platforms. Muhajir's observation of activity on Baduda's Facebook page revealed that they rarely engaged with any of Nanoe Biroe's several "official" Facebook pages.

4. In later press interviews, Nanoe Biroe referred to this concert as a bid to focus authorities' attention on the need to clean the river, but the show was also a publicity stunt that earned him a fourth listing in the Indonesian Museum of Records (MURI). Previous listings were earned for having the longest CD sleeve, singing for eighty hours straight, and personally signing the most CD covers ever signed (TrashStockBali 2015).

REFERENCES

Published Works

Abbott, Jason. 2013. "Introduction: Assessing the Social and Political Impact of the Internet and New Social Media in Asia." *Journal of Contemporary Asia* 43, no. 4: 579–590.

"Aku Lahir Membawa Dosa dan Kejahatan" [I was born bearing sin and evil]. 1970. *Aktuil* 57:44–46.

Allen, Pamela, and Carmencita Palermo. 2003. "Ajeg Bali: Multiple Meanings, Diverse Agendas." *Indonesia and the Malay World* 33, no. 97: 239–255.

Anderson, Benedict. 1990. "Sembah-Sumpah: The Politics of Language and Javanese Culture." In *Language and Power: Exploring Political Cultures in Indonesia*, 194–237. Ithaca, NY: Cornell University Press.

——. 1983. *Imagined Communities*. London: Verso.

Anggraini, Adisty Dwi. 2008. "Pembentukan identitas Slankers melalui pemaknaan terhadap simbol-simbol budaya musik Slank" [The formation of Slankers' identities: Signifying the symbols of Slank's music]. Undergraduate thesis, Bogor Agriculture Institute.

Annabella, M. 1973. "Situ Harus Tahu, Ah!" [You need to know this!]. *Aktuil* 127:6.

Antara. 2006. "Cerita Sedih di Balik Semarak Nada Sambung Pribadi Telkomsel" [The sad story behind the success of Telkomsel ringback tones]. www.scribd.com/doc/86084799/Certa-Sedih-Di-Balik-Semarak-Nada-Sambung-Pribadi-Telkomsel.

Antara News. 2011. "Telkom incar Rp1,5 triliun dari musik digital" [Telkom eyeing Rp1.5 trillion from digital music]. May 2. https://www.antaranews.com/berita/256767/telkom-incar-rp15-triliun-dari-musik-digital.

Appadurai, Arjun. 2010. "How Histories Make Geographies: Circulation and Context in a Global Perspective." *Transcultural Studies* 1:4–12.

——. 1996. *Modernity at Large: The Cultural Dimensions of Globalization*. Minneapolis: University of Minnesota Press, 1996.

Ardianto, Danny, Jeremy Aarons, and Frada Burstein. 2014. "Can Twitter Enhance Food Resilience? Exploring Community Use of Twitter Using Communicative Ecology." In *Proceedings of the Twenty-Fifth Australasian Conference on Information Systems, 8th–10th December, Auckland, New Zealand.* aut.researchgateway.ac.nz/handle/10292/7977/discover.

Aribowo, Bill. 2002. "Dangdut, Identitas Bangsa" [Dangdut, identity of a nation]. *Kompas Minggu*, July 28. http://mellowtone.multiply.com/journal/item/105.

Aspinall, Edward. 2013. "The Triumph of Capital? Class Politics and Indonesian Democratisation." *Journal of Contemporary Asia* 43, no. 2: 226–242. https://doi.org/10.1080/00472336.2012.757432.

——— . 2005. *Opposing Suharto: Compromise, Resistance, and Regime Change in Indonesia.* Stanford, CA: Stanford University Press.

——— . 1993. *Student Dissent in Indonesia in the 1980s.* Melbourne: Centre of Southeast Asian Studies, Monash University.

Aveling, Harry. 1975. "Contemporary Indonesian Poetry." In *Contemporary Indonesian Poetry*, xvii–xxiii. St. Lucia: University of Queensland Press.

Bang, H. 2009. '"Yes We Can": Identity Politics and Project Politics for the Late-Modern World.' *Urban Research and Practice* 2, no. 2: 1–21.

Barendregt, Bart. 2006. "Cyber Nasyid: Transnational Soundscapes in Muslim Southeast Asia." In *Medi@asia: Communication, Culture, Context*, edited by T. Holden and T. Scrase, 171–187. London: Routledge.

Barendregt, Bart, and Wim van Santen. 2002. "Popular Music in Indonesia since 1988, in Particular Fusion. Indie and Islamic Music on Video Compact Discs and the Internet." In *Yearbook for Traditional Music* 34:67–113.

Baudrillard, Jean. (1970) 1998. *The Consumer Society: Myths and Structures.* London: Sage.

Baulch, Emma. 2017a. "The Everyman and the Dung Beetle: New Media Infrastructures for Lower-Class Cultural Politics." *Cultural Politics* 13, no. 2: 202–226.

——— . 2017b. "Mobile Phones: Advertising, Consumerism and Class." In *Digital Indonesia: Connectivity and Divergence*, edited by Edwin Jurriëns and Ross Tapsell, 38–55. Singapore: ISEAS and ANU Press.

——— . 2016. "Genre Publics: *Aktuil* Magazine and Its Role in Shaping Critical Middle Class Youth in 1970s Indonesia." *Indonesia*, October, 85–113.

——— . 2014. "Pop Melayu vs. Pop Indonesia: Marketeers, Producers and New Interpretations of a Genre into the 2000s." In *Sonic Modernities in the Malay World: A History of Popular Music, Social Distinction and Novel Lifestyles (1930s–2000s)*, edited by Bart Barendregt, 187–216. Leiden: Brill.

——— . 2013. "Longing Band Play at Beautiful Hope." *International Journal of Cultural Studies* 16, no. 3: 289–302.

———. 2012. "God Bless Come Back: New Experiments with Nostalgia in Indonesian Pop." *Perfect Beat* 12, no. 2: 129–146.

———. 2010. "Music for the pria dewasa: Change and Continuity in Class and Pop Music Genres." *Journal of Indonesian Social Sciences and Humanities* 3:99–130.

———. 2007a. "Cosmopatriotism in Indonesian Pop Music Imagings." In *Cosmopatriots: On Distant Belongings and Close Encounters*, edited by Edwin Jurriëns and Jeroen de Kloet, 177–204. Amsterdam: Rodopi.

———. 2007b. *Making Scenes: Punk, Reggae and Death Metal in 1990s Bali*. Durham, NC: Duke University Press.

———. 2002a. "Alternative Music and Mediation in Late New Order Indonesia." *Inter-Asia Cultural Studies* 3, no. 2: 219–234.

———. 2002b. "Creating a Scene: Balinese Punk's Beginnings." *International Journal of Cultural Studies* 5, no. 2: 153–177.

Bennett, Andy. 2006. "Even Better Than the Real Thing? Understanding the Tribute Band Phenomenon." In *Access All Eras: Tribute Bands and Global Pop Culture*, edited by Shane Homan, 19–31. Berkshire, UK: Open University Press.

Benson, Phil. 2013. "English and Identity in East Asian Popular Music." *Popular Music* 32: 23–33.

Beta, Annisa. 2016. "Socially Mediated Publicness in Networked Society for Indonesian Muslim Women." *Jurnal Ilmu Komunikasi* 13, no. 1: 19–30.

———. 2014. "Hijabers: How Young Urban Muslim Women Redefine Themselves in Indonesia." *International Communication Gazette* 74, no. 4–5: 377–389. http://doi.org/10.1177/1748048514524103.

Blaustein, Jessica. 2004. "How Publics Matter: A Handbook for Alternative World-Making." Review of *Publics and Counterpublics*, by Michael Warner. *American Quarterly* 56, no. 1 (March): 171–181.

Bolter, J. David, and Richard Grusin. 1996. "Remediation." *Configurations* 4, no. 3: 311–358.

Browne, Susan. 2000. *The Gender Implications of dangdut kampungan: Indonesian "Low Class" Popular Music*. Monash University Insititute for Asian Studies Working Paper 109. Melbourne: Centre of Southeast Asian Studies.

Buchanan, Ian. 2007. *Jameson on Jameson: Conversations on Cultural Marxism*. Durham, NC: Duke University Press.

Cahyono, Aris Danu. 2009a. "Erwin Gutawa Anggap Pop Melayu 'Jadul'" [Erwin Gutawa considers pop Melayu passé]. Accessed August 19, 2009. http://artis.inilah.com/berita/2009/05/08/105434/erwin-gutawa-anggap-pop-melayu-jadul/.

———. 2009b. "Ridho 'Slank' Malu Musik Melayu" [Ridho Slank is ashamed of Melayu music]. Accessed August 19, 2009. http://artis.inilah.com/berita/2009/05/08/105331/ridho-slank-malu-musik-melayu/.

Carr, J. 1970. "Kemanakah Generasi Kami Tuan Bawa" [Where are you taking our generation, sir?]. *Aktuil* 52:8–9.

Cartwright, Lisa, and Stephen Mandiberg. 2009. "Obama and Shepard Fairey: The Copy and Political Iconography in the Age of the Demake." *Journal of Visual Culture* 8, no. 2: 172–176.

Castells, Manuel. 2010. *The Rise of the Network Society*. Malden, MA: Wiley-Blackwell.

Cholid, Mohamad, Ardian Suseno, and Ekram H. Atamimi. 1989. "Kisah Isabela" [The story of Isabela]. *Tempo*, November 25–December 1.

Cody, Francis. 2011. "Publics and Politics." *Annual Review of Anthropology* 2011, no. 40: 37–52.

Crosby, Alexandra. 2013. "Remixing Environmentalism in Blora, Central Java 2005–10." *International Journal of Cultural Studies* 16, no. 3: 257–269.

——. 2010. "Alternative Arts Collectives and the Festival Phenomenon." Paper presented at "Cultural Performance in Post–New Order Indonesia: New Structures, Scenes, Meanings," Sanata Dharma University, Yogyakarta, June 28–July 1.

Crouch, Harold. 1986. "The Missing Bourgeoisie: Approaches to Indonesia's New Order." In *Nineteenth and Twentieth Century Indonesia: Essays in Honour of Professor J. D. Legge*, edited by David Chandler and Merle Rickleffs, 41–56. Melbourne: Centre of Southeast Asian Studies, Monash University.

Crouch, C. 2004 *Post-democracy*. Cambridge: Polity.

David, Bettina. 2014. "Seductive Pleasures, Eluding Subjectivities: Some Thoughts on Dangdut's Ambiguous Identities." In *Sonic Modernities in the Malay World: A History of Popular Music, Social Distinction and Novel Lifestyles (1930s–2000s)*, edited by Bart Barendregt, 249–270. Leiden: Brill.

——. 2003. "The Erotics of Loss: Some Remarks on the Pleasure of Dancing to Sad *Dangdut* Songs." Paper presented at the Workshop "Pop Music in Southeast Asia," Leiden, December 8–12.

Dean, Jodi. 2008. "Communicative Capitalism: Circulation and the Foreclosure of Politics." In *Digital Media and Democracy: Tactics in Hard Times*, edited by Megan Boler, 101–122. Cambridge, MA: MIT Press.

——. 2001. "Cybersalons and Civil Society: Rethinking the Public Sphere in Transnational Technoculture." *Public Culture* 13, no. 2: 243–265.

DeLuca, Kevin Michael, and Jennifer Peeples. 2002. "From Public Sphere to Public Screen: Democracy, Activism, and the 'Violence' of Seattle." *Critical Studies in Media Communication* 19, no. 2: 125–151.

Denny MR. 2009a. "In God We Trust." *Rolling Stone* 49:22–29.

——. 2009b. "Raksasa yang Menyendiri" [Solitary giant]. *Rolling Stone* 49:30–36.

Derrida, Jacques. 1995. *Archive Fever: A Freudian Impression*. Chicago: University of Chicago Press.

Dethu, Rudolf. 2011. *Blantika Linimasa* [Music of an era]. Denpasar, Indonesia: Matamera Books.

Deuze, Mark, and John Banks. 2009. "Co-creative Labour." *International Journal of Cultural Studies* 12, no. 5: 419–431.

Dick, H. 1990. "The Rise of the Middle Class and the Changing Concept of Equity." In *The Politics of Middle-Class Indonesia*, edited by Richard Tanter and Kenneth Young Glen Waverly, 71–92. Monash Papers on Southeast Asia No. 19. Melbourne: Centre of Southeast Asian Studies, Monash University.

——. 1985. "The Rise of a Middle Class and the Changing Concept of Equity in Indonesia." *Indonesia* 39:71–92.

Didiek W. 1970. "Kau Laki Laki Pengecut, Hendra" [You are a cowardly man, Hendra]. *Aktuil* 57:12–13.

Djatmiko, Harmanto Edy. 2004. "Rich and Famous, Yeah . . ." *SWA*, May 13–26, pp. 24–25.

Doron, Assa. 2012. "Consumption, Technology and Adaptation: Care and Repair Economies of Mobile Phones in North India." *Pacific Affairs* 85, no. 3: 563–585.

Duara, Prasenjit. 2015. "The Agenda of Asian Studies and Digital Media in the Anthropocene." *Asiascape: Digital Asia* 2:11–19.

——. 2010. "Asia Redux: Conceptualizing a Region for Our Times." *Journal of Asian Studies* 69, no. 4: 963–983.

Endah. 2003. *1001 KD*. Jakarta: Gramedia.

"Esia HP Edisi Slank 30s.mpeg" [Slank edition of Esia mobile phone]. 2010. YouTube video, 0:29, uploaded January 25, 2010. www.youtube.com/watch?v=upTDzoD_k2k.

Fabbri, Franco. 1981. "A Theory of Musical Genres: Two Applications." In *Popular Music Perspectives*, edited by David Horn and Philip Tagg, 52–81. Gothenburg, Sweden: International Association for the Study of Popular Music (IASPM).

"Fans Slank Sambut Jokowi di Potlot" [Slank fans greet Jokowi at Potlot]. 2014. Detiknews. http://news.detik.com/berita/2593408/fans-slank-sambut-jokowi-di-potlot.

Farid, Hilmar. 2011. "Meronta dan Berontak: Pemuda dalam Sastra Indonesia" [Breaking away and rebelling: Youth in Indonesian literature]. *Prisma* 30, no. 2: 72–82.

——. 2005. "Indonesia's Original Sin: Mass Killings and Capitalist Expansion, 1965–66." *Inter-Asia Cultural Studies* 6, no. 1: 3–16. http://dx.doi.org/10.1080/14623940420003 26879.

Ferry, Megan. 2003. "Advertising, Consumerism and Nostalgia for the New Woman in Contemporary China." *Continuum: Journal of Media and Cultural Studies* 17, no. 3: 277–290.

Finnegan, Ruth. 1989. *The Hidden Musicians: Music-Making in an English Town*. Cambridge: Cambridge University Press.

Firdanianty. 2004. "Purwartjaraka Musik Studio: Menjajakan Musik ke Sekolah-Sekolah"

[Purwartjaraka Musik Studio: Selling musik from school to school]. *SWA*, May 13–26, pp. 42–44.

Ford, Michele, and Thomas B. Pepinsky. 2013. "Beyond Oligarchy? Critical Exchanges on Political Power and Material Inequality in Indonesia." *Indonesia* 96 (October: "Special Issue: Wealth, Power, and Contemporary Indonesian Politics," edited by Michele Ford and Thomas B. Pepinsky): 1–9.

Fornas, Johan. 1995. "The Future of Rock: Discourses That Struggle to Define a Genre." *Popular Music* 14, no. 1: 111–125.

Fraser, Nancy. 1990. "Rethinking the Public Sphere: A Contribution to the Critique of Actually Existing Democracy." *Social Text*, no. 25–26: 56–80.

Frederick, William. 1982. "Rhoma Irama and the *Dangdut* Style: Aspects of Contemporary Indonesian Popular Culture." *Indonesia* 32:103–130.

Frith, Simon. 1996. *Performing Rites: The Value of Popular Music*. Cambridge, MA: Harvard University Press.

Fuhr, Michael. 2016. *Globalization and Popular Music in South Korea: Sounding Out K-pop*. Oxon: Routledge.

Fung, Anthony, ed. 2013a. *Asian Popular Culture: The Global Discontinuity*. New York: Routledge.

——— . 2013b. "Deliberating Fandom and the New Wave of Chinese Pop: A Case Study of Chris Li." *Popular Music* 32, no. 1: 79–89.

Fushiki, Kaori. 2013. "Social and Political Effects of Pop Bali Alternatif on Balinese Society: The Example of XXX." *IJAPS* 9, no. 1: 37–67.

——— . 2010. "Ajeg Bali to Pop Bali: Local identity wo meguru bunka undo to Bali-tono popular ongaku no" [Ajeg Bali and pop Bali: Cultural movement on local identity and the change of Balinese popular music]. In *Asia no popular ongaku: Global to Local no sokoku* [Asian popular music: Overcoming global and local], edited by T. Inoue, 79–101. Tokyo: Keiso Shobo.

——— . 2009. "Media conglomerate niyoru image sehryaku: Pop Bali to Local Identity" [An image strategy of media conglomerate: Pop Bali and inspired local identity]. *Tokyo Gijutsudaigaku Ongakugakubu Kiyo* [Bulletin of Tokyo University of the Arts, Faculty of Music] 34:139–156.

——— . 2008. "Ajeg Bali to sono jissen: Indonesia Bali-to no kodomotachino geino" [The practice of "Ajeg Bali": Children's gamelan activities, for example]. *Tetusgaku* 119:429–455.

Gantini, N. 1973. "Kapan TE-VE-ER-I mau konsekwen?" [When will TE-VE-ER-I be consistent?]. *Aktuil* 123:6.

Gaonkar, Dilip Parameshwar, and Elizabeth A. Povinelli. 2003. "Technologies of Public Forms: Circulation, Transfiguration, Recognition." *Public Culture* 15, no. 3: 385–397.

Gehl, Robert. 2009. "YouTube as Archive: Who Will Curate This Digital Wunderkammer?" *International Journal of Cultural Studies* 12, no. 1: 43–60.

Gjelstad, Lars. 2003. "The World of Sparkling Lights: Popular Music and Teenage Culture in Solo, Central Java." Paper presented at the workshop "Pop Music in Southeast Asia," Leiden, December 8–12.

Gontani. 1969. "Porno di Denmark." *Aktuil* 30:42–43.

Habermas, Jürgen. 1991. *The Structural Transformation of the Public Sphere: An Inquiry into a Category of Bourgeois Society.* Cambridge, MA: MIT Press.

Hadi Jaya. 1999. "Dari Redaksi." In *Kelas Menengah Bukan Ratu Adil,* vii–xxvi. Yogyakarta: PT Tiara Wacana Yogyakarta.

Hadiz, Vedi R. 2013a. "The Rise of Capital and the Necessity of Political Economy." *Journal of Contemporary Asia* 43, no. 2: 208–225.

——— . ed. 2013b. "Special Feature Section: Capitalism and Indonesia's Democracy." *Journal of Contemporary Asia* 43, no. 2.

——— . 2010. *Localising Power in Post-authoritarian Indonesia: A Southeast Asia Perspective.* Stanford, CA: Stanford University Press.

Hadiz, Vedi R., and Daniel Dhakidae. 2005. Introduction to *Social Science and Power in Indonesia,* 1–30. Jakarta: Equinox and Institute of Southeast Asian Studies.

Hadiz, Vedi R., and Richard Robison. 2013. "The Political Economy of Oligarchy and the Reorganization of Power in Indonesia." *Indonesia* 96 (October): 35–56.

——— . 2005. "Neo-liberal Reforms and Illiberal Consolidations: The Indonesian Paradox." *Journal of Development Studies* 41, no. 2: 220–241.

Hamayotsu, Kikue. 2013. "The Limits of Civil Society in Democratic Indonesia: Media Freedom and Religious Intolerance." *Journal of Contemporary Asia* 43, no. 4: 658–677.

Hara-Hara, MN Sofian. 1974. "Jerry Pengen Beken." *Aktuil* 139:6.

Hariman, Robert, and John Louis Lucaites. 2007. *No Caption Needed: Iconic Photographs, Public Culture, and Liberal Democracy.* Chicago: University of Chicago Press.

Harnish, David. 2005. "Teletubbies in Paradise: Tourism, Indonesianisation and Modernisation in Balinese Music." *Yearbook for Traditional Music* 37:103–123.

Hasanta. 1970. "Tidak Mau Banjak Diberi Komentar" [Not interested in providing much commentary]. *Aktuil* 52:45.

Hatley, Barbara. 2008. *Javanese Performances on an Indonesian Stage: Contesting Culture, Embracing Change.* Singapore: NUS.

——— . 1990. "Contemporary Indonesian Theatre as Cultural Resistance." In *State and Civil Society in Indonesia,* edited by Arief Budiman, 321–348. Melbourne: Monash Asia Institute.

Heins, Ernst. 1975. "*Keroncong* and *Tanjidor*: Two Cases of Urban Folk Music in Jakarta." *Asian Music* 7, no. 1: 20–32.

Hemmings, Clare. 2005. "Invoking Affect." *Cultural Studies* 19, no. 5: 548–567.

HEN/DDN. 2008. "TVS Motor gandeng Iwan Fals" [TVS Motor teams up with Iwan Fals]. Detikfinance, July 24. finance.detik.com/read /2008/07/24/104202/977032/.

Hendrik Z. 1969. "Tjorat-tjoret Ernie: Kita Mampu Menandingi Artis Eropa" [Notes from Ernie: We can compete with European artists]. *Aktuil* 30:3–4.

Hendriyani, Ed Hollander, Leen d'Haenens, and Johannes Beentjes. 2014. "Views on Children's Media Use in Indonesia: Parents, Children, and Teachers." *International Communication Gazette* 76, no. 4–5: 322–339.

——— . 2011. "Children's Television in Indonesia." *Journal of Children and Media* 5, no. 1: 86–101. https://doi.org/10.1080/17482798.2011.535404.

Heryanto, Ariel. 2014. *Identity and Pleasure: The Politics of Indonesian Screen Culture.* Singapore: NUS.

——— . 2010. "Entertainment, Domestication, and Dispersal: Street Politics as Popular Culture." In *Problems of Democratisation in Indonesia: Elections, Institutions and Society,* edited by Edward Aspinall and Marcus Mietzner, 181–198. Singapore: Institute of Southeast Asian Studies (ISEAS).

——— . 2008. "Pop Culture and Competing Identities." In *Pop Culture in Indonesia: Fluid Identities in Post-authoritarian Politics.* London: Routledge.

——— . 2006. *State Terrorism and Political Identity in Indonesia: Fatally Belonging.* London: Routledge.

——— . 2003. "Public Intellectuals, Media and Democratization." In *Challenging Authoritarianism in Southeast Asia: Comparing Indonesia and Malaysia,* edited by A. Heryanto and S. K. Mandal, 24–59. London: RoutledgeCurzon.

——— . 1999. "The Years of Living Luxuriously: Identity Politics of Indonesia's New Rich." In *Culture and Privilege in Capitalist Asia,* edited by Michael Pinches, 159–187. London: Routledge.

——— . 1996. "The Student Movement." *Inside Indonesia,* no. 48 (October–December): 10–12.

Hidayat, Taufik. 2004. "Pongki Jikustik: Bayaran Mencipta Lagu Kian Menggiurkan" [Pongki Jikustik: Fees for song composition becoming increasingly attractive]. *SWA,* May 13–26, pp. 52–55.

Hill, David T. 1994. *The Press in New Order Indonesia.* Nedlands: University of Western Australia Press.

Hills, Matt. 2001. "Intensities Interviews Henry Jenkins @ Consoling Passions, University of Bristol, 7th July." Intensities.org/Essays/Jenkins, accessed January 17, 2013.

Hirschkind, Charles. 2006. *The Ethical Soundscape: Cassette Sermons and Islamic Counterpublics.* New York: Columbia University Press.

Hobart, Mark. 2006. "Entertaining Illusions: How Indonesian Élites Imagine Reality TV Affects the Masses." *Asian Journal of Communication* 16, no. 4: 393–410.

Hoesterey, James B. 2016. *Rebranding Islam: Piety, Prosperity, and a Self-Help Guru*. Stanford, CA: Stanford University Press.

Holt, Fabian. 2007. *Genre in Popular Music*. Chicago: University of Chicago Press.

Homan, Shane, ed. 2006. In *Access All Eras: Tribute Bands and Global Pop Culture*. Berkshire, UK: Open University Press.

Hoo, Oey Hian. 1970. "Vivi Sumanti." *Aktuil* 56:6.

Hotline Production. 2009. "Iklan Kartu As Telkomsel, Promo Kartu As Slank Versi Konser (30 second)" [Ad for Telkomsel's Kartu As, Slank concert version of Kartu As promotion 2009]. YouTube video, 0:40, uploaded March 18, 2009. www.youtube.com/watch?v=373q-TnPWlU.

Hughes-Freeland, Felicia. 2007. "Charisma and Celebrity in Indonesian Politics." *Anthropological Theory* 7, no. 2: 177–200.

"Iklan Yamaha Vega ZR Versi Slank" [Ad for Yamaha Vega ZR, Slank version]. 2014. YouTube video, 0:45, July 17. www.youtube.com/watch?v =IYCqCh3S9Lc.

ITU (International Telecommunications Union). 2019. ICT Statistics Home Page. https://www.itu.int/en/ITU-D/Statistics/Pages/default.aspx.

Ivy, Marilyn. 1995. *Discourses of the Vanishing: Modernity, Phantasm, Japan*. Chicago: University of Chicago Press.

Iwabuchi, Kōichi. 2010. "Undoing International Fandom in the Age of Brand Nationalism." *Mechademia* 5:87–96.

———. 2002. *Recentering Globalization: Popular Culture and Japanese Transnationalism*. Durham, NC: Duke University Press.

Jain, Kajri. 2011. "Divine Mass-Reproduction." In *Medium Religion*, edited by Peter Weibel and Boris Groys, 142–154. Karlsruhe: Zentrum für Kunst und Medientechnologie.

———. 2007. *Gods in the Bazaar: The Economies of Indian Calendar Art*. Durham, NC: Duke University Press.

Jameson, Fredric. 1991. *Postmodernism, or the Cultural Logic of Late Capitalism*. Durham, NC: Duke University Press.

———. 1984. "Postmodernism, or the Cultural Logic of Late Capitalism." *New Left Review* 146:54–92.

Jayanti, Tri Sapti, Mohamad, Djemdjem Djamaludi, and Melly Latifah. 2011. "Persepsi, Pengetahuan dan Perilaku Remaja dalam Pembelian Compact Disc.". *Jurnal Ilmu Keluarga dan Konsumen 4, no. 2*. http://dx.doi.org/10.24156/jikk.2011.4.2.190.

Jenkins, Henry. 1992. *Textual Poachers*. New York: Routledge.

Jones, Carla. 2010. "Materializing Piety: Gendered Anxieties about Faithful Consumption in Contemporary Urban Indonesia." *American Ethnologist* 37, no. 4: 617–637.

Jones, Carla, and Martin Slama. 2017. "Introduction: Piety, Celebrity, Sociality." In "Piety, Celebrity, Sociality: A Forum on Islam and Social Media in Southeast Asia," edited by Martin Slama and Carla Jones. *American Ethnologist* website, November 8.

http://americanethnologist.org/features/collections/piety-celebrity-sociality/intro
duction.

Juliastuti, Nuraini. 2018. "Limits of Sharing and Materialization of Support: Indonesian
Net Label Union." *Inter-Asia Cultural Studies* 19, no. 1: 87–102.

Jung, Sun, and Doobo Shim. 2014. "Social Distribution: K-pop Fan Practices in Indonesia
and the 'Gangnam Style' Phenomenon." *International Journal of Cultural Studies* 17,
no. 5: 485–501.

Karib, Fathun. 2007. "Kesadaran Kolektif dan Identitas dalam Komunitas Punk Jakarta:
Kasus Bunga Hitam" [Collective consciousness and identity in the Jakarta punk community: The case of Bunga Hitam]. Undergraduate thesis, Universitas Indonesia.

Keane, Webb. 2009. "Freedom and Blasphemy: On Indonesia Press Bans and Danish
Cartoons." *Public Culture* 21, no. 1: 47–76.

Kelly, William W. 1986. "Rationalization and Nostalgia: Cultural Dynamics of New
Middle-Class Japan." *American Ethnologist* 13, no. 4: 603–618.

KPL/DIS/NPY. 2010. "Wali band terima penghargaan dari MURI" [Wali band receives an
award from the Indonesian Museum of Records]. Kapanlagi.com, February 5, www.
kapanlagi.com/foto /berita-foto/indonesia/11193wali_band_di_moi _kelapa_gading-
20100207-003-deni.html.

Kuwado, Fabian Januarius. 2014. "Tiba-tiba jokowike Potlot, Bimbim kaget" [Suddenly,
Jokowi visits Potlot, Bimbim was caught unawares]. Kompas.com, July 9. entertainment.
kompas.com/read/2014/07/09/131831510/Tiba-tiba.Jokowi.ke.Potlot.Bimbim.Kaget.

Larkin, Brian. 2004. "Degraded Images, Distorted Sounds: Nigerian Video and the Infrastructure of Piracy." *Public Culture* 16, no. 2: 289–314.

Lawson, Dom. 2014. "Joko 'Jokowi' Widodo's Metal Manifesto." *Guardian*, July 11. http://
www.theguardian.com/music/2014/jul/11/joko-jokowi-widodos-metal-manifesto.

Lee, Doreen. 2015. "Absolute Traffic: Infrastructural Aptitude in Urban Indonesia." *International Journal of Urban and Regional Research* 39, no. 2: 234–250. https://doi
.org/10.1111/1468-2427.12212.

——— . 2011. "Styling the Revolution: Masculinities, Youth, and Street Politics in Jakarta,
Indonesia." *Journal of Urban History* 37:933–951.

Lee, Jung-yup. 2009. "Contesting the Digital Economy and Culture: Digital Technologies
and the Transformation of Popular Music in Korea." *Inter-Asia Cultural Studies* 10,
no. 4: 489–506.

Leo, Bens. 1974. "Obrolan Dengan Gitaris Senioren Jopie Item" [Conversation with senior
guitarist Jopie Item]. *Aktuil* 138:2–3.

Lev, Dan. 1990. "Intermediate Classes and Change in Indonesia: Some Initial Reflections."
In *The Politics of Middle Class Indonesia*, edited by Richard Tanter and Kenneth Young,
25–43. Monash Papers on Southeast Asia no. 19. Melbourne: Centre of Southeast Asian
Studies, Monash University.

Lewis, Tania, Fran Martin, and Wanning Sun. 2016. *Telemodernities: Television and Transforming Lives in Asia*. Durham, NC: Duke University Press.

Liddle, William. 1990. "The Middle Class and New Order Legitimacy." In *The Politics of Middle-Class Indonesia*, edited by Richard Tanter and Kenneth Young, 49–52. Monash Papers on Southeast Asia no. 19. Melbourne: Centre of Southeast Asian Studies, Monash University.

Liechty, Mark. 2003. *Suitably Modern: Making Middle-Class Culture in a New Consumer Society*. Princeton, NJ: Princeton University Press.

Lim, Merlyna. 2014. "Seeing Spatially: People, Networks and Movements in Digital and Urban Spaces." *IDPR* 36, no. 1: 51–72.

Lindsay, Jennifer. 2005. "Performing in the 2004 Indonesian Elections." Asia Research Institute Working Paper Series no. 45. Singapore: Asia Research Institute, National University of Singapore.

Lockett, Hudson. 2016. "Indonesia Motorbike Sales Hit the Brakes in April." *Financial Times*, May 13. www.ft.com/content/a0473631-fa72-3a8b-b13f-35bd266f7dc3.

Lukose, Ritty. 2009. *Liberalization's Children: Gender, Youth, and Consumer Citizenship in Globalizing India*. Durham, NC: Duke University Press.

Luvaas, Brent. 2013a. *DIY Style: Fashion, Music and Global Digital Cultures*. London: Bloomsbury Academic.

——— . 2013b. "Exemplary Centers and Musical Elsewheres: On Authenticity and Autonomy in Indonesian Indie Music." *Asian Music* 44, no. 2: 95–114.

——— . 2009. "Dislocating Sounds: The Deterritorialization of Indonesian Indie Pop." *Cultural Anthropology* 24, no. 2 (2009): 246–279.

Ma, Eric Kit-Wai. 2000. "Readvertising Hong Kong: Nostaligia Industry and Popular History." *Positions* 9, no. 1: 131–159.

Mackie, Jamie. 1990. "Money and the Middle Class." In *The Politics of Middle-Class Indonesia*, edited by Richard Tanter and Kenneth Young, 96–122. Monash Papers on Southeast Asia no. 19. Melbourne: Centre of Southeast Asian Studies, Monash University.

Manabe, Noriko. 2015. *The Revolution Will Not Be Televised: Protest Music after Fukushima*. New York: Oxford University Press.

Manopol, Yuyun. 2004a. "BNG, Si Jago Peralatan Musik." [BNG, leader in music equipment. *SWA*, May 13–26, pp. 46–48.

——— . 2004b. "Gemuruh Thunder di Bisnis Sewa Alat Pentas." [Rumblings in the music equipment hire business. *SWA*, May 13–26, pp. 48–49.

Martin-Iverson, Sean. 2014. "Bandung Lautan Hardcore: Territorialisation and Deterritorialisation in an Indonesian Hardcore Punk Scene." *Inter-Asia Cultural Studies* 15, no. 4: 532–552.

——— . 2012: "Autonomous Youth? Independence and Precariousness in the Indonesian Underground Music Scene." *Asia Pacific Journal of Anthropology* 13, no. 4: 382–397.

Mazzarella, William. 2003. *Shoveling Smoke: Advertising and Globalisation in Contemporary India*. Durham, NC: Duke University Press.

McCarthy, Paul. 2003. "The Case of Jakarta, Indonesia." In *Understanding Slums: Case Studies for the United Nations Global Report on Human Settlements 2003*. London: Development Planning Unit, University College London. https://www.ucl.ac.uk/dpu -projects/Global_Report/cities/jakarta.htm.

McIntosh, Jonathon. 2010. "Dancing to a Disco Beat: Children, Teenagers and Localizing of Popular Music in Bali." *Asian Music* 41, no. 1: 1–35.

McRae, Dave. 2014. "The 2014 Indonesian Elections and Australia-Indonesia Relations." Centre for Indonesian Law, Islam and Society, Policy Paper 7.

Metro hari ini (Metro TV News). 2014. "Jokowi-JK bertemu Slank di Potlot" [Jokowi and JK meet Slank at Potlot]. YouTube video, 11:25, May 29. www.youtube.com/watch?v=_beGSnGrmnw.

Mishra, Smeeta. 2016. "Media Convergence: Indian Journalists' Perceptions of Its Challenges and Implications." *Convergence: The International Journal of Research into New Media Technologies* 22, no. 1: 102–112.

Mitchell, T. 1996. *Popular Music and Local Identity: Rock, Pop and Rap in Europe and Oceania*. London: Leicester University Press.

Moore, Rebekah E. 2015. "Indie Music in Post-bomb Bali: Participant Practices, Scene Subjectivities." PhD diss., Indiana University.

——— . 2013a. "Elevating the Underground: Claiming a Space for Indie Music among Bali's Many Soundworlds." *Asian Music* 44, no. 2: 135–159.

——— . 2013b. "MyMusic, MyFreedom(?): The Troubled Pursuit of Musical and Intellectual Independence on the Internet in Indonesia." *Asian Journal of Communication* 23, no. 4: 368–385.

Mōri, Yoshitaka. 2005. "Culture = Politics: The Emergence of New Cultural Forms of Protest in the Age of Freeter." *Inter-Asia Cultural Studies* 6, no. 1: 17–29.

Muhajir, Anton. 2014. "Nanoe Biroe, Terus Menyanyi untuk Bali" [Nanoe Biroe, keeps on singing for Bali]. *Bale Bengong*. http://balebengong.net/kabar-anyar/2014/05/01 /nanoe-biroe-terus-menyanyi-untuk-bali.html. Accessed March 3, 2016.

——— . 2013. "Riset Mobile Indonesian. Analisis Hasil Pemantauan Aktivitas Facebook dan Log Book." Report prepared for the Mobile Indonesians project on Baduda's Facebook use, based on self-reporting and monitoring.

Mulyadi, Muhammad. 2009. *Industri musik Indonesia: Suatu sejarah* [Music industry: A history]. Bekasi: Koperasi Ilmu Pengetahuan Sosial.

Murray, Alison. 1991. "Kampung Culture and Radical Chic in Jakarta." *Review of Indonesian and Malayan Affairs* 25, no. 1: 1–16.

Negus, Keith. 1999. *Music Genres and Corporate Cultures*. London: Routledge.

Oakley, Kate. 2004. "Not So Cool Britannia: The Role of the Creative Industries in Economic Development." *International Journal of Cultural Studies* 7, no. 1: 67–77.

"150 Album Indonesia Terbaik Sepanjang Masa" [150 of the best Indonesian albums ever]. 2007. *Rolling Stone* 32 (December).

Ong, Aihwa. 2006. *Neoliberalism as Exception: Mutations in Citizenship and Sovereignty.* Durham, NC: Duke University Press.

Palupi, Dyah Hasto. 2004. "Menjual Artis Peranti Industri" [Selling artists and the industry machine]. *SWA*, May 13–26, pp. 60–62.

"Panen dangdut, dangdut, dangdut" [Dangdut, dangdut, dangdut harvest]. 1975. *Tempo*, March 22. http://mellowtone.multiply.com/tag/koes%20plus.

Pangestu, Mari Elka. 2009a. "Cetak Biru Industri Musik Nasional, Bagian 1" [Blueprint for the national music industry, part 1]. *Rolling Stone* 54:66–70.

——— . 2009b. "Cetak Biru Industri Musik Nasional, Bagian 2" [Blueprint for the national music industry, part 2]. *Rolling Stone* 55:52–8.

Peters, Robbie. 2009. "The Assault on Occupancy in Surabaya: Legible and Illegible Landscapes in a City of Passage." *Development and Change* 40, no. 5: 903–925.

Picard, Michel. 1996. *Bali: Cultural Tourism and Touristic Culture.* Singapore: Archipelago.

Pinney, Christopher. 2003a. "Introduction — 'How the Other Half . . .'" In *Photography's Other Histories*, edited by Christopher Pinney and Nicolas Peterson, 1–14. Durham, NC: Duke University Press.

——— . 2003b. "Notes from the Surface of the Image: Photography, Postcolonialism, and Vernacular Modernism." In *Photography's Other Histories*, edited by Christopher Pinney and Nicolas Peterson, 202–220. Durham, NC: Duke University Press.

Pioquinto, Ceres. 1995. "*Dangdut* at *Sekaten*: Female Representations in Live Performance." *Review of Indonesian and Malayan Affairs* 29, no. 1–2: 59–89.

Piper, Suzan, and Sawung Jabo. 1987. "Musik Indonesia, dari 1950-an hingga 1980-an" [Indonesian music from the 1950s to the 1980s]. *Prisma* no. 5, Tahun 16: 8–19.

Prahalad, Coimbatore Krishnarao. 2004. *The Fortune at the Bottom of the Pyramid.* Upper Saddle River, NJ: Pearson Education.

PT Agung Nusantara. 2015. "Iklan TV So Nice versi 'SLANK RAME-RAME.'" [So Nice TV ad, Slank Rame-Rame (All Together) version]. YouTube video, 0:53, January 16. www.youtube.com /watch?v=njoESi2_Wmk.

Puisi Mbeling Remy Sylado [Remy Sylado's Puisi Mbeling]. 2004. Jakarta: Kepustakaan Populer Gramedia.

Purbaya, Rio. 1970a. "Balada Sebuah memori" [Ode to a memory]. *Aktuil* 52:37–39.

——— . 1970b. "Balada Sebuah memori" [Ode to a memory]. *Aktuil* 52:44–46.

Putranto, Wendi. 2009a. "Inilah musik Indonesia hari ini" [This is the Indonesian music industry today]. *Rolling Stone* 47:64–71.

—— . 2009b. *Musik Biz: Manual Cerdas Menguasai Bisnis Musik* [Music Biz: Manual for understanding the music business]. Yogyakarta: B-First.

—— . 2008. "Noxa." *Rolling Stone* 4:41.

—— . 2006. "'Tambang Emas Nada Tunggu" [The ringback tone gold mine]. *Rolling Stone* 19:50–55.

Qiu, Jack. 2009. *Working-Class Network Society: Communication Technology and the Information Have-Less in Urban China.* Cambridge, MA: MIT Press.

Rafick, Ishak. 2004. "Sony Music: Raja Industry Rekaman di Tanah Air." *SWA*, May 13–26, pp. 58–59.

Rahayu, Eva Martha. 2004. "Grup band Padi: Tak Menyangka Masuk Papan Atas" [Padi: Unexpectedly enters the upper echelons. *SWA*, May 13–26, pp. 50–52.

Ratna Press. 1969. "Ellya Lindawati jang Bertjita-tjita Gede" [Ellya Lindawati and her big dreams]. *Aktuil* 30:47.

Rednib, Cal. 2014. "Joko Widodo Loves Napalm Death, Devil Horns, and Sticking Up for the Little Guy." *Vice*, April 1. http://www.vice.com/read/meet-jokowi-indonesias-probable-next-president.

Richter, Max. 2012. *Music Worlds in Yogyakarta.* Leiden: Brill.

Robison, Richard. 1996. "The Middle Class and the Bourgeoisie in Indonesia." In *The New Rich in Asia: Mobile Phones, McDonald's and Middle Class Revolution*, edited by Richard Robison and David S. G. Goodman, 70–104. London: Routledge.

—— . 1990. "The Problems of Analysing the Middle Class as a Political Force in Indonesia." In *The New Rich in Asia: Mobile Phones, McDonald's and Middle Class Revolution*, edited by Richard Robison and David S. G. Goodman, 137–147. London: Routledge.

—— . 1986. *Indonesia: The Rise of Capital.* Sydney: Allen & Unwin.

Romano, Angela. 2003. *Politics and the Press in Indonesia: Understanding an Evolving Political Culture.* London: RoutledgeCurzon.

Ryter, Loren. 1998. "Pemuda Pancasila: The Last Loyalist Free Men of Suharto's Order?" *Indonesia* 66:45–73.

Saefullah, Hikmawan. 2010. "Punk Rock as Counter-hegemony: A Case Study in Indonesia." Master's thesis, Research School of Pacific and Asian Studies, Australian National University.

Sakrie, Denny. 2009. "Ellya Khadam Telah Pergi (1928–2009)" [Ellya Khadan has left us]. http://dennysak.multiply.com/tag/dangdut.

—— . 2008a. "Betulkah Dangdut Is the Music of Our Country?" [Is it true dangdut is the music of our country?]. http://dennysak.multiply.com/tag/dangdut.

—— . 2008b. "Ketika Achmad Albar Berdangdut" [When Achmad Albar performs dangdut]. http://dennysak.multiply.com/tag/elvy%20sukaesih.

Sarang Slankers. 2009. "Filosofi Logo Slank" [The philosophy of Slank's logo]. slanker-community blogspot.com.au/2009/01/filosofi-logo-slank.html.

Scherer, Savitri. 1981. "Yudhistira Ardi Noegraha: Social Attitudes in the Works of Popular Writer." *Indonesia* 31:31–52.

Schmidt, Leonie. 2017. *Islamic Modernities in Southeast Asia: Exploring Indonesian Popular and Visual Culture*. London: Rowman & Littlefield.

Schneider, Florian. 2015. "Searching for 'Digital Asia' in Its Networks: Where the Spatial Turn Meets the Digital Turn." *Asiascape: Digital Asia* 2:57–92.

Sen, Krishna. 2003. "Radio Days: Media-Politics in Indonesia." *Pacific Review* 16, no. 4: 573–589.

Sen, Krishna, and David T. Hill, eds. 2010. *Politics and the Media in Twenty-First- Century Indonesia: Decade of Democracy*. New York: Routledge.

———. 2000. *Media, Culture and Politics in Indonesia*. Melbourne: Oxford University Press.

Setiyono, Budi. 2001. "Ngak, Ngik, Ngok." *Pantau* Tahun II, no. 18 (October): 38–47.

Shin, Hyunjoon. 2009. "Have You Ever Seen the Rain? and Who'll Stop the Rain? The Globalizing Project of Korean Pop (K-pop)." *Inter-Asia Cultural Studies* 10, no. 4: 507–523.

Siegel, James. 1986. *Solo in the New Order*. Princeton, NJ: Princeton University Press.

Simatupang, AM. 1973. "Di Balik Layar Remaco." *Aktuil* 127:6.

Simatupang, G. R. Lono Lastoro. n.d. "Kisah Sebuah Nama: 'Orkes Melayu' dalam Dangdut" [The story of a name: "Orkes Melayu" in dangdut]. http://wa-iki.blog spot.com/2010/11/kisah-sebuah-nama-orkes-melayu-dalam.html. Accessed June 4, 2011.

Simone, Abdoumaliq. 2013. "Cities of Uncertainty: Jakarta, the Urban Majority, and Inventive Political Technologies." *Theory, Culture & Society* 30, no. 7–8: 243–263.

Slamet, Mohamad. 1990. "Comment on Jamie Mackie's 'Money and the Middle Class.'" In *The Politics of Middle-Class Indonesia*, edited by Richard Tanter and Kenneth Young, 123–126. Monash Papers on Southeast Asia no. 19. Melbourne: Centre of Southeast Asian Studies, Monash University.

Slank.com. 2014. "Indonesia Wow!" September 8. slank.com/potlot/indonesia-wow/.

Smith, Christina. 2009. "Iconic Images and the Visual Public Sphere." *Review of Communication* 9, no. 1: 72–75.

Soelaeman, Henni T. 2004. "Gemerlap yang Menciptakan Bisnis-Bisnis Baru" [The razzle-dazzle creating new business]. *SWA*, May 13–26, pp. 26–39.

Solihun, Soleh. 2010. "Nada sambung bawa untung" [Ringback tones are creating profits]. *Rolling Stone* 59:30–36.

———. 2004. "Perjalanan Majalah Musik di Indonesia" [The journey of Indonesian music magazines]. Undergraduate thesis, Padjadjaran University.

Sopiann, Agus. 2002. "Lima Raksasa Internasional di Indonesia.". *Pantau* Tahun III, no. 25 (May): 40–47.

———. 2001a. "From Kebonsari with Rock." *Pantau* Tahun II, no. 20 (December): 42–47.

———. 2001b. "Putus Dirundung Malang" [Shut Down, dogged by bad luck]. *Pantau* Tahun II, no. 16 (August).

Spyer, Patricia, and Mary Margaret Steedly. 2013. "Introduction: Images That Move." In *Images That Move*, edited by Patricia Spyer and Mary Margaret Steedly, 3–40. Santa Fe, NM: School for Advanced Research Press.

Steele, Janet. 2005. *Wars Within: The Story of Tempo, an Independent Magazine in Soeharto's Indonesia*. Jakarta: Equinox and Institute of Southeast Asian Studies.

Strassler, Karen. 2014. "Seeing the Unseen in Indonesia's Public Sphere: Photographic Appearances of a Spirit Queen." *Comparative Studies in Society and History* 56, no. 1: 98–130.

———. 2010. *Refracted Visions: Popular Photography and National Modernity in Java*. Durham, NC: Duke University Press.

———. 2009. "The Face of Money: Currency, Crisis, and Remediation in Post-Suharto Indonesia." *Cultural Anthropology* 24, no. 1: 68–103.

Street, John. 2012. "Do Celebrity Politics and Celebrity Politicians Matter?" *BJPIR* 14:346–356.

———. 2004. "The Celebrity Politician: Political Style and Popular Culture." *British Journal of Politics and International Relations* 6, no. 4: 435–452.

Subianto, Benny. 1990. "Konsep Kelas Menengah Indonesia: Konsep yang Kabur" [The concept of the middle class in Indonesia: A vague concept]. In *Kelas Menengah Bukan Ratu Adil* [The middle class is not a saviour], edited by Hadi Jaya, 17–24. Yogyakarta: PT Tiara Wacana Yogyakarta.

Sudarmadi. 2004. "Original Production Memburu Margin 10% dari Bisnis Pertunjukan" [Original productions chasing 10% profit margins in the performance business]. *SWA*, May 13–26, pp. 40–41.

Sugiono MP. 1973. "Wawancara Dengan Anna Manthovani" [Interview with Anna Manthovani]. *Aktuil* 128:30.

Suhendra. 2008. "TVS Motor Gandeng Iwan Fals" [TVS Motorbikes holding hands with Iwan Fals]. Detikfinance. http://finance.detik.com/read/2008/07/24/104202/977032/4/tvs-motor-gandeng-iwan-fals. Accessed June 23, 2016.

Sujana. 2009. *Rahasia Kangen Band: Kisah Inspiratif Anak Band* [The secret of Kangen Band: An inspirational story of a boy band]. Jakarta: RM Books.

Sulaksono, Sugeng. 2009. "Rancu antara Melayu dan Pop" [Hard to tell the difference between Melayu and pop]. *Jawa Pos*, April 26, 10.

Sundaram, Ravi. 2004. "Uncanny Networks: Pirate, Urban and New Globalisation." *Economic and Political Weekly* 39, no. 1 (January 3–9): 64–71.

"Supermie 'Slank' Mountain." 2008. YouTube video, 1:00, March 27. www.youtube.com/watch?v=7awVjvNVnQk.

Surya, S. 1969. "Musik Pop: Media jang Telah Melahirkan Kreatifitas Serta hasil Seni dan

Revolusi" [Pop music: Media that is giving rise to creativity and revolution]. *Aktuil* 30:10–11.

SWAOnline. 2008. "Bait Baru Industri Musik Indonesia" [New chapter in the Indonesian music industry]. SWA, June 12. https://swa.co.id/swa/listed-articles/bait-baru-industri -musik-indonesia. Accessed June 21, 2019.

———. 2007. "Rahasia Dedengkot Musik Tetap Eksis" [Secrets of music industry leaders live on]. SWA, August 9. https://swa.co.id/swa/listed-articles/rahasia-dedengkot -musik-tetap-eksis. Accessed June 21, 2019.

Sylado, Remy. 2004. *Puisi Mbeling Remy Sylado* [Remy Sylado's Puisi Mbeling]. Jakarta: Kepustakaan Populer Gramedia.

Tanter, Richard, and Kenneth Young. 1990. Introduction to *The Politics of Middle Class Indonesia*, 7–21. Monash Papers on Southeast Asia no. 19. Melbourne: Centre of Southeast Asian Studies, Monash University.

Taufiqurrahman M. 2011. "Long Live 1970s Indonesian Rock and Roll." *Jakarta Post*, April 1. http://www.thejakartapost.c om/news/2011/04/10/long-live-1970s-indonesian-rock -and-roll.html.

Thajib, Ferdiansyah. 2011. "Bhs Sgktn di SMS" [SMS abbreviations]. *Kulturcell,* January 7. kulturcell. kunci.or.id/?p=361.

"Tinny." 1970. *Aktuil* 52:3.

Toynbee, Jason. 2000. *Making Popular Music: Musicians, Creativity and Institutions.* London: Bloomsbury.

TrashStockBali. 2015. "Nanoe Biroe: Menginspirasi, Bukan Menggurui" [Nanoe Biroe: Inspiring, not lecturing]. Bale Bengong. http://balebengong.net/kabar-anyar/2015/06/14 /nanoe-biroe-bukan-menggurui-tapi-menginspirasi-2.html. Accessed March 3, 2016.

Truitt, Alison. 2008. "On the Back of a Motorbike: Middle-Class Mobility in Ho Chi Minh City, Vietnam." *American Ethnologist* 35, no. 1: 3–19.

Vickers, Adrian. 1989. *Bali: A Paradise Created.* Melbourne: Penguin.

Wallach, Jeremy. 2007. *Modern Noise, Fluid Genres: Popular Music in Indonesia, 1997–2001.* Madison: University of Wisconsin Press.

———. 2002. "Exploring Class, Nation and Xenocentrism in Indonesian Cassette Outlets." *Indonesia* 74:79–102.

Wallach, Jeremy, and Esther Clinton. 2013. "History, Modernity, and Music Genre in Indonesia: Popular Music Genres in the Dutch East Indies and following Independence." *Asian Music* 44, no. 2: 3–23.

Wallis, Cara. 2013. *Technomobility in China: Young Migrant Women and Mobile Phones.* New York: NYU Press.

Wang, Jing. 2008. *Brand New China: Advertising, Media, and Commercial Culture.* Cambridge, MA: Harvard University Press.

Warner, Michael. 2002a. *Publics and Counterpublics.* New York: Zone Books.

———. 2002b. "Publics and Counterpublics." *Public Culture* 14, no. 1: 49–90.

Warren, Carol. 1998. "Mediating Modernity in Bali." *International Journal of Cultural Studies* 1, no. 1: 83–108.

Weintraub, Andrew N. 2017. "Titiek Puspa: Gendered Modernity in 1960s and 1970s Indonesian Popular Music." In *Vamping the Stage: Female Voices of Asian Modernities*, edited by Andrew N. Weintraub and Bart Barendregt, 144–173. Honolulu: University of Hawai'i Press.

———. 2014. "Melayu Popular Music in Indonesia, 1968–75." In *Sonic Modernities in the Malay World: A History of Popular Music, Social Distinction and Novel Lifestyles (1930s–2000s)*, edited by Bart Barendregt, 165–186. Leiden: Brill.

———. 2013. "The Sound and Spectacle of Dangdut Koplo: Genre and Counter-genre in East Java, Indonesia." *Asian Music* 44, no. 2: 160–194.

———, ed. 2011. *Islam and Popular Culture in Indonesia and Malaysia.* London: Routledge.

———. 2010. *Dangdut Stories: A Social and Musical History of Indonesia's Most Popular Music.* New York: Oxford University Press.

———. 2008. "'Dance Drills, Faith Spills': Islam, Body Politics, and Popular Music in Post-Suharto Indonesia." *Popular Music* 27, no 3: 367–392.

———. 2006. "Dangdut Soul: Who Are 'the People' in Indonesian Popular Music?" *Asian Journal of Communication* 16, no. 4: 411–431.

Wieringa, Saskia. 2003. "The Birth of the New Order State in Indonesia: Sexual Politics and Nationalism." *Journal of Women's History* 15, no. 1: 70–91.

Wingo, Scot, and Alex Rued. 2014. "Indonesia's Future Trajectory under Joko Widodo: An Interview with Marcus Mietzner." *Georgetown Journal of Asian Affairs*, Fall/Winter: 149–156.

Winters, Jeffrey A. 2013. "Oligarchy and Democracy in Indonesia." *Indonesia* 96 (October): 11–33.

Yampolsky, Philip. 2013. "Three Genres of Indonesian Popular Music: Genre, Hybridity, and Globalization, 1960–2012." *Asian Music* 44, no. 2: 24–80.

———. 1989. "Hati yang Luka: An Indonesian Hit." *Indonesia* 47:1–17.

Yang, Ling. 2009. "All for Love: The Corn Fandom, Prosumers, and the Chinese Way of Creating a Superstar." *International Journal of Cultural Studies* 12, no. 5: 527–543.

Zt. 1973. "Renny Konstantin." *Aktuil* 127:19.

Zulkarnaen, Happy Bone, Faisal Siagian, and Laode Ida. 1983. "Kelas Menengah Digugat: Catatan Editor." In *Kelas Mengenah Digugat*, edited by Happy Bone Zulkarnaen, Faisal Siagian, and Laode Ida, 9–26. Jakarta: PT Fikahati Aneska.

Zurbuchen, Mary, ed. 2005. *Beginning to Remember: The Past in the Indonesian Present.* Singapore and Seattle: Singapore University Press and University of Washington Press.

Interviews (by Author)

*participated in a focus group discussion on September 8, 2013.

Ameng, Indra. White Shoes and the Couples Company (band). June 13, 2009.

Andaresta, Oppie. Solo artist. March 3, 2004.

Andhika. Vocalist, Kangen Band. April 24, 2010.

Annash, Eka. The Brandals (band). June 11, 2009.

Ardiesyah, Hasief. Writer, *Rolling Stone*. October 8, 2009.

Audy. Solo artists. April 28, 2004.

Azis MS. Jamrud (band). May 9, 2004.

Boer, Harlan. Manager of Efek Rumah Kaca. May 22, 2009.

Burgerkill (band—all members). March 12, 2004.

Decker, Lesley. Programmer, MTV Indonesia. May 28, 2004.

Dek Gun (*Aktuil* reader). October 12, 2003.

Denny MR. Music writer. February 6, 2005, and July 1, 2009.

Dethu, Rudolf (manager of Superman Is Dead and co-owner of Glam Punkabilly Inferno) and Sarah Forbes (co-owner, Glam Punkabilly Inferno). January 20, 2005.

Dhani, Ahmad. Founder of Dewa (band). April 3, 2004.

Djayadiningrat, Dimas. Music video producer. May 25, 2004.

Djuhana, Yan. A and R Sony Music Entertainment Indonesia. April 6, 2004.

Fariz RM. Composer. June 30, 2009.

Fernandez, Edward. Founder of Sova (music duo). April 2, 2004.

Gitomartoyo, Wening. Writer, *Rolling Stone*. October 7, 2009.

Handi. A and R, Musika Records. March 29, 2004.

Hidayat, Adib. Editor, *Rolling Stone*. October 6, 2009.

*Indrawan, Putu Billy. Baduda. September 8, 2013.

*I Nyoman Agus Swanjaya. Baduda. September 8, 2013.

*I Nyoman Widarta. Baduda. September 8, 2013.

Ivan, John Paul. Boomerang (band). February 4, 2005.

*I Wayan Ariawan. Baduda. September 8, 2013.

*I Wayan Sugiyaksa. Baduda. September 8, 2013.

Iin. A and R, Aquarius Musikindo. May 11, 2004.

Jadugar (band—all members). May 29, 2004.

*Januar, Iwan. Baduda. September 8, 2013.

Karto, David. Founder, De Majors. May 28, 2009.

Lubis, Feby. Musika Group marketing and promotions. May 12, 2004.

Makki, Ungu (band). March 3, 2004.

*Man Agus. Baduda. September 8, 2013.

Man Danoe. Baduda. December 14, 2015.

Mantovani, Rizal. Music video and filmmaker. May 19, 2004.

Maulana, Armand. Gigi (band). February 5, 2005.

Mocca (band—all members). April 10, 2004.

Natadiningrat, Tagore. Executive creative director, Dream Team (advertising agency). February 8, 2005.

*Ni Luh Made Indah Widyasari. Badudawati. September 8, 2013.

*Ni Putu Dewi Suyastini. Badudawati. September 8, 2013.

Noya, Andy F. President director, *Rolling Stone*. October 9, 2009.

Nymphea (band—all members). June 12, 2009.

Oka. Solo rap artist. March 19, 2004.

*Parliawan, Agus. Baduda. September 8, 2013.

Pas (band—all members). March 12, 2004.

Putri, Ade. Former manager, Superman Is Dead. March 4, 2004.

Putranto, Wendi. Writer, *Rolling Stone*. June 26, 2009.

Rocket Rockers (band—all members). February 1, 2005.

Satriyo Yudi Wahono (Piyu). Padi (band). April 2, 2005.

7 Kurcaci (band—all members). March 10, 2004.

Siahaan, Ricky. Writer, *Rolling Stone*. October 8, 2009.

Soebari, Monika. Vice president, *Rolling Stone*. October 9, 2009.

Solihun, Soleh. Writer, *Rolling Stone*. October 6, 2009.

Sujana. Manager, Kangen Band. April 27, 2010.

Superman Is Dead (band—all members). January 18, 2005.

Tanasputra, Hendra. Programmer, MTV Indonesia. May 2, 2004.

The Trees and the Wild (band—all members). June 29, 2009.

Uci. Organizer for Kerawang chapter of Kangen Band fan club. April 28, 2010.

Varma, Mishal. Programming and Talent, Artist Relations, MTV Singapore. June 4, 2004.

Yudhis. Sony Music Entertainment Indonesia. March 8, 2004.

Zhelebour, Log. Executive director, Logiss Records. March 9, 2004.

Albums

Kangen Band. *Yang Sempurna* (*Tentang Aku, Kau dan Dia* repackaged). Warner Music. 2007.

——— . *Bintang 14 Hari*. Warner Music Indonesia. 2008.

Krisdayanti. *Terserah*. Hemagita Records. 1995.

Slank. *Suit Suit He he*. Project Q. 1990.

——— . *Kampungan*. Project Q. 1991.

——— . *Generasi biru*. Piss Records. 1994.

——— . *Mata hati reformasi*. Slank Records. 1998.

——— . *PLUR*. Pulau Biru. 2004.

ST12. *P.U.S.P.A.* Trinity Optima Production. 2007.

Superman Is Dead. *Kuta Rock City*. Sony Music Entertainment Indonesia. 2003.

——— . *The Hangover Decade*. Sony Music Entertainment Indonesia. 2004.

Tribute to Ian Antono. Jakarta, Sony Music Entertainment Indonesia. 2004.

Wali. *Orang Bilang*. Nagaswara. 2008.

——— . *Cari Jodoh*. Nagaswara. 2009a.

——— . *Ingat Sholawat*. Nagaswara. 2009b.

Video Clips

"Muka Tebal." Sony Music Entertainment Indonesia. 2004.

"Punk Hari Ini." Sony Music Entertainment Indonesia. 2003.

"Rock and Roll Band." Sony Music Entertainment Indonesia. 2004.

Rumah Kita. Indonesian Voices. Sony Music Entertainment Indonesia. 2004.

"Selingkuh." Kangen Band. Warner Music Indonesia. 2008.

INDEX

MUSIC / CULTURE

A series from Wesleyan University Press
Edited by Deborah Wong, Sherrie Tucker, and Jeremy Wallach
Originating editors: George Lipsitz, Susan McClary, and Robert Walser

Marié Abe
*Resonances of Chindon-ya:
Sounding Space and Sociality in
Contemporary Japan*

Frances Aparicio
*Listening to Salsa: Gender, Latin Popular
Music, and Puerto Rican Cultures*

Paul Austerlitz
*Jazz Consciousness: Music, Race,
and Humanity*

Emma Baulch
*Genre Publics: Popular Music,
Technologies, and Class in Indonesia*

Harris M. Berger
*Metal, Rock, and Jazz: Perception and the
Phenomenology of Musical Experience*

Harris M. Berger
*Stance: Ideas about Emotion, Style,
and Meaning for the Study
of Expressive Culture*

Harris M. Berger and
Giovanna P. Del Negro
*Identity and Everyday Life: Essays
in the Study of Folklore, Music,
and Popular Culture*

Franya J. Berkman
*Monument Eternal: The Music
of Alice Coltrane*

Dick Blau, Angeliki Vellou Keil,
and Charles Keil
*Bright Balkan Morning: Romani Lives and
the Power of Music in Greek Macedonia*

Susan Boynton and Roe-Min Kok, editors
*Musical Childhoods and the
Cultures of Youth*

James Buhler, Caryl Flinn,
and David Neumeyer, editors
Music and Cinema

Patrick Burkart
Music and Cyberliberties

Jonathan Pieslak
*Radicalism and Music: An Introduction
to the Music Cultures of al-Qa'ida, Racist
Skinheads, Christian-Affiliated Radicals,
and Eco–Animal Rights Militants*

Lorraine Plourde
*Tokyo Listening: Sound and Sense
in a Contemporary City*

Matthew Rahaim
*Musicking Bodies: Gesture and
Voice in Hindustani Music*

John Richardson
*Singing Archaeology:
Philip Glass's Akhnaten*

Tricia Rose
*Black Noise: Rap Music and Black Culture
in Contemporary America*

David Rothenberg and
Marta Ulvaeus, editors
*The Book of Music and Nature:
An Anthology of Sounds, Words, Thoughts*

Nichole Rustin-Paschal
*The Kind of Man I Am: Jazzmasculinity
and the World of Charles Mingus Jr.*

Marta Elena Savigliano
*Angora Matta: Fatal Acts of
North-South Translation*

Joseph G. Schloss
*Making Beats: The Art of
Sample-Based Hip-Hop*

Barry Shank
*Dissonant Identities: The Rock 'n' Roll
Scene in Austin, Texas*

Jonathan Holt Shannon
*Among the Jasmine Trees: Music and
Modernity in Contemporary Syria*

Daniel B. Sharp
*Between Nostalgia and Apocalypse:
Popular Music and the Staging of Brazil*

Helena Simonett
*Banda: Mexican Musical Life
across Borders*

Mark Slobin
*Subcultural Sounds: Micromusics
of the West*

Mark Slobin, editor
*Global Soundtracks: Worlds
of Film Music*

Christopher Small
The Christopher Small Reader

Christopher Small
*Music of the Common Tongue:
Survival and Celebration
in African American Music*

Christopher Small
Music, Society, Education

Christopher Small
*Musicking: The Meanings of
Performing and Listening*

Maria Sonevytsky
*Wild Music: Sound and Sovereignty
in Ukraine*

Regina M. Sweeney
*Singing Our Way to Victory:
French Cultural Politics and Music
during the Great War*

ABOUT THE AUTHOR

Emma Baulch researches Indonesian media and popular culture. She is an associate professor of media and communications at Monash University Malaysia. Baulch is the author of *Making Scenes: Reggae, Punk, and Death Metal in 1990s Bali* (Duke University Press, 2007) and coeditor (with Adrian Athique) of *Digital Transactions in Asia: Economic, Informational, and Social Exchanges* (Routledge, 2019).